"The School on the Hill"

Memories of Three Hundred Years of
Friends' School, Saffron Walden
1702 – 2002

*by those who taught, learned
and grew up there*

Published by The Friends' School, Saffron Walden, Essex

2002

"The School on the Hill"

These words were coined by Albert C Linney as the title for an article he wrote for Past and Present, *A Journal for Scholars, Old and Young, of Friends' Schools, 15 July 1907.*

He wrote: "Here we have a School built specially for a School, something extraordinary among our Quaker Educational Establishments. It is within convenient distance of London, amid interesting and picturesque country, in a healthy situation. The Headmaster has a staff of unusual ability under him, and the premises are splendid (though I am told that if any one wants to benefit the School, there is still lacking a forge, an art-room, and a separate hospital).

For myself, having seen Walden in its ordinary aspect, two feelings stand clear. One, that of admiration for the well-appointed School, possessed as it is of so many attractive features; two, that of amazement because it is not always packed to overflowing. I do not know to what extent the Committee seek to attract pupils who are not Friends (of course, always supposing that they do not exclude those for whom the School was primarily founded), but I cannot understand why, if only they knew of its existence, scores of middle-class London parents should not be hurrying to place their sons and daughters at Walden.
. . . ."

An earlier report, to a joint committee of Friends in 1876, when the School was looking for a new home, speaks of ". . . The Principal Building Developments 'Situated on an open breezy hill' . . ."

Published in 2002 by Friends' School,
Saffron Walden, Essex CB11 3EB
Copyright © 2002 Friends' School

British Library Cataloguing in Publication Data
A catalogue record for this book is available from the British Library
ISBN No 0-9542413-0-4

All rights reserved. No part of this publication may be reproduced, stored in a retrieval system or transmitted in any form or by any means, electronic, mechanical, photocopying, recording or otherwise, without the prior permission in writing of the publishers.

Typesetting by Hilary R Halter
Printed in Hong Kong by C & C Printers

Contents

Foreword	i
Editorial	i
Notes and Acknowledgements	ii
Three Hundred Years of Friends' School A Four-site Saga	1
List of Stewards, Masters, Superintendents and Head Teachers	11
The Complaints Book of Richard Hutton	12
A short account of the last annual treat given to the children of Croydon School	16
Principal Building Developments 1879 - 2002	17
Junior House 1930-1948	26
FSSW and the Friends' Ambulance Unit	30
Crime and Punishment at Walden	33
A Good Idea? Well it seemed like it at the time	37
The Staff	38
Home for the Homeless	51
Informal Pastimes	58
Food	59
Marygold's Diary	63
One Family's Sporting Links with Walden	69
Theatre at Friends' School 1977-2002	72
Half a Century of Music Making at Walden	75
Eminent Alumni	78
The Squash	90
100 Years of the OSA	91
While in their spare time . . .	98
The Night We Saved the Girls' Honour	106
The Present Generation	108
Still Inclusive, Still Thriving	111
A New Head for a New Century	112
A Vision for the Future	112

All interspersed with the memories of Staff and Students

Foreword

This book is published to mark three hundred years of the Friends' School at its four locations, Clerkenwell, Islington Road, Croydon and Saffron Walden.

It is not a history: it does not seek to replicate or replace David Bolam's *Unbroken Community*, published for the 250th anniversary in 1952. It is, rather, a montage: a mix of archive, recollection and snapshot – both literal and metaphorical – combining to give a fascinating picture of life at the School over the years.

Hilary Halter, herself at the School from 1941-47, has put it together with skill, enthusiasm, persistence and determined sleuthing. The result is something which few connected with FSSW will not gain both enjoyment and interest from reading – or just dipping into from time to time.

For those of us who learned or taught there it will stir some memories, bring some surprises, and remind us of people who have left a mark on our lives. For everyone it will bring fresh insights into the story of an institution which has helped to shape so many people over three centuries as, still flourishing, it enters its fourth.

Tony Newton
The Rt Hon Lord Newton of Braintree, OBE

Editorial

Photo Michael Gee

When Jane Laing asked me to undertake this project, my first reaction was to question if it was right for a practising Jew to chronicle three hundred years of Quaker education. And then I thought that perhaps it was. If not a member of the immediate family I am a close friend, able to look in with affection on a unique institution where I spent six happy years. After all, Quakerism is all about inclusiveness.

This has not been an academic exercise. It comprises the memories and sentiments of a wide variety of people. Some of it is light hearted, some serious, much very thoughtful. It is intended to be an easy read.

Thank you to everyone who has sent in stories and photographs. In the end, it was a struggle to find room for absolutely everything, but I hope that anything which has not appeared may be used in future publications.

It might seem that a good proportion of the stories cover the Forties and Fifties. There could be two reasons for this – many of us came to the School to escape the bombing in the big cities, others were escaping persecution. Either way, we would not have experienced Friends' School had it not been for the external pressures and there was a very interesting mix of scholars there at the time. Also, the older one gets, the more one thinks back to one's childhood and the influences that shape a person – the wartime generation are at that age.

This project has been a joy to me. It has brought me into contact with lovely people – some I have not met in fifty years, others I have never met at all. I hope it gives you as much pleasure as it has given me.

Hilary Hockley

Notes on the Text

When assembling a publication with so many contributors and so many different names being mentioned, there is an editorial dilemma. To include all information about every name every time it is mentioned risks cluttering the text and taking up too much space. It has therefore been decided to use names when at School throughout, as these will be more readily recognised. Details of present names, dates at School and any other relevant information are listed at the end of the book.

Photographs have been attributed only where the photographer is definitely known. It is almost certain that names like Maurice Haselgrove and Uwe Gerstl would probably arise in several instances but it is difficult to be certain at this time.

Acknowledgements

I have many individuals to thank for special help and support. It is always difficult to include absolutely everybody, but here, in no particular order, are those without whom this Book could not have come to fruition: Roger Buss, OS Archivist who, apart from contributing a thoroughly researched article, has been the source of much of the illustrative material. Roger Bush has done sterling work in the field of editorial advice, writing and proof reading. Wilfrid Hayler has been a tower of strength with his encyclopaedic knowledge of who's who. He has spent many hours compiling information regarding Old Scholars and Staff which has been invaluable, quite apart from his meticulous proof-reading. For advice on content, I have called on Naomi Sargant who has given a considerable amount of time. Martin Hugall has been our liaison with the School. Charles Davey, from his home in New York, has organised and advised on the actual production of the Book. I would like to express my special thanks to Michael Gee for his photography. Tom Robinson, with his excellent website, has ensured that there has been plenty of cyber publicity and encouragement. Andrew and Nigel McTear, Treasurer and Secretary respectively of the OSA, have given enormous encouragement and taken on the burden of business management. Mark Bertram, has given much encouragement, as well as valuable contributions to the Book.

There may well be others whom I have not mentioned. Please know how grateful I am. It has been an honour to be associated with this project.

Three Hundred Years of Friends' School
A Four-Site Saga

Farrand Radley

When I first used this title for my Presidential address to the Old Scholars' Association in 1967 a television adaptation had made Galsworthy a little more topical than today – but those four sites are still there all right. Clerkenwell 1702, Islington Road 1786, Croydon 1825 and Saffron Walden 1879. And when it came to planning an Appeal for a 'Tercentenary' in 2002 and I was on the Committee which organised it, I had a head start in drafting its objects. I suggested "to commemorate 300 years of the oldest continuously surviving community in the British Isles providing a Quaker education".

The Committee agreed, very kindly.

But first there are a few questions to be answered. Exactly what was started in 1702 to justify a tercentenary in 2002? If, as first described, it was a 'workhouse', did it also qualify as a school – at least enough to justify the description given it by David Bolam in his book, *Unbroken Community*, published for the 250th anniversary in 1952? And if so, is there any other current Quaker establishment that has existed without any gap for 300 years or more, here or anywhere else in the world. And, lastly, was there in 1702, and is there now, such a thing as a Quaker education?

This chapter is an attempt to answer those questions.

Perhaps I ought, first of all, to state my family connections with all this. My grandfather, Alexander Radley, married a Farrand, originally a French name meaning just Smith – the maréchal ferrant (from fer, iron), that is a farrier or blacksmith. Some came over with the Huguenots but my lot definitely escorted the Conqueror! And one John, a baker, got married in 1720 at Peel Meeting House, where the Clerkenwell Boys went on Sundays. Joseph Farrand, 'last and patten maker', accepted the discharge to his care from Clerkenwell of Edward Sweatman in 1781. There were six Farrands at Islington Road and two Radleys, one of whom, Mary Ann, had, according to the Admission Register, "hardly learned anything sixteen months ago when she came to School" – a good academic start for the family!

There were eighteen Farrands and ten Radleys (including Joseph, later Head of Lisburn in Ulster) at Croydon. A Farrand, Isabella, taught at Saffron Walden before, sadly, ending up at The Retreat. At Walden again, my father, John Charles, was the first (1883-89) to take London Matric, and was a Junior Master (1891-94); and yours truly (1927-33) was in the first Sixth Form to take Higher School Certificate.

My cousin Philip, later Head of Ackworth, was arrested at Walden as a Student Master in 1916 for being a Conscientious Objector, and always claimed to have been the first Quaker to spend a night in The Tower since William Penn. And my father came back for an Old Scholars' Weekend in 1914 and met my mother, Helen Louise Howell, who taught music and had done so before at Ayton. Not for nothing did a law firm recently write to me as Messrs H A Farr & Radley.

Quaker education up to 1702

George Fox was "much exercised with schoolmasters and schoolmistresses", warning them to teach their children sobriety in the fear of the Lord, that they might not be nursed and trained up in lightness, vanity and wantonness". In 1668, having also given attention to the problems of marriage satisfactorily, he passed out of London "into the counties" again and came to Waltham (Abbey), where he "established a school for teaching of boys" and "ordered a women's school to be set up in Shacklewell (in Hackney) "to instruct young lasses and maidens in whatsoever things were civil and useful in the creation". This had gone by 1677, alas. The boys school lasted not more than ten years after moving to Edmonton in 1679. But it taught two sons of Isaac Penington, one of Robert Barclay, and a grandson of Margaret Fell. The master, Christopher Taylor, left for Pennsylvania, as did his successor, George Keith, who, although a founder of the Penn Charter School there in 1689, blotted his copybook and was finally disowned both in Philadelphia and Britain. So that was the end of Fox's personal contribution, though it came after an early start by George Whitehead in 1653 and at least two schools run by Friends in prisons, at Stafford and Ilchester, for their comrades there.

By 1690 London Yearly Meeting was warning Friends "not to send their children to the World's schools to corrupt them by learning Heathen Authors and the names of their gods. Schoolmasters and Schoolmistresses (where they are capable) should take care that they train them in the language of truth and the plainness that becomes the Truth". Leonard Kenworthy asked us in 1983 to "imagine a small group of people, many of them illiterate, starting schools in a century where education was considered a monopoly of the rich and powerful. Yet the Quakers did just that". In 1691 there were 27 day schools in England, three in each of Scotland and Ireland, with a published list of fifteen boarding schools – "scholes kept by Friends". One of these was Penketh, which must be examined with care, since it affects the FSSW claim to unique continuous survival, along with other contenders opened before 1702.

Penketh was a Preparative Meeting boarding school in 1688. One of its later pupils was John Bright, better remembered as an old scholar of Bootham. But in 1834 it was replaced by an entirely distinct foundation under the joint management of Hardshaw East and West Monthly Meetings. This lasted until 1934, when it fell foul of the Depression, though its Old Scholars Association lasted until 2000. Penketh therefore cannot defeat FSSW. Nor can Stramongate in Kendal, to which my father brought me as a child, as he did to Penketh, since he was on the Committee of both. Opened in 1698, it too died from the Depression in 1932. As the Old Scholars' magazine, The Old Stramonian, movingly put it: "our school is to close, the oldest of its kind. We believe that her passing will be regretted by a wider company than ours which has known her from the inside." In the end, the school went down fighting: "the school tradition taught the school at least – to play the game."

Lancaster was around by 1700, operating for long in the wings of the Meeting House, until selling out to a non-Friend body in 1969. (This at least had the decency to name it the George Fox School, though it fails now to provide a Quaker education). Another non-competitor is Sidcot. Although it apparently stole a march on FSSW by announcing its Tercentenary in 1999, that was only an anniversary of its foundation as a Monthly Meeting School under William Jenkins Jun, which closed when he retired in 1728. There was then a gap of more than half a century before John Benwell opened a private school there from about 1784 to 1805. The Headmaster in 1994 confirmed that the school "ceased to exist at Sidcot for some years". So, although it was refounded in 1808 as a Quarterly Meeting School, it loses out to FSSW on continuity. (Some personal regret here, as I have a small claim to have founded it myself. In 1935, as a Student Master at Sidcot, I played a part in Evelyn Roberts' *Sidcot Pageant*. I was William Jenkins.)

Turning to the New World, the official list of US boarding schools compiled by the Friends Council of Education in Philadelphia traces two already operating before 1702 and still doing so. William Penn had followed in Fox's footsteps as a thinker on education: "Let my children be husbandmen and housewives; it is healthy, honest and of good example". Abington Friends School, Pennsylvania, of 1697, and the William Penn Charter School, Pennsylvania, of 1689, both still flourish. So, as you will see, our claim to be the oldest continuously surviving community providing a Quaker education is only valid on this side of the Atlantic.

> ## Quaker Committee and 'Meeting' Boarding Schools
>
> ### Long-term Pre-1702
> Penketh I (1688-1834); Stramongate (1698-1932); Sidcot I (1699-1728); Lancaster (1700-1969)
>
> William Penn Charter, USA (1689-present); Abington, USA (1697-present)
>
> ### 1702 and After
> Clerkenwell (1702) – Islington Road (1786) – Croydon (1825) – Saffron Walden (1879)
>
> Leeds (1756-1838); Gildersome (1882-1815); Lisburn, Ireland (1774-present); Ackworth (1779-present); The Mount (1784-1814; 1831-present); Mountmellick, Ireland (1786-1921); Newtown, Ireland (1798-present); Ipswich (1790-1800); Sidcot II (1808-present); Wigton (1815-1984); Bootham (1823-present); Rawdon (1832-1921); Penketh II (1834-1934); Brookfield, Ireland (1836-1921); Ayton (1841-1997); Sibford (1842-present); Newton-in-Bowland (1884; 1868-1911); Leighton Park (1890-present)
>
> In the year 2000 there were 73 in USA, 7 in Great Britain and two in Ireland. *(Source: Friends House, London. Library Guide 7 – Quaker Schools in Great Britain and Ireland)*

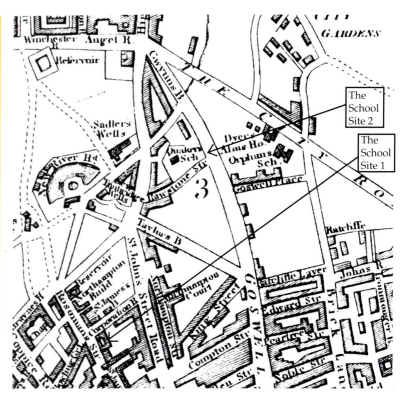

CLERKENWELL 1702 – The First of the Four Sites

The key name here is John Bellers (1645- 1725). He was a Quaker cloth merchant, a philosopher and polymath who was made a Fellow of the Royal Society in 1798 (eight years after his son!). Bellers has been described as "one of those who never sees a wrong without wanting to smite it down – whose minds are ever engaged in shaping schemes for the regeneration of humanity – schemes, alas, too often incapable of being realised". He certainly smote, anticipating the European Union, the National Health Service, fair parliamentary elections, and turning his mind to a scheme to provide "Profit for the Rich, a Plentiful Living for the Poor and a Good Education for Youth". These last were his *Proposals for Raising a Colledge of Industry of all Useful Trades and Husbandry* (1695, with a second, and definitive, edition in 1696).

Bellers had already had experience of working for the poor in Bristol and now sought a wider field, presenting a version of his proposals to London Yearly Meeting on 29 May 1697. They were recommended "to the further consideration and amendment of the morning meeting and our Meeting for Sufferings" and on 19 June 1699 were finally approved. London and Middlesex Quarterly Meeting was entrusted with implementing the project. After being gazumped for one site and rejecting "a vinegar house to lett in Islington", they found a "hous in Clerkenwell" which, on 18 August 1701, was felt to be a "very proper and convenient hous". A lease was signed by John Bellers, Merchant, and John Hopes, Cornfactor, from the executors of Sir Thomas Rowe, who had run 'The College of Infants' in part of the property from 1686 until his death in 1696, something that obviously endeared it to Bellers. It had been a Corporation Workhouse from the 1660s, paid for by local parishioners and accommodating 600 paupers, and a County House of Correction – something Bellers was anxious not to replicate – but had been closed in 1673 as too expensive. It has been described as "a commodious and airy building, ideally suited to the use of which it was put", ie at the minimum to house the 'Antient Friends' and teach the children trades which would help them to be apprenticed and provide saleable articles; all in one community.

Was it a workhouse or a school?

The terms of the 2002 Appeal were carefully chosen. FSSW celebrates 300 years of a Community, a word used in case any challenge should be raised that the establishment at Clerkenwell – at least at the outset – did not fall under the description of a School. Mind you, in the 200th anniversary booklet written in 1902 by James Backhouse Crosfield, Clerk to the School Committee, it was categorically quoted that on 27 July 1702 "two women aged 83 and 75 were come in from the Bull meeting" and "John Staploe give account one boy from the Peele is come in", this being taken to indicate the date of commencement of the original School. It was a claim echoed by Campbell Stewart in 1957: "this school (FSSW) had its beginning in 1702, a very oblique result of the remarkable suggestion of John Bellers. It was St James Workhouse in Clerkenwell, London, refuge for a few old and infirm people and a boarding school for some young children."

Yet the actual title of the community at its beginnings was undoubtedly a Workhouse. In the minutes of a 'Meeting for the business of the poore' a reference to 'the hous in Clerkingwell' is noted in the margin as simply 'Worke Hous'. And Richard Hutton, a Lancastrian who was Steward from 1711 to 1737 and kept a voluminous 'Complaints Book', refers habitually to the 'hous' but has the management committee of thirty meet at "the workhouse of the people called Quakers at Clerkenwell". By 1739 Maitland's *History of London* made a distinction between the 'Quaker Workhouse, being both an Hospital and Workhouse' and the 'Quakers School' (belonging to it!) and in 1746 another book, by Timothy Revan, is called, 'with the full support of the Committee', *An Account of the Rise, Progress and Present State of the School and Work – house maintained by the people called Quakers in Clerkenwell*. A committee minute of 2 December 1772 simply refers to 'the Charity called the Quakers School and Workhouse situate in Clerkenwell'. And every boy on leaving after 1775 was given a paper: 'Advice on quitting the Friends' School and Workhouse at Clerkenwell, London'.

This would have pleased Bellers, who never liked the word 'Workhouse' and already in 1718 had written in an epistle to the Quarterly Meeting of London and Middlesex that he "felt it necessary to change its name from a Workhouse to either an Hospital or a College, but rather the latter: because some parents will not put their children to so Contemptible a place of Education as a Workhouse or an Hospital, the first sounding too much like a Bridewell (the local Prison) and the second like an Almshouse, whereas a College bespeaks a more Liberal Education". Unfortunately, his suggestion was not taken up.

Was the Education a Quaker Education'?

John Bellers, like Penn before him, had practical views on education: "beyond Reading and Writing a multitude of Scholars is not so useful to the Public as some think". But his biographer, George Clarke, writing in 1987, feels that "his proposals regarding education were the most serious attempts made during the late 17th and early 18th centuries to provide for a full and caring education for all children, rich and poor".

The children went to Meeting at Peel, in St John's Lane, which, until it was destroyed by enemy action in World War Two, was London's oldest Meeting House. A schoolmaster and a schoolmistress taught them the three Rs in two-hour periods, and the Committee was able to report, on 1 January 1707/8 for example, that "the children have a suitable education". As David Bolam writes: "the fundamental aim of all teaching was religious. Both the technique and aims were the same as those of the contemporary charity schools except that the catechisms used set forth a distinctive Quaker interpretation of life". The material included questions like this: "Q. What saith the Apostle of the Righteous undergoing Tribulation? A. We must through much Tribulation enter into the Kingdom of God. Yea, and that all that will live Godly in Christ Jesus shall suffer Persecution". This must have spoken closely to the condition of children with parents under duress or in jail.

A Committee Order of 1709 asks "for the benefit of the Family and the advancement of Piety and Godliness therein, that after the boys are dressed at the direction of the Steward they read as many chapters in the Bible as he shall see meet. The same also to be observed in the evenings, and as often as may be, to be called together to wait upon and Worship God".

Clerkenwell Assessed

John Bellers was highly regarded as a social economist by Karl Marx. In *Capital* (1867) he sees him as a "veritable phenomenon in the history of political economy".

This opinion must have received a greater world-wide circulation than anything published by Quakers, and it is hardly surprising that the contemporary Russian academic Tatyana Pavlova adds her tribute. She does, however, ascribe his lack of recognition in his own lifetime and his "assignation to oblivion until Marx" to "his tragedy in attempting to fuse two incompatible things, maximum advantage for the rich and welfare for the poor". He did not "think in terms of undermining the pillars of the existing set-up", but she gives him credit for his pedagogic ideas, which were "more democratic and humanistic than those of the contemporary philosopher John Locke".

Bellers's first scheme was certainly ambitious. Children were to be educated in the college, a simple book education being combined with training in handicrafts, but, as Ruth Fry pointed out in 1935, "his later editions omit mention of children and the place becomes a labour colony". And George Clarke finds the Workhouse, both in name and application, "a pale shadow of Bellers's all-embracing concept". The Board of Education Report on its 1905 inspection of FSSW is rather dismissive: "it was originally a Workhouse School for poor London children, but in this form it does not seem to have been very successful."

As to its influence, commentators differ in their assessment of this early experiment in inspiring imitations or affecting the general course of Quaker education. But Campbell Stewart praises "the minority of schools founded 1695 to 1725" for "playing a vital part in the educational history of the Society in keeping alive the spirit of an earlier enthusiasm during the period of decline around the 1720s". This was caricatured in a cartoon of the day showing a Quaker leaning on two sticks marked 'Sinless Perfection' and 'Infallibility' – the caption was "Quakerism Drooping"! At that time, John Wesley and his followers were enjoying the kind of popular favour which George Fox had had in the previous century, and from him comes perhaps the strongest tribute of all. He is quoted as saying that he regretted time did not allow a visit to the Quakers' Workhouse but that it was said "to be the best to take a plan from of any in London".

The Clerkenwell Site after 1786

When the Committee decided to find a new home because the numbers of Antient Friends were felt to be inhibiting the development of the children's school, the Clerkenwell premises suffered neglect, and by 1803 were described as the "ruins of the Quakers' Workhouse" which had "fallen into decay many years past, and what remains is let to poor occupants at very low rents". Two years later these ruins were pulled down and the site was used for a series of prisons. There had been a Bridewell in Clerkenwell since 1616, hived off from the original at Blackfriars, and this was replaced first by a New Prison in 1775 and then by a new New Prison in 1818, which became the Middlesex House of Detention from 1845 to 1877. It was this building that was the scene of a terrorist incident in 1867 – the outer wall was blown to pieces in an attempt to free some Irish Fenian prisoners and a row of houses opposite destroyed. The ringleader of this Gunpowder plot, Michael Barrett, was the last man to be publicly executed in this country.

The site was subsequently cleared for a new London Schools Board Secondary School, opened in 1893 and named after Hugh Myddelton, whose nearby New River of 1616 was a pioneer enterprise in bringing fresh water to London. Nearly a hundred years later, in 1981, the school started sharing premises with the Kingsway Princeton Further Education College, which got into debt, and by 1998 both had to vacate the site and sell it to developers, who started turning the building into luxury flats and offices. Only an Infants school at the Woodbridge Street end of the site survives as the Rosemary School for special needs. The dungeons, which had been taken over for School staffrooms, photographic darkrooms and the like, became for a short while a tourist attraction as the 'House of Detention 1616-1990 – London's Underground Prison'. Now this too has gone, not even its impressive doorway remains. One thing John Bellers would have applauded – at least the site was occupied for a time by a College!

ISLINGTON ROAD – 1786-1825

You would think that Islington Road means the road to Islington. And so it did, but the best contemporary map-maker, John Rocque (1744-46), shows several roads with that name, and they include St John Street and Goswell Road, both in Clerkenwell. Between them lay our second site. Although the School Report of 1817 calls it Islington Road, both Crosfield (1902) and Bolam (1952) put just

FRIENDS' SCHOOL, ISLINGTON.
(Lent by Benjamin J. Winstone.)

Islington on their title pages, adding the word Road in the text. And without question the site was Islington Road Estate on Hermitage Fields, in the area of present-day Rawstorne Street.

The community took over the remaining 148 years of a lease from the owners, the Worshipful Company of Brewers, in 1786. The new site was in an academic area. The Hermitage from which the fields took their name was a 10 acre estate that had belonged to Dame Alice Owen and on which she had built almshouses and a school in 1613. The Dame Alice Owen Boys' School moved to a new building in the 1840s and, in 1886, was joined by a Girls' School, blitzed in 1940, rebuilt in 1963, and now, as the Dame Alice Owen Building, a department of the City University (the former Northampton Poly). Both Dame Alice schools moved out in 1976 to Potters Bar.

The building was beautiful, with a Robert Adam style bay window. According to an 1803 description it "had the appearance of a villa, surrounded as it is by pleasure grounds, gardens and trees". Although only just around the corner from the old Workhouse it was in a Spa area with Sadler's and Bagnigge Wells nearby. And it was here that emancipation took place, both from the Antient Friends (only seven of them left by then) and from the name of Workhouse. In 1811 it became the 'Friends School, under the care of the Quarterly Meeting of London and Middlesex' – even the local maps changed its description from 'Quaker Workhouse' to 'Friends Schools'.

Despite the earlier account of a building in which "the cielings (sic) were remarkably high, and the windows large, consequently the rooms are perfectly dry and well aired", it may not have been entirely satisfactory. An 1828 history of the area tells a different story: "The ceilings of all the rooms are not remarkable for their height, and it is a fact that the Society have been induced to remove the institution to Croydon, in Surrey, partly, at least, on account of the dampness of the lower apartments, and their fears for the health of those who occupied them. This removal took place at Midsummer 1825, since when the structure has been deserted." The Committee had given a building lease to one Christopher Cockerton, who pulled the building down and constructed a labyrinth of streets and slums, the rent from which helped sustain the school at Croydon. And when the 148-year lease was up, in 1934, there was enough of a windfall to enable the School, by then at Saffron Walden, to have a new Assembly Hall and to get Paul Mauger (architect and Old Scholar) to turn the old Lecture Hall into a Library.

If you go back to the Islington Road site now you will find a Friend Street on its northern boundary. Is that a memorial? Well yes, but to one George Friend who ran the Finsbury Dispensary for the Poor on the corner there! The Brewer's Society, the ground landlords, are still evident in the line of restored 19th century tenements along Rawstorne Street.

CROYDON – 1825-1879

The Committee took over another beautiful house in Croydon, and one nearly as old (1708) as the date we started from. But they had learned: a minute of 1824 says "it is desirable that the rooms in the wings (the new additions to be built) be not less than thirteen feet in height and those of the dormitories not less than twelve feet". Some splendid glass negative pictures taken before it left in 1879 by Bedford Lemere (Old Scholars' President and Architectural Photographer to Queen Victoria) show its spaciousness and that of the beautiful long garden stretching away into the distance.

My uncle, Alfred Alexander Radley, who later emigrated to Canada and became President of their Methodist Conference, was there and wrote to me of his experience as a child "during five years (1867-72) in a boarding school under the control of the Society of Friends. Games were encouraged. Cricket, football, shinny, paperchase and others. Nature study was stimulated by long walks into the country and the collecting of specimens: plants, butterflies, shells, birds' eggs. Budding literary genius found its opportunity in the 'Select Society' to which the older boys were admitted on the approval of the Teachers' Meeting. All of which was good. But

FRIENDS' SCHOOL, CROYDON
from the field opposite

over against this put the fact that we had no organised physical drill or athletics; anything like the Boy Scouts or Cadets would have been frowned upon; dramatics were taboo, as also was the singing of secular songs (and even hymns for a while); no music, vocal or instrumental, was taught or even allowed; novels were absolutely forbidden; theatre-going and public entertainment (except lectures) were not to be thought of and anything like games of chance, such as cards etc, were equally regarded."

The School was one of a motley collection of educational establishments in Croydon, from the Military Seminary of the East India Company through a Dame School, a 'School of Industry' (very much up our street), a Ragged School sponsored by Lord Shaftesbury, and the Warehousemen and Clerks' School similarly by the 1st Earl in 1879. After a series of lesser schools in the building came the solid prep school, St Anselm's, in 1904, which pulled down the wings but left the 1708 core and added a Memorial Hall for World War One. And then, in September 1940, it all went, along with the Head's House and the Friends Meeting House. Providentially the school had by that time been evacuated.

What happened was this: the Germans had dropped a landmine captured at Dunkirk from British stores and, out of respect for its origins, it refused to explode on landing; but on removal it did, though luckily no-one was hurt. Of the property the only survival was the 1708 front gate, which had allowed the blast to whistle through it. And it was a notable survivor, very likely the work of Thomas Robinson, who was responsible for work at St Paul's Cathedral and for two local masterpieces at Carshalton Park and Beddington, both now in the USA. The Beddington Gates were replaced by a replica, insisted on as part of the deal, and they share with our gates a U motif, which certainly points to ours being by Robinson. He has been described by the ironwork expert Raymond Lister, in his 1957 *Decorative Ironwork in Great Britain*, as "representing the greatest achievement of pure English blacksmithery".

During the war the gate had been carefully guarded by Ernest Allen, a Croydon Friend. But when it came to its reinstatement, there was nowhere to put it. Croydon Council had built its new high-rise municipal offices on the site, and the Meeting House had lost ground through a road-widening scheme, which includes the delightfully named Friends Road. So the gates ended up at Saffron Walden. A plaque commemorates their 1976 re-opening by Duncan Fairn, Clerk of London and Middlesex General Meeting, in the presence of two former Clerks of London Yearly Meeting, Redford Crosfield Harris and Godfrey Mace (an Old Scholar), and the acknowledged pioneer in tracing these four sites, George Edwards.

SAFFRON WALDEN 1879

Sir William Temple Bt (1628-99), a diplomat and contemporary of George Fox, wrote of this successful medication: "The spirit of Saffron is of all others the noblest and yet the most innocent virtue. I have known it restore a man out of the very agonies of death when left by physicians as wholly desperate." It's doubtful whether this old opinion weighed with the choice of a more healthy location, but in a way saffron has always been with the School. There is a Saffron Hill in Clerkenwell, and the very name of Croydon has been defined as the valley where the wild saffron or crocus grows. The market town of Chipping Walden was saffronised in the mid-14th century, and saffron was cultivated here to the mid-18th', adding extra wealth to the wool trade. For it remains one of the most expensive herbs, needing a whole field to make a pound's weight because only the stamens are used for the yellow colour. Though the Old Scholars' badge of the 1930s had the flower itself yellow, the saffron on the 2002 Appeal has gone for the more correct purple.

When Croydon became too unhealthy from typhoid, and even a death from rheumatic fever, the Committee had explored other locations, among them Alton and Chelmsford, both – like Walden – outside the area of London and Middlesex Quarterly Meeting, the School's owner. But, in 1876, came an irresistible offer from a Walden Friend, the banker and former Mayor of the town, George Stacey Gibson, of a site – and a free one too! "It is beautifully situated . . . on an open breezy hill above the town, near the railway station and within a very easy distance of the Meeting House." And what clinched it, after the Croydon experience, was that it had "a good supply of water from a deep artesian well".

It was breezy all right. Early photos show it in splendid isolation with nothing even remotely near it. The architect was Edward Burgess (1847-1929), who also built the local Grammar School in 1881 and a Training College in 1884. None of these counted for much with Pevsner, who wrote in his *Buildings of England*: "the three educational buildings are of red brick, in a Tudor style, and have little to recommend them architecturally". But Croydon had bequeathed its 1872 clock, which had graced the garden front, and can now be proudly seen from The Avenue, in the view immortalised in the Quaker Tapestry panel depicting all the Friends' Schools of its day. The School also inherited the Barometer, one of the group given to all the Friends' Schools in 1871 by the first Quaker MP, Joseph Pease. But the real treasure remains the 1787 clock, made two years before the French Revolution, and that came from Islington Road in the famous clock-making district of Clerkenwell.

The School's Old Scholars' Association, of which my grandfather Alexander Radley had been a founder member in 1869, played a large part in the Bicentenary Appeal of 1902. The tangible result was the Swimming Pool, and the main target of the 2002 Appeal is its refurbishment. It is of some sorrow to me that there is no possibility of restoring one of its main pleasures, the diving board, officialdom having proclaimed, long ago, that the depth of the pool was too shallow. But no-one ever had an accident from it, and we are deprived of that most magnificent sight – a weighty Friend doing a Honeypot off the top board and splashing everyone near!

An article in *Past and Present*, the only magazine ever to cover all the Friends' Schools, commented in 1907 that the "premises are splendid, though I am told that if anyone wants to benefit the School there is still lacking a forge, an art room and a separate hospital". The art room came in 1921 when Fred Rowntree built one over the new Boys' Teaching Block, and the Sanatorium, again by Burgess, was completed in 1913, again with help from the Old Scholars in providing furnishings for the convalescent wards. It is now the flourishing Junior Branch, Gibson House, for Infants and Juniors. But we still await the forge, which would have given me, Farrand, the maréchal ferrant or blacksmith, a unique chance to shine!

One of the extra things for which we have to thank the donor of the site was the enlargement of the 1791 Meeting House in the town to allow the School's participation en bloc every Sunday morning. During World War One it became, for a while, a canteen for troops, who also took over the entire School for a few months in 1915. The Committee were advised to put in a large bill for damages in the expectation that they would get half; in the event they submitted what they considered a strictly fair estimate, and got it in full Of the other alterations since then, one charming detail stands out as typical of the care shown over all this time for human, even Quaker, values. When Burgess was called back, though in his seventies, to make additions, he built a new spur, housing the boys' music cubicles. They were far enough away from the main block to be *almost* sound-proofed.

QUAKER EDUCATION NOW — HOW DOES SAFFRON WALDEN STAND?

Does the School still 'provide a Quaker education' and thus justify the Appeal wording in every respect – if you allow that I have satisfactorily dealt with the claim to be 'the oldest surviving community' doing just that in the British Isles?

The Old Scholar John R Reader, who became Head of Ayton, delivered the Swarthmore Lecture in 1979 with the title *Of Schools and Schoolmasters*: "The point has been made that Friends have not produced a distinctive philosophy of education throughout their history and that they are divided in their views today. They have always been clear, however, about the spirit in which education should be practised even if they have fallen short at times in the way they have expressed it."

Britain Yearly meeting is now actively concerned with establishing Quaker Values in Education, and the former FSSW Head, Sarah Evans, was a speaker at a recent Conference. She had already, in the Annual Report of 1994, declared that "at the heart of the School's aims is to see that of God in every one". And London and Middlesex General Meeting, which must surely have the last word, minuted in 1996 that "despite a minority of Friends on the staff and among the scholars or residents it maintains a distinctive Quaker ethos which all who become involved recognise. There is a palpably happy atmosphere and a determination that everyone within the environment should be treated equally: it is seen to be essentially Quaker."

Based on the Presidential Address given as a Magic Lantern Lecture during Britain Yearly Meeting, 28 May 2000, and printed in the Friends' Historical Society Journal, Vol 59, No 2, 2001.

I have always nursed my private definition of education as e-ducat-ion, the art of extracting ducats, or cash, out of parents. And if you look at an old wall board at Walden you may indeed wonder what the parents of ninety years ago thought they were paying for. The board bears the names of (boy) Senior Scholars (including my father) and Athletic Champions from 1885 onwards - until 1910, that is, when it just said 'Co-education', drew a line and ended. So, with no more studies and no more sport, were they just paying to get their offspring into boarding care?

List of Stewards, Masters, Superintendents and Head Teachers

Clerkenwell, 1702-1786

The earliest Heads of the Institution were known as Stewards. From 1737 the Committee made joint appointments of Steward and Stewardess.

1702-1704	George Barr
1704-1709	John Powell
1709	John Davis
1709-1711	Samuel Trafford
1711-1737	Richard Hutton
1737-1742	George Reynolds "and his wife"
1742-1753	Nicholas Davis "and his sister Elizabeth"
1753-1760	Leonard Snowden "and wife"
1760-1778	Robert Letchworth "and wife"
1778-1783	Scrivenor and Mary Alsop
1783-1786	Josiah (died 1784) and Elizabeth Collier

Islington Road, 1786-1835

In 1786 the "ancient Friends" were removed to Plaistow in the care of John and Ann Withers; Elizabeth Collier was Stewardess until they were brought to Islington. In 1808 the offices of Steward and Schoolmaster were combined in one person to be called Master. The Master's wife usually acted as Housekeeper and Mistress of the Family.

1786-1792	Elizabeth Collier
1792-1808	John and Ann Withers
1808-1809	Thomas Salter
1809-1816	Edmund Gower (at times assisted by Mary, his wife)
1816-1818	William and Mary Baker
1818-1825	Abigail Binns

Croydon, 1825-1879

From 1825 the Head of the School was known as the Superintendent. In joint appointments the wife continued to act as "Mistress of the Family".

1825-1833	Henry and Edith Dymond
1833-1838	Edward and Elizabeth Brady
1838-1842	Elizabeth Brady
1842-1853	John and Hannah Sharp
1853-1854	Charles and Sarah Fryer
1854-1860	Sarah Fryer (assisted after 1856 by William Robinson as Principal Officer and General Superintendent on the boys' side)
1860-1869	William and Mary Ann Robinson
1869-1879	George F and Lucy Linney

Saffron Walden, 1879-2002

Headmasters/Heads

The title Head Master replaced that of Superintendent in 1891.

1879-1890	George F and Lucy Linney
1890-1922	John Edward and Anna Phillis Walker
1922-1934	C Brightwen Rowntree BA
1934-1955	Gerald Littleboy MA(Cantab)
1955-1968	Kenneth Nicholson MA(Cantab)
1968-1989	John Woods BA(Manchester)

From 1985 the title Head replaced that of Head Master

1989-1996	Sarah Evans BA(Sussex) MA(Leicester)
1996-2001	Jane Laing BA(Reading)
2001-	Andy Waters BEd(London) MA(Hertfordshire)

Senior Mistresses/Head Mistresses

Shortly after the introduction of co-education in 1910 the Senior Mistress became known as Head Mistress. Her status was recognised by the Association of Head Mistresses in 1931.

1894-1920	Lucy Fairbrother
1920-1937	Florence D Priestman BA
1937-1944	M Sylvia Clark BA
1944-1964	Jennie Ellinor MA(Durham)
1965-1972	Joy Dupont (née Ashford) GRSM(London) ARCM

(Until 1968 Head of Girls' Side)

Deputy Heads

1964-1965	Phyllippa D M Brown
1964-1972	Cyril A Mummery MA(Oxon)
1972-1977	Ena W Evans BScHons(Lond)
1977-1984	A Margaret Brandon (BA (UBC)
1984-1987	Christine J Weston BEd(Oxon)
1988-1989	Trina Davies BA (Wales)
1988-	Martin J Hugall BSc(Bristol) (Deputy Head/Senior Teacher)
1990-1995	Jane Laing BA(Reading)

The information up to 1952 is taken from **Unbroken Community** *by David W Bolam*

The Complaints Book of Richard Hutton

John Woods recalls an early hero of the FSSW story

One of the treasures of the school's archives, now stored in ideal conditions in the Record Office at Chelmsford, is the Complaints Book of Richard Hutton, who was Steward at Clerkenwell from 1711 to 1737. It is a large, leather bound book with nearly 190 folio pages, containing, in Richard Hutton's handwriting, a collection of documents relating to his service as Steward. The London Record Society thought the work to be so important for knowledge of London life, that they obtained permission for Timothy Hitchcock to transcribe, edit and print the book, which was published in 1987 as Volume 24 of their publications of primary sources of London life.

The purpose of the Institution, the brainchild of the Quaker pioneer, John Bellers, was outlined in his *Proposals for Raising a Colledge of Industry*. Friends in the Quarterly Meeting of the London Monthly Meetings established it in 1702. A community, housing poor people, a family of both old and young, admitted on the recommendation of Friends, was to be governed by a committee of Friends, supported financially by Monthly Meetings and the profits gained from the trade in yarn – cotton worsted and linen – spun in the house.

Most of the entries are copies of papers that were prepared for other purposes. There is no way of discovering the criteria that Richard Hutton used to select his entries. Some do not relate to his time of office. The inclusion of a copy of a letter, dated 1683, about consanguinity signed by, among others, George Fox, and a series of entries, dated 1681, about taking oaths, do not, on the face of it, have much to do with the Institution.

Together, however, the entries give a fascinating glimpse into the details of life in the house during his Stewardship. It is as though Richard Hutton uses the Complaints Book to get things off his chest or to create a record of his side of the story. But it is not a journal or a diary. There is no systematic or chronological account. He records, almost randomly, the daily situations, the recurring difficulties and the occasional problems of the family. Indirectly, he shows that he brought effective administrative skills to the complex task of managing an institution that had an amalgam of personnel problems, trading business, educational responsibilities, public and Quaker relationships, community health matters and financial solvency to resolve. But he tells us very little about himself or his family. We know from elsewhere, not from the Complaints Book, that he was born into a Quaker family in Lancaster in 1662, was apprenticed as a tailor, married Sarah Steed, and with her had nine children, all of whom died before they were eighteen months old. He died while still Steward of Clerkenwell in 1737 and is buried in Bunhill Fields, where George Fox is buried.

Throughout we find we are in touch with a man who was determined to rescue the reputation of the institution to which he was appointed Steward nearly ten years after it was founded. He shows that he had an eye for detail and a command of all the various elements involved in running what was, in effect, a great experiment. He recognised that the committee was responsible for the existence of the institution, deferred to its wisdom and worked very hard on its behalf. If some of the entries feel a little tetchy, it is because the situations recorded were exasperating. Perhaps writing in the Com-plaints Book enabled him to deal better with the matters than he might otherwise have done.

Even on their own, without reference to any other document, such as the best and rough minutes of the Committee, the entries in the Complaints Book give a very comprehensive picture of the Institution. They show most aspects of the management of a community housing both old people (ancients) and children. There are details of the finances of trading in yarn, of tending to sick inmates, of receiving, or not, the legacies due to the House. There is evidence of the continual tightrope walked in dealing with interested Friends and relatives of inmates. Accounts of indiscipline and of the predicaments of individual inmates bring a very personal touch. There is reference to the bill of fare, central to the welfare of an institution at that time, which was the cause of argument, complaint and rumour. There are copies of the documents that Richard Hutton used to negotiate his own salary from a committee keen to make ends meet and glad to have the service of two, Richard and Sarah, for the price of one. The qualifications and duties of teachers are included. And for good measure there is an extract from a sermon of Bishop Tillotson, Archbishop of Canterbury, and an essay by Richard Hutton on methods for being *"a dextrous and ready penman and accurate accomptant"*. The details are different but the situations are recognisable from experience over two hundred years later, though there is no Complaints Book for 1968-1989 to prove it!

Let Richard Hutton describe the House, mostly, in the words of his own entries. By May 1718: *After 17 years continuance (the House) hath 75 persons maintained in it (including steward & servant).*

But they caused problems:
Two of them, a man and the other a woman, are lame and use crutches, and another woman friend is blind. The rest are mostly aged and weak, of whom several have kept their beds pretty much this last winter and three of the women friends who are usually sent into the house now are not of ability to be nurses as formerly they were. And our children are generally now small and several of them have been sickly and weak most part of last winter. One girl in particular was ill near six months, who had been sorely afflicted with convulsion fits to such a degree as had made her incapable of walking but by use of crutches; and she had a fire in her chamber constantly for several weeks and one to sit up or be with her in her chamber all the time, the fits being often upon her and suddenly taken.

And:
. . . .there are so many small children and 17 or 18 of them are girls, who are more trouble than boys. . . .

Attending to ancients and children simultaneously with very different needs presented real problems.

To keep in good order a family made up partially of men and women who are aged and too liable to be discontent, also boys and girls whose parents and other relations. . . . has and yet may give much uneasiness, seems to be very difficult to keep in good order. . . .

This situation was only one reason for discontent. One ancient, William Brady, had complained that he was starved while he was in the house. Richard Hutton had to write a long report to the committee refuting the allegations. William Brady was not alone.
Our family have generally speaking consisted of dissatisfied persons very unfit for a community, also having amongst us as a people such who are very unskillful in their sentiments relating to the managing such an affair. . . .

Older residents had been granted special favours before Richard Hutton became Steward. They resisted change.
. . . .many other difficulties I could mention which we have and do still lay under. And it seems to us very unlike it should be, otherwise, whilst persons are placed here on a different foot to the rest, who esteem themselves not only equal but superior to us, and we but as their servants. . . .

William Townsend caused many headaches. He objected to the bill of fare, wanted repayments if he stayed away from the house, demanded special treatment and alleged that the Steward was cruel, did not give good value and lined his own pocket from the inmates' payments. He took his complaints to the committee on three occasions. Richard Hutton expected redress from the committee, but there is no record of the outcome:
We do think that if the committee were sensible how hard it is for us. . . . to reside constantly amongst a dissatisfied people. . . . you would conclude our post very uncomfortable.

Richard Hutton found that he and Sarah had little privacy.

So we hope it may not be thought unreasonable if, with submission, we desire the little parlour and kitchen to ourselves. . . . We desire it not for ostentation, but. . . . that the business which requires privacy may be done accordingly, also to have a place to retire to as occasion requires. . . .

Some inmates wanted special attention, such as fires in their chambers and constant attendance.

Some had higher expectations because they made greater payment and demanded separate rooms. These demands caused difficulties within the house and damaging accounts of it outside. The choice was between a charge for such services and a poor reputation for inadequate attention. Richard Hutton proposed action to quell both difficulties. He could improve matters by increasing contentment within the house from the better bill of fare that he had introduced in 1713:
they are allowed each: 8 oz of butter and 16 oz of cheese per week, about 14 oz of bread (it not being weighed except Daniel Rosier's, who has 18 oz) per day, 8 oz of flesh per meal & if not enough they are desired to send for more, 19 oz of pudding per meal, and more if they can eat it (which is 10 oz per meal more than the former allowance), furmenty, milk etc a sufficient quantity.

The committee could also play their part by visiting once a week to see that things were in good order, by giving regular reports to meetings and by discouraging false reports. The Steward could try to manage affairs within the house, but he could not control what went on outside. A recurring difficulty was the spread of these reports, which did such damage to the reputation of the house, especially among the meetings that sent the inmates to it. He clearly thought that the committee should tackle this:
Complaints were taken out of the house that the poor were oppressed, the aged and sick wanted due

tendance. Which complaints were a disadvantage to the house in discouraging friends from coming in who might have been helpful and likewise thankful for so comfortable a provision. . . .

There has lately been many false stories spread abroad to the defaming of the house and those who have the care thereof and hurt of the children already here, to whom such reports have been privately brought. Which to prevent for the future we see no way at present,.. unless . . . a minute . . . from the committee be directed to each monthly meeting requesting such reports may be discouraged so often as they are related. And also that at the taking children into the house the parents have both orders (rules) and bill of fare read to them and report thereof made to the committee before such child be admitted into the house.

But there was appreciation. Richard Hutton records a letter of thanks from Thomas Sands:
Kind steward
These are to acquaint thee that I am safe arrived at my uncle's house where I was kindly received. My love to thee and thy wife, also to all the friends of the committee and to my master that taught me to write. My love to all the ancient friends and all the children of the workhouse which were my school fellows. . . . My uncle is about placing me at Exeter to Arthur Purchas, a tucker. I am in all due respects thy friend.

And in 1721 Richard and Sarah would have been pleased to receive this:
Ed. H. Said thou and thy wife are brave folks indeed, and much valued. This great undertaking has been a great success under your management,

Perhaps these commendations helped the Steward to deal with the problems of discipline, which challenged his authority.
It would be tedious, also unpleasant, to hear the whole of the provocations rehearsed; also here are too many to mention the particulars of those who in their turns are addicted unto, But, the ground of it all is their being under any obligation, either with respect to the orders of the house, bill of fare and the diet therein mentioned,

He certainly needed his wits to deal with John Gorden, a boy who got up to much mischief

The story of John Gorden as it appears in Hutton's own handwriting

before he broke into the storeroom.

. . . .At another time he got a candle over night and got up about twelve o'clock at night and took a pane of glass out of the storeroom window and got in, from whence he took four pounds of plum pudding, although he, as well as the rest of the big boys, had a full pound for dinner besides their suppers. And he ate so much in the storeroom he could not come thence without leaving behind what is not fit here to mention..,

The servants were not an unmixed blessing either! Elizabeth Rand refused to carry out instructions, complained about her Work, was reported to the committee, apologised and then negotiated with the Steward and his wife the basis of a return to work. Other servants employed as teachers were given detailed directions for the schoolmaster and schoolmistress to observe.

The Steward had to negotiate his own salary with the committee and produced papers to justify his requests. In 1720 he wrote to the committee:

Friends, It's not pleasant to use this to apply, yet think ourselves under a necessity to let you understand that we are not thoroughly satisfied with our present salary, it being now going on nine years since we came to serve the committee. . . .

He had been engaged for £20 per annum in 1711, which was increased to £25 next year and to £30 in 1714. He felt that he deserved more than the £40 paid since 1719. In 1725 he asked for £60 arguing that this was for the service of two people, that they had no other income, had no time for other employment and had improved the reputation of the house. He reminded the committee of his duties: buying wool, spinning yarn, trading in spun yarn, keeping accounts, drawing bills, clothing the family, buying provisions. The committee agreed that he deserved £60, but in February decided to advance £10 now and £10 some time after, as that would be easier for them than to find £20 at one time. Richard Hutton renewed his case and in September

1725 the committee agreed to the full £60.

. . . .in consideration of his care and pains with respect to the trade and his wife's conduct and service in the family, ... himself and his wife having assured us that they will not at anytime hereafter ask any farther advance to said salary and that they will continue their service so long as they live and are able.

There are several entries that relate to the finances of the house. The Steward:
negotiated the price of bread
(8s 6d per hundredweight),
recorded the costs of supplying clothes for members of the family
(26 new hats brought of Thomas Pittflow £2 12s),
and entered schedules of the earnings and gains from the work of the children *(earnings and gains over 12 years £2590 3s 6 $\frac{1}{4}$d).*

When John Wilson was sick, he received a special diet. Over six months his supply of 71 oysters cost 10d and $1\frac{3}{4}$ lbs of chocolate cost 6s $1\frac{1}{2}$d. There is an estimate for repairs of the Workhouse at Clerkenwell, which was not new when Friends leased it.

*Ripping and tiling the whole in the
same form as it is now in, being
158 square at 15s per square   £118.10s
Materials and carpenter's
work shoring and repairing
the rafters and eaves boards   £20.00s
                                    £148.10s*

The house made its own beer to provide sufficient for the inmates. Richard Hutton tells us how.

Take about 2 ounces of the finest & clearest isinglass beat or cut very small, put it into an earthen vessel with as much vinegar. . . . as will cover the isinglass. Brush it very well with a whisk twice or thrice a day till it be quite dissolved & as it grows thick put a little more vinegar to it till it becomes a very thick syrup, then strain through a cloth about a pint thereof, ...Then open the bung of the cask. With a whisk then pour in the strained isinglass, stirring it very well also & bung the cask very close & in 24 hours your drink will be very clear.

There is a recipe for a lotion to apply to sore eyes and a recipe to deal with an incipient problem, bedbugs.

Take of the highest rectified spirit of wine. . . . half a pint; newly distilled oil or spirit of turpentine, half a pint; mix them together and break into it, in small bits, half an ounce of camphor, which will dissolve in it in a few minutes. Shake them well together, and with a sponge. . . . wet very well the bed or furniture wherein those vermin harbour or breed, and it will infallibly kill and destroy both them and their nits. . . .

A paper of this length cannot do full justice to the riches in the Complaints Book. Together, the entries give a comprehensive view of the issues involved in managing an institution in the eighteenth century. It was a community of old and young, the ancients needing shelter, support and some nursing, the children needing nurture, learning and some training. But it is also a human document about a family. Individuals come vividly to life: mischievous John Gorden, cantankerous William Townsend, grumbling William Brady and grateful Thomas Sands. So also, despite his dry, sometimes long-winded reports, does the Steward: anxious, serious, diligent, meticulous, purposeful, determined that the inmates should have comfort and no cause for complaint within the house and concerned that the committee should promote its reputation for fairness and good-order without. Surely the institution is able to celebrate its tercentenary partly because Richard Hutton established such a firm foundation in those early years between 1711 and 1737.

John Woods was a Student at the School from 1941 to 1949 and Headmaster from 1968 to 1989

A short account of the last annual treat given to the children of Croydon School

by Albert J Edmunds
Copied by E Freelove

Many memories of the old school will be treasured up by those who have known and loved it, and few, perhaps, more so than the remembrance of our grand old "treats". I would fain use the more polished word "excursions", but "treat" is a Croydon word; therefore I stick to it.

Though in times of greater wealth we were wont to have these outings twice a year instead of once (though they were called "annual treats" all the same), yet those which we do get now are as good as ever; and the one which I am going to speak of now is reckoned by most the best we have ever had. Looking back over thirteen years, I cannot pick out a time when the great bulk of children and teachers more thoroughly enjoyed themselves than we did at Brighton, on a day that will live long in memory, June the Tenth, 1879.

Some Croydon Friends had made up their minds that we should wind up our days at this school with an excursion that should be remembered, and we most heartily own that they have won their end. Owing to their kindness we set out, on the morning of the day aforesaid, to ride to Brighton.

One of them, Henry Tylor, was kind enough to be with us and help in the doings of the day, as did also his daughters. So we met him at Brighton. The day settled on was made on purpose for us, as it has been before; for both the former and the following days were showery. But this day was sunny all through. Great cliffs of cloud were piled up on the horizon as we whirled along, but they sank and sank, till only a few lonely scrolls could be seen against the bright blue of summer. Having taken some lunch at the meeting house, we made for the Aquarium where a pleasant hour was spent in watching "the monsters of the deep at their uncouth gambols". The sea-lions roared, porpoises floundered, alligators winked, sea anemones lay in stillness in the waters, and a hundred other things did a hundred things, which we will not linger to tell.

On leaving those shadowy courts, the main body of the boys went to bathe, while the girls went out and enjoyed the sight of the open sea for an hour, receiving from kind hands a recompense for not being able to bathe. The bathing, it should be said, was not in the sea, but in closed baths. Then followed dinner at the meeting house, at which the tables were decked with shining rows of flowers. After which the meal - the children were very pleased when they were told that they might help themselves there to which they did without stint, as many of their buttonholes bore witness for the rest of the day. Oranges freely given round were also prized by them.

This done, we all got into wagonettes, and started for a place called by the darkened heathenish name of "Devil's Dyke". Though the road thither was not through the most enchanting country, yet it was enlivened by the lively youthfulness of lively youth, and was not long in being passed. Then burst upon our sight the long, long stretch of country that sweeps northward and westward from the Dyke; it broke upon us in the twinkling of an eye – an overwhelming sight to such as had not witnessed it before. On the hill-top were sundry kinds of sports, into which many entered with much warmth, while a few strolled in quietness along the slope to watch and gaze upon the scene which nature had spread out for them.

Tea-time came, and in a small grassy close we took the evening meal, as the sunbeams came shining sweetly and softly through the leaves that hedged us in round about. After tea, three lusty cheers were sent ringing into the summer air for the kind Friend who had been helping us so busily, and one more for the others who had done the same. A few more minutes were spent at the Dyke. Some went tearing ... wildly down it, where it pitches straight into the plain, like an earthen wall, while the greater deal were content to look on at these neck-riskers.

The sun was now lowering its head and lighting up the endless plain with those lovely beams which summer evenings alone know the glory of. We got again into the wagonettes and journeyed Brighton-wards, the sea lying to our right, pale and smooth and silent. Except that a tired member tried to break his toe, the homeward ride was as pleasant as the outset, and we all got safely to the station.

A ride of forty miles in the fair white light of a fine June day, whose beams came spiking from the unclouded west, and glowing through thousands of trees into our carriage windows as we flew northward wound up the day, and I am sure that the "three cheers for Henry Tylor" which had long ago died away on the slopes of the mighty Dyke, had not died away in our thankful hearts.

Albert J Edmunds' dates at the School appear to be 1866-1873 and he was living in Philadelphia in 1914.

Eleanor J Freelove, who copied out the story in beautiful copperplate handwriting, was at the School 1887-1891. She lived in Kingston-on-Thames.

Principal Building Developments 1879 - 2002

Roger Buss
FSSWOSA Archivist

Introduction

It is interesting to note that, despite all the developments that have taken place on the School site, the exterior of the main building is immediately recognisable as the same structure that was designed by Edward Burgess about 125 years ago.

The basic information in this article, comes mainly from two sources. These are the annual reports presented by the Heads and Governing Body to the School's parent body, the London and Middlesex Quarterly (now General) Meeting, and from reports published in the Annual Reports of the Old Scholars' Association.

In general only the larger extensions and additions to the school premises are described. Smaller works are not included and neither are the internal alterations made to the original building or to subsequent buildings, except in a few cases. Many parts of the fabric have undergone changes of use if not physical alteration, sometimes more than once. These changes were often the result of and complemented the concurrent major building projects. Such changes have progressively improved the School and the careful planning that was required to implement them should not be underestimated.

Visible objects with links with the School's past are described in Farrand Radley's article.

NOTE: *The numbers in square brackets refer to position on the plan opposite*

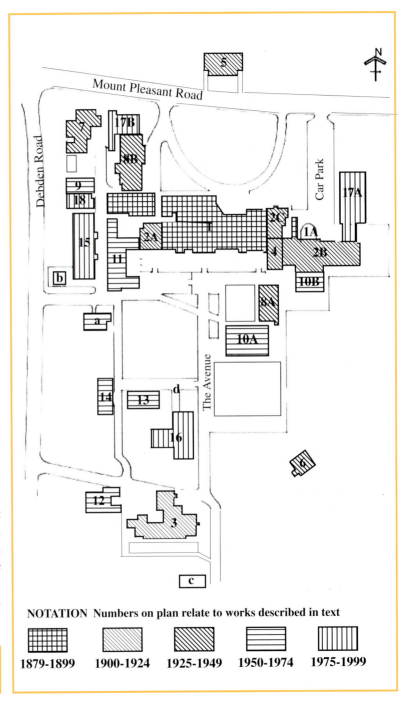

NOTATION Numbers on plan relate to works described in text

1879-1899   1900-1924   1925-1949   1950-1974   1975-1999

The Principal Building Developments
The move to Saffron Walden

There were serious outbreaks of typhoid fever in 1875, which followed other epidemics; the threat to health demanded a radical solution. Farrand Radley, in his article, explains the reasons for the choice of Saffron Walden. The School Committee (the forerunner of the Board of Governors) felt "the liberality of George (Stacey) and Deborah Gibson in presenting the land required for the School should be recorded and gratefully acknowledged". The availability of a supply of clean water from the adjacent reservoir was probably also an important consideration. David Bolam (in *Unbroken Community*) comments that almost without the Committee knowing it, he (George Stacey Gibson) had a school dining room planned, more baronial in size or style than many of the Friends' would have approved. Incidentally, the original balcony in the hall provided the access from the boys' side to the only baths in the building.

A further 10 acres (4 ha) of land was purchased for £2060. The total outlay, including land, was £30,400, nearly all of which was provided by the sale of the estate at Croydon which realised £27,800.

Progress on the "New Schools in Saffron Walden"[1], "which are arranged for 150 children" (90 boys and 60 girls) was reported (tender price £16,545). There were, indeed, two separate sets of teaching accommodation. In the event there were 58 boys and 32 girls when the School opened in the new premises in August 1879. The architect was Edward Burgess (1847-1929), a Quaker who had attended Bootham School in York. He also designed the nearby former teacher training college in South Road (now Bell Language School), the former grammar school in Ashdon Road (now Dame Bradbury School) and the extensions to Saffron Walden Town Hall. The builders of the school were Wm Bell & Sons (est. 1794) a local firm which carried out work all over East Anglia (colleges, churches etc).

Bedford Lemere 1920s

Bedford Lemere 1920s

Three Major Schemes at the turn of the Century

At the end of the 19th Century, a chemistry laboratory was provided in 1892 and music teaching and practice rooms and a darkroom were constructed at the boys' (east) end (completed 1898) [1A]. In 1899 the need for a swimming bath and gymnasium and for accommodation for teachers of both sexes was reported. Edward Burgess was again the architect. An appeal for £7000 was launched and about £8000 was raised by donations. The resulting schemes were: -

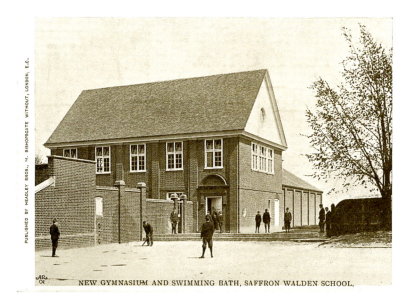
NEW GYMNASIUM AND SWIMMING BATH, SAFFRON WALDEN SCHOOL.

- an extension comprising classroom, workshop, dormitory and four staff studies and bedrooms [2A] at the girls' (west) end, completed in 1901.

- the gymnasium and indoor swimming bath [2B] completed in 1902, the School's Bicentenary. The inscription on a plaque recorded the contribution made to this by Old Scholars. The chalk from the excavations for the bath was used to make the bank running between the school field and Mount Pleasant Road. The chlorinating plant was added in 1936. Substantial repairs were carried out to the bath roof in 1949 as it had deteriorated because of intensive use by the US Air Force during the war. The gymnasium became a drama studio in 1984 when the sports hall was completed.

- At the boys' (east) end, the Masters' Block, Science Laboratories and Lecture Room and a Workshop [2C] were completed in 1903.

The total cost of the three schemes was about £12,000.

The "New Hospital"
The health of pupils was a major anxiety for the School Committee until the separate sanatorium [3] building was completed in 1913 as a variety of diseases were commonplace and serious. Although unlike the main building in appearance, this was also designed by Edward Burgess and was built by Wm. Bell & Sons. It cost about £3200 and was funded by gifts of about £2600. Old Scholars provided part of the furniture. It was built on part of the land given to the School by James B Crosfield. In the influenza epidemic of 1919, when 150 scholars and 18 adults were affected, the 'San' proved its value. The building became Gibson House (named after the original benefactor, George Stacey Gibson), a boarding house for junior boys, in 1966 when a new sanatorium was erected (see below). It now accommodates part of the Junior Department.

A "Building Scheme"
In order to meet Board of Education accommodation requirements the School Committee commissioned Fred Rowntree and Ralph W Thorpe, architects, to prepare plans for two classrooms and an art room [4] on the site of the Fives Court at the boys' end. Appeals for building funds were made in 1921 and 1923 and this block was completed in 1922 (cost of this and related works was £15,000). The builders were Wm Bell and Sons. It is interesting to note that at one time Fred Rowntree worked for Edward Burgess. He also designed a number of Friends' Meeting Houses and works at various schools as well as the Quaker village of Jordans in Buckinghamshire.

Better Living Quarters
At the beginning of the 1920s, a pair of semi-detached houses opposite the school in Mount Pleasant Road was purchased. The first (west) was used to accommodate the Headmaster and his family. The second (east) was adapted as a hostel for 20 girls. The combined building was called *Hillcroft* [5]. Subsequently, in 1937, another house, adjoining the school field, *Robin's Acre*, was purchased for the new

The San   *Bedford Lemere 1920s*

Hillcroft *Bedford Lemere 1930s*

Headmaster and the remainder of Hillcroft adapted for scholars and staff. Robin's Acre in 1991 was sold and Hillcroft in 1994.

A Sporting Gesture

The Cricket Pavilion [6] was a gift of the Old Scholars' Association in 1925 and paid for by an appeal. It cost £400. The architect was Paul Mauger FRIBA MRTPI DipTP (Lond) (died 1982), a former pupil (1906-13) and President of the Old Scholars Association in 1939/40. In addition to other work for the School, his career covered private houses, housing schemes and churches and he was in demand as an adviser on town and country planning. He was greatly respected by Saffron Walden Borough Council, for which he designed housing estates.

A Major Venture for the Jubilee

The School Committee decided to mark 50 years at Saffron Walden with an appeal for £1200, later raised to £1900 (donations totalled £1920). The Committee had identified the lack of a preparatory school for the under 10s. Flint House (1840) at the corner of the estate came on to the market. It was an ideal site, and was purchased, altered and extended to form the Junior School [7]. Architects, Johns and Slater of Ipswich, designed the extensions. The school was opened in September 1930 with eight boys (six boarders) and five girls and by 1933 was full (thirteen boarders and thirteen day scholars). As a result of plans for the two-stream School made in 1946 (see below) it was decided that, because of the need for more accommodation for the main school, the Junior School should be closed. Thereafter the premises were renamed Croydon House after the former site of the School and used for domestic science and needlework teaching and a mistresses' study on the ground floor and as bedrooms for girls on the first floor. More recently the use has changed again to accommodation for sixth formers.

Science and the Arts

In 1935 Trustees of the Islington Road Estate, where the School was formerly situated, handed over the School's share of the capital sum arising from the termination of the 148-year lease of 0.7ha (1.75 acres) of property. This made it possible for the School Committee to consider the provision of some needed extensions of the premises (£39,000 was realised). A building programme to include a biology laboratory and geography room [8A] (tender price £1998) and a School assembly hall [8B] (seating 500) (tender price £4238) were sanctioned. The architects for both schemes were Johns & Slater (Martin J Slater FRIBA was at the time of these projects Chairman of the Suffolk Association of Architects). Both projects were completed in 1936. As a result, the former Lecture Room in the centre of the School was converted into a library (designed by Paul Mauger).

Cricket Pavilion *Donald Peverett 1925*

Assembly Hall Interior Bedford Lemere c1936

Post-War Optimism

A report, following a full Board of Education inspection of the School in 1940, made some favourable comments but stated that day rooms and recreation rooms were badly needed and that classrooms could not serve a double purpose. In 1945, the Post-War Development Committee considered plans for a two stream school giving a school population of 240 up to School Certificate age and a 6th form of about 30 (with about 25% day pupils). It was recognised that this would require a considerable building programme to provide adequate living and teaching accommodation. Kenneth Bayes of the Design Research Unit (DRU) was appointed as architect. The DRU, formed in 1943, was at about this time involved in design work for the Britain Can Make It Exhibition (1946) and the Festival of Britain, South Bank Exhibition (1951).

Provisional plans for the school extensions, mainly a group of buildings on the field near to Mount Pleasant Road, were approved in principle in 1946. The architect's report commented that the existing accommodation was far below, in terms of both size and convenience, that recognised as desirable. A 42% increase in accommodation was estimated to be needed. The building designs were in a modern style and a report stated: "I hope that when Old Scholars see the interesting drawings they will like the freshness of the scheme and not be put off by the departure from what has so far been thought of as Friends' School architecture." An appeal, the *Post-War Fund for Extension and Modernisation*, was launched in 1947/8. This sought £35,000 for the first stage but only £12,000 was raised. In the event the scheme was not implemented. Major improvements, resulting from earlier proposals, were carried out to the kitchens in 1949-50.

More Teaching Space

Although no progress was made with the major scheme, it was decided to initiate a limited appeal. This was to fund the provision of two additional classrooms [9], which were required because of the increased numbers in the School and pressure on space, and also towards the refurnishing of some classrooms to make them better fitted for service as living rooms as well as classrooms. These classrooms, to the west of the assembly hall, were completed in 1950 and used by the junior forms. Flint faced concrete blocks were used in the construction to reflect the appearance of Croydon House. In 1967 the classrooms were transformed into craft, design and technology (CDT) workshops and an extension was erected in 1987. At the same time as the erection of the classrooms, a house (The Laurels, 55 Debden Road)[a], designed by Kenneth Bayes, was constructed for the Bursar. It is now occupied by the Head and his family.

New Science Facilities and Changing Room

Paul Mauger was appointed architect for a new block "in the middle of what is left of the boys' playground" to accommodate chemistry and physics laboratories [10A], and also for the girls' changing room block [10B] attached to the swimming bath. These two projects, estimated cost £16,800, were both completed in 1955. The Friends' Education Committee made a grant of £9000. The physics laboratory was gutted by fire during its first term of use. Insurance covered the cost of renewal. These science laboratories were extensively rebuilt and refurbished in the summer of 2000 at a cost of £225,000.

The Largest Extension to the Original Building

A review in 1957 resulted in a further building programme for "more accommodation for (i) feeding, (ii) teaching and (iii) sleeping". Extra bedroom accommodation was constructed for boys in the roof space in 1959. In the same year it was decided to build a new classroom block with an art room and staff common room, on the south side of the main building, at an estimated cost of £40,000. Kenneth Bayes was the architect. An appeal, *The Development Fund Campaign* was launched. The building was completed in 1961 at a cost of £35,864. The block was later named the Essex Wing [11] in recognition of the grant of £25,000 made by Essex Education Committee.

The Essex Wing — *John Maltby c1961*

A Medical Centre and More Classrooms

In 1964 the Building Development Committee was considering what could be done with the limited funds available to it. Subsequently approval was given to the construction of a new and smaller sanatorium, in order to convert the existing one into a junior house for 35-40 boys, and the building of 4 classrooms on a site to the south of the Essex Wing. In addition the workshops were to be transferred to the 1950 classrooms. The New Sanatorium [12], with 14 beds was completed in 1966 and the Sanatorium became Gibson House. The new classrooms designed by the Black, Bayes & Gibson partnership, and named Crosfield [13] after a family which had given much service to the School, were completed in 1967. These works were partly funded by an appeal, partly by a grant of £5,000 by Essex Education Committee, and the remainder (£30,000) by a loan from the Friends' Provident and Century Life Office. After completion, the structure of the first floor of Crosfield showed signs of crumbling. This was as a result of the use of high-alumina cement in its construction. It was closed for repairs during 1974.

Recycled Buildings

The old Water Tower (built in 1913) [b] adjoining Debden Road and the adjacent reservoir (constructed in 1862) became redundant and were purchased by the School in 1968. The cost was £250 plus legal expenses. In the same year, temporary classrooms, which had originally been part of a group of wartime buildings erected at the Isolation Hospital in Hilltop Lane, and were sited near the Water Tower, were moved to a site near Crosfield and adapted and improved. They provided a room for Girl Guides and a Music Room [14] that was named after Helen Radley in special memory of this former devoted member of the staff.

The *Appeal for the 70s* launched in 1971 sought to raise £60,000 for the conversion of the reservoir into a recreation centre and to build a new Teaching Block (see below). The target was reached in 1972 (partly as a result of a share of the proceeds from the sale of Junior House School at Walden Grove) but the money raised did not cover the combined costs (£77,000). The remainder was financed from School funds. The architect for both the reservoir conversion and the new Teaching Block was Philip M Cowell MA FRIBA AIArb of Bedford.

The Reservoir Recreation Centre [15] was completed in 1975. In 1991 it was transformed into an art exhibition area - The Octopus Gallery.

Specialist Teaching Rooms

A new teaching block to the south of Crosfield containing six specialised classrooms (two Modern Languages, two Mathematics, one History, one English) was completed in 1975. It was named Leicester [16] in memory of Mark Leicester one of the generous benefactors to the School at Saffron Walden. The Head commented that the completion of this Teaching Block would result in the final separation of academic and recreation areas as envisaged in the 1940s.

The Reservoir (now the Octopus Gallery) — *Farrand Radley c1970*

The Croydon Gate

The wrought iron gate [d], the sole survivor of the School's former premises at Croydon following World War II, was installed, between new brick piers which reproduced the original ones, close to the garden surrounding Leicester and formally re-opened in 1976. The gate, a fine example of 18th century craftsmanship, is described by Farrand Radley in his article.

Two Big Projects

The highest priority identified in the early 80s, and the subject of the subsequent appeal, was the provision of indoor sports facilities (estimated cost £275,000) and for accommodation where the work of the music department could be co-ordinated under one roof (estimated cost £175,000). The *Appeal for the Eighties* sought to raise £175,000, which was surpassed by at least £5000, towards the eventual total cost of £524,848. The sale of the land to the south of Gibson House and the medical centre, which was not used or required by the School, raised £208,000 at auction. The Sports Hall [17A] and Music School [17B] were both completed in 1984. They were designed by the architects Jolly and Millard (B H Jolly & R E Millard, had their head office in Bishop's Stortford and designed a variety of projects). The main room in the Music School has taken the name Radley from the former building.

Bursar, Eric Brown,..by the Croydon Gate (1976)
Cambridge Evening News

The new Sports Hall, completed 1984. Compare this with the illustration on page eighteen.

Continuing Developments

An addition to the 1950 classrooms, that had been converted into workshops, to provide a further CDT building (Craft, Design, Technology) [18] was completed in 1987. Gibson House was adapted to accommodate the new Junior Department in 1992. This department expanded to take over the whole of the former Medical Centre building in 1995. The result of this was a return of medical facilities to the main school building. The most recent major projects were the works to the science laboratories (already referred to) and the works to the swimming bath, which were the subject of the tercentenary appeal. The roof of the swimming bath was reconstructed in 2000.

With acknowledgements to Richard Wright, Margaret Brinkworth, Martin Hugall and Farrand Radley and special thanks to Eric Brown for advice and many informative insights.

Of Flu, Flight and Apple Pie

At the end of the 1914-18 War came the 'Flu Epidemic. Nearly all the School succumbed, only about six of the boys escaping. Stanley Pumphrey, who had served throughout the war on ambulance trains in northern France, returned to his post as Science Master, just in time to render sterling service as a ward orderly, while Dorothea Waring, the boys' Matron, was tireless. A big supply of oranges came the School's way, the gift of Mr Welch. No child in the School died in that epidemic. Dr John Atkinson, the School's Medical Officer, attended conscientiously. When an inspector from the Government, visiting the School on his sad rounds, enquired brusquely "How many have you lost?", Dr John squared up to him, in broad Essex mode, and replied "None, and we ain't a-goin' to!"

Shortly after the end of the War, about 1919, a light single-seater biplane (of the sort used in the War) landed on the School Field. Coming from the direction of the Isolation Hospital the pilot espied this welcome extent of grass, and landed, having lost his way to Duxford. It was most timely of him to arrive during morning recess. We all rushed over to see the plane, and he was given directions, in effect "straight on, mate ". So one or two boys swung the propeller for the pilot, and he took off, aiming for the gap between the last house in Mount Pleasant Road and the 'pepper pot' windmill. He cleared the road, but only by a modest margin, and we assumed he got to Duxford all right as we heard no more of him. It is amazing to recall how short a runway those slow old-fashioned planes needed in order to become airborne.

One prank went too far. Four boys collected one of Turner's long ladders, propping it up from the (then) drying ground (behind the laundry) and against a window in the girls' long corridor. One boy held the ladder, two 'kept cavey', while the fourth made his way to the Headmistress' bedroom where he made her an Apple-pie bed. So far so good, but Lucy Fairbrother, Headmistress since 1894 and no great enthusiast for coeducation, was outraged when she discovered the happening. No member of staff condoned this exploit, and the perpetrator was identified and sent home forthwith. To his credit, he did not split on his accomplices.

Henry Rowntree

Memories of the 1920s

Fire Drills
We were warned when this would take place. If the bell sounded at night we put on dressing gowns and shoes and were led across the upper landing through a door onto a grating between the roofs, though another door to the boys' side, down their stairs to the playground where our names were called.

On a lighter note, one evening some girls found that the door to the fire escape was unlocked. They took some mugs of water and were able to reach the "pit "bedroom on the boys' side and gave them a soaking. This escapade was never discovered or if it was, no action taken.

Discipline
This was based on self-discipline. We were encouraged to respect everyone and the environment. It was therefore understood that we were in honour to obey rules. (This was a very hard concept, especially for the very young). Offences from this were gently reprimanded by Miss Priestman the Head with "I'm surprised at you, you of all people". Smaller offences were given "words" 5-10-20. If the total amounted to 20 in a week, we had to write out words from a spelling book a hundred times.

Pocket Money
Each term we were allowed to take 16s pocket money and this was given out on a Saturday morning. We presented our account book and could withdraw 3d for sweets and 3d for fruit, (total 2.5p in modern money) This money also paid for subscriptions for any society we belonged to and for pens, pencils, nibs, etc (all exercise books were provided). We had to keep 2s so that at the end of term we could pay for our luggage to get home.

Quarantine
If we were in quarantine for any infectious disease, a list was made for sweets and fruit and two prefects went and collected them from Mrs Fitch's shop where they would be made up into little packages and individually labelled.

Cicely Rawlings

1930-1948
Junior House

Friends' School

for pupils aged seven to ten

In 1990

Jean Stubbs

collected memories from over forty of them, covering the whole period, which she then used to write a Supplement for the FSSW OSA Annual Report. She has based this article on that earlier record.

Throughout its existence the children's impressions of the life at Junior House in the company of the resident adults shows a striking consistency – it was "a happy school where time passed quickly", lessons merged into activities, and communal mealtimes moulded friendships.

The junior school opened in the autumn of 1930 – a knapped flint and grey brick house, standing squarely in its garden, high above the Debden Road corner: lawn, backyard, kitchen garden, orchard; a pump, no longer in working order, by the scullery door.

With the Teacher Jeanne Barrie, Margaret Stubbs the Matron-Housekeeper, six boy boarders, two day-boys, five day-girls – lessons commenced, using Senior School space.

Meanwhile foundations for the redbrick extension were laid and building went ahead. By Easter 1931 the playground had been levelled and concreted, also the backyard after a second well shaft had been discovered – and filled.

The Summer Term 1931 brought Joyce Harris the Headmistress, and two girls to board in the increased space. The ground floor now had additionally two classrooms, a cloakroom, extended dining area – and the covered way with its three fire-buckets.

Rapidly numbers grew to full complement of over thirty children, thirteen of them boarders fairly divided between boys and girls. The school flourished through peace and war, but the plans for further enlargement were never carried out; and eventually the 1944 Education Act, with the 11+ entrance, obliged the School Committee to review and alter the nature of the main School, absorbing the premises, which were renamed Croydon House.

The four years of transition up to 1948 saw the Intermediate Class, with Betty Morland as teacher, accommodating the ten-year-olds; Joyce Harris married and left in 1946; then Margaret Stubbs retired, and in 1948 Jeanne Barrie set up independently in the town, forming Junior House School.

Junior House itself from the word go in 1930 became a viable entity – several of the children had siblings in the main School, and subsequent new entrants were rapidly absorbed. Play in the sandpit or a special welcome in mid-term overcame initial shyness and offered security. Some were refugees from oppression; others, later, were escaping the air-raids. Home-sickness was rare, and treated with sympathy – and chocolate! Only a few never felt at ease.

Classroom walls dutifully displayed charts with 'stars' marking progress at multi-plication tables, and bore illustrations of the three principal styles of Greek architecture. Shelves at the back were stocked with reading books . . .

The day began with Morning Assembly – one of the boys, a skilful pianist, accompanying the hymns: Songs of Praise (and when a note couldn't be reached with his fingers he played it with his nose.)

Throughout, the impact was on the imagination, not the intellect: learning to spell, moving up or down a line according to one's prowess; making things with Miss

The new extension in 1931
Standing in front are l-r
A visitor, Tom Marsh, Stephen Mattingly,
David Prentice, Jean Lyons, Catherine Webb,
James Brereton, Harold Mattingly,
John Dewhurst

Barrie – a robin's pincushion or ornaments out of beech mast; decorating poems with letters in coloured crayons and producing loops in f's and b's to the rhythm of the wind-up gramophone; doing a map of the classroom; making models of the Market Stalls complete with fruit and groceries; forming farmyard animals from soggy bread squeezed into shape and painted; studying the coal-fields of Britain, producing a single handwritten copy of a Form Magazine, striking flints to burn autumn leaves, or cooking flapjacks; growing hyacinths in vases; sowing carrot seeds; gardening at Hillcroft; learning to weave, in winter; refusing to play on the triangle one day during a thunderstorm; sports on the lawn (which was usually out of bounds); giving puppet shows with homemade puppets or miming while the choir sang; or again, Music and Movement on the wireless with Ann Driver! Lessons were easy and relaxed, expanding into leisure activities.

In addition to Music Teachers – Stanley Thorne who came over for singing lessons and Miss Bird who gave piano lessons to some in her School Study – the main School lent facilities and staff for Art, Gym, Games and Swimming, for which the children recall the long trek to and fro via School asphalts or playgrounds. A keen swimmer learnt from Barney Jacob how to lob one's arms for maximum pull in the crawl, and 'a lady in a wet-suit' sometimes assisted Jeanne Barrie with the beginners. Stanley King Beer even used the Field for history rambles (and they found out how cavemen set traps for animals).

The main School also invited Junior House to Saturday evening Films which included *Captains Courageous*, and once to a Gilbert and Sullivan concert. They themselves produced *Hiawatha* and a mime on the Lawn Tennis Court. Even *Doctor Dolittle* was enacted, the boy being cast as Jip having a very realistic costume which itched, so that in one respect acting was automatic.

Memories run on: the rest period after dinner – day-scholars confined to the big classroom, boarders on their beds with books (and three sweets from their tins). 'Bouncing', a silent joy, led to broken springs, charged at sixpence each on school bills.

War-time with the blackout: window-panes criss-crossed with strips of old sheeting pasted on to protect from flying glass; blast-proof walls and sandbags – Aircraft activity; searchlights at night; Joyce Harris's study transferred upstairs and beds brought down into the front room where the ceiling was reinforced with planks supported on pine-trunks; gas-masks always at hand in their small boxes with carrying strings . . .

At table good manners included looking after one's neighbour – and expecting reciprocated attention; however, 'one brown slice first, before the white' was an irksome rule; nor was war-time diet all that interesting; but overall, food was pronounced to be good and a birthday occasioned personal choice – Mrs Stubbs's sausages and mash, then All Bran cakes with golden syrup; or, for one, toad-in-the-hole and bubble-and-squeak followed by chocolate pudding with chocolate sauce! Two day children could also be invited to tea.

Margaret Stubbs was Matron as well as Housekeeper: she watched over health and hygiene on the principle of 'what one needed, all got'. Once, when colds were particularly prevalent, this applied to mustard baths; similarly, when *Snow White and the Seven Dwarfs* came to the cinema, they went to see it – all sucking throat pastilles. Snuffling salty water was a panacea; and senna pods existed, as in the main School. Accidents occurred now and then, from which roller-skating was not immune. Witch-hazel for mere bruises; the doctor called in when stitches were needed – once for a hand, another time for a leg. Falling from a tree caused a broken arm; disturbing a wasps' nest during a walk occasioned a mass arrival of casualties at the San; a bad cold usually led to a few days in the sick-room; or a fever, to that lovely ride on a stretcher to the San for a week or so . . . Mrs Stubbs to the rescue: of course they were fond of her – she was always so kind (they said) – so lovely to them all . . .

Joyce Harris was Headmistress from 1931 to 1946. Her reports were searching, at times reproving, perhaps requiring a more serious effort. Yet, balancing any criticism, the children had the joy of being allowed to raid her bookshelves, the delight of listening to *Swallows and Amazons* or *The Far Distant Oxus*, on Sunday evenings, or the treat of her musical box with its endless tunes.

. . . And, all things considered, they judged that the four staff truly complemented each other, being fair and kind and working in well together as a good and dedicated team.

It was, however, Jeanne Barrie who won all hearts: who had wax fruit in her room that looked real, and a bed that folded upwards into a curtained cupboard; a canvas-strap fire-escape from her tall window lowered everybody one by one during practices. She cheered one child up with chocolate, or helped another over reading difficulties with extra tuition. She was, they said, a veritable presence, an almost larger-than-life, caring, loving and jolly person, whom they certainly loved dearly. . .

They recalled her reading them *Biggles*

and *Doctor Dolittle* on Sunday evenings, and bagging her hands for Sunday afternoon walks, so that they could listen to her stories – or sitting at her table at dinner and playing word-games, geography and spelling in particular; she taught them how to walk on stilts and entered into their games of marbles, sevenses, waves, tincan, rounders. She encouraged their first efforts on roller-skates, admired their fine marble-runs in the sandpit and enjoyed their exploits in racing their model yachts. No wonder they remembered her.

Moreover she kept two goats which lived in the orchard and grazed on the old Reservoir or along the New Avenue. One job was helping to look after them. A parent made them kennels, and tethers which had to be moved daily; he also taught one or two how to milk. Eventually, they were mated and produced kids.

But the Walks! Setting off in a crocodile and then the freedom of romping over the fields, playing lovely imaginative games . . . the Copse, the Battle Ditches, the Park, the Mazes, the Dungeon, the Claypits, Everlasting Walk, the Beeches; picking blackberries for jam, gathering sweet chestnuts and roasting them at Mrs Stubbs's gas-fire and, of course, collecting conkers for the goats.

Some were inveterate collectors: stamps, caterpillars, the Claypits' burnet moth cocoons – a vapourer moth caterpillar, carefully fondled all the way back to Junior House, brought the bearer out in a rash. The Claypits were a treasure trove with the deep pond, its water-boatmen and newts. . . .

They did not feel over-supervised, but were free to be themselves: one brought a live crab back, and recalled watching the lightning strike the conductor on the Water Tower; two set up a club to protect the weak from bullying; another, sitting under the trees in the orchard, committed to memory *The Walrus and the Carpenter*; some, on a wintry walk, made a huge snowball, rolling it all the way back; or again peeled and ate the beech nuts which fell from the magnificent tree against the wall. . .

Wednesday shopping outings – when threepences would purchase ice-creams or marbles; day-scholars inviting boarders round to play, or for tea; one mother's unforgettable Hallowe'en Parties; and at Junior House making faces from pumpkins and lanterns from turnips, bobbing for apples, hunting for ghosts outside after dark. . . .

Indoor games figured at all seasons, with fun groups; and listening to *Children's Hour*: Uncle Mac, *War of the Worlds*, *Exploits of Professor Challenger and his Team*. . . .

On wet Sunday afternoons, the dining-room became a café, with desk-tops levelled for tables; menus, cardboard coins. . . . waitresses.

They were mostly out of doors: role-playing in the summer house; the backyard for marbles, sevenses or hopscotch; sandpit; the little pond. Sports, vigorous team games; football, cricket; also rounders and netball, in which all joined. . . .

But roller-skating for ever! And once mastered, joining in with the best, circling the playground, then fast through the gap into the back yard and twizzle round. Once one boy took a header into a fire-bucket.

Michael King Beer with goat

Joyce Harris (l) and Jeanne Barrie

Faces and scenes flooding back: the coconut through the post, the address painted on the husk; a parent providing bananas, unobtainable during the war; or another offering trips to Whipsnade and fireworks for November Fifth. . . . and those who staged a sit-in till Gerald Littleboy, having accepted their older daughter in the main School, also made space in Junior House for their younger one bargaining that she should meanwhile bring key skills up to standard.

What was it like, at an age when time stood still? To be always fully occupied, never lonely or bored. Day-scholars knew that their boarder friends were happy to be there. Adaptability flourished alongside a feeling of independence and freedom. All this allowed for resolving of personal anxieties, the reconstructing of lives, even while bending to the norm.

Perhaps adults rarely know what children are actually thinking, but there was stability and it could be felt. For the refugees this was a haven of kindness in a harsh, unpredictable and incomprehensible world; for a Jewish child, the two years in Junior House were a wonderfully happy time; for the parents of another, who had no Christian attachments, it was deemed the best form of Christianity to be found. All agreed that Junior House prepared one for life in the main School.

One former pupil wrote: "With so much of our lives strongly influenced by our experience before we are ten, the three years in Junior House must have been very significant" and again: "The relative triviality of our conscious memories must conceal deep and lasting impressions which steered our future".

The last and youngest of them all describes the Junior House experience as a purely happy time, coming as she did, at six, for the final term, from a large, scary school, to such a lovely place.

And Miss Barrie? We continue the quotation: "She was a remarkable person who definitely had a strong and very positive influence on us all. Large built, with a strong face, she did not have to command attention but got it without much effort. She did not lay down the law or talk down at us. Instead she explained everything even if this took a lot of time. Though we greatly respected and admired her we were able to communicate and ask questions, and she patiently and without any condescension responded, so that one can truthfully say there was dialogue between us.

"In this way she taught us the importance of being receptive to the views of others, and of the adjustments required to be made by individuals living in even the smallest social group. . . . The goats typified her desire to be in touch with the whole environment and to live a life of simplicity and integrity with Nature. . . . Jeanne Barrie was an unusually gifted and successful teacher, and I am glad to have this opportunity to record what she meant to me."

And so we salute a much-loved little school, opened in the time of Brightwen Rowntree – Mr Rowntree, still remembered by the children for his sprightly step when he came over to visit them all.

Peter Joselin's Memories of Junior House, 1942

I was just over eight when I started a boarder in Junior School in September 1942. When, later, we sang Forty Years On at end-of-term concerts, I never once thought that I would be writing this memoir sixty years on. Forty years was forever then and sixty years was unimaginable. How time flies!

One of my clearest memories of Junior House is the homesickness of the first few days. This lessened with time due to the kindness of the staff, but it didn't go completely all year, nor even for another couple of years. The boys' bedroom I was in was downstairs on the left at the bottom of the stairs. There were about half a dozen or so of us in the room. It had pine tree trunks, the bark still on them, which supported the ceiling in the hope that they would prevent the upper floor from collapsing in the event of a bomb hitting nearby. When I studied structural engineering some ten years later, I realised just how little support those quite flimsy props would have given had they ever been put to the test. Wooden blackout shutters and heavy curtains covered the windows each night. The girls had a similar bedroom down the hallway.

There was a playground on the south (water tower) side of the building with a fair sized sand pit in the south west corner. There was grass on the west side of the building and a border of shrubbery and small trees against the wall to Debden Road; good for playing in and on. From the wall at the corner of Debden and Mount Pleasant roads one could see down the hill towards town and see the smoke from the 'cranks' as they passed under the bridge. Train buffs start early in life! On Saturday afternoons we would all walk together, in file and in pairs, down the hill to town, but that memory may be from a year or two later, in Intermediate or Upper 3. At the corner where the road bears right to the War Memorial, was a sweet shop, on the far side of the road, where I used parts of many a monthly sweet ration. Those sweets, and anything else I might want, came out of the 10/- pocket money for each term that was given out a few pennies or a shilling at a time, on request each week. That pocket money also had to do for stamps for the compulsory letter home each week. It seems such a small pocket money amount now but I do not recall ever feeling really hard done by or penniless, although one had to be thrifty. There were also the Sunday afternoon walks, shorter in Junior School than in the upper school, around the countryside and across the fields.

I cannot recall anything particular about the food. No doubt we all thought it was terrible as it was boarding school and not our mother's cooking, but it couldn't have been that bad or one would remember it as being so. I guess it was because no food in wartime was that spectacular, even at home. And it was good enough to keep us regular, because after breakfast and bed making each day, there was an inspection by Matron of our performance.

In early December 1942 I came down with chickenpox. I remember being carried on a stretcher by two sixth formers under the trees, along Mistresses Walk, to the San. I was more concerned at having to stay there over Christmas than anything else. I know I had to miss the Squash (the train to London) home but how I did get home I don't recall. I suppose my mother had to come down for me because an eight-year-old *could not go by himself on a train, let alone cross London from Liverpool Street to London Bridge.*

I will always be grateful to the staff who looked after, and mothered, us and who did such a great job because, despite homesickness and other growing up pains, we returned for further years at Walden. Whatever we thought at the time, and there were many complaints and names for the School and the town, we must have loved it to be writing this book of memories of The School on the Hill *so many years later. I know I did. FSSW was a memorable experience I will never forget and I am sure all contributors and readers of this book feel likewise.*

Peter went on to get a B.Sc.(Eng.) degree from London University and a Fulbright Scholarship to the USA. He had asked to go to a university in New England but was sent to Tulane University in New Orleans. It worked well, however, for he was three years in the city, obtained an M.S. degree in structural engineering and married a New Orleanean. They now live near Niagara Falls, Canada. Their three daughters and four grandchildren also live in Canada. Peter's career was as a consulting engineer, mostly in hydroelectric power station design and power system planning. During that career he worked in or visited about 25 countries, including every country in eastern Africa south of the Sudan. He is now retired and lives near the south shore of Lake Ontario, where he sails in summer and curls in winter.

Jean Sleight

I was very grateful to FSSW for introducing me to the *Sunday Times* newspaper and to knitting on Sundays. I had a Methodist upbringing and neither Sunday newspapers, nor knitting, nor riding bicycles, were allowed on Sundays. Although we never had a Sunday newspaper at home, I was, after a term at FSSW, allowed to knit.

I remember an occasion when we were in our classroom at 11.00 am, in readiness for a lesson with Mr Hindle – possibly Geography or Biology. A note was passed round saying that, at 11.20, Harper would faint. This he duly did. It was, of course, to cause a diversion which we all enjoyed.

James Allward

Before War was declared (September 1939), time at FSSW was most pleasant. I remember being introduced to traditions such as:
- Bell ringing to get one up from bed before the last step down was accomplished – otherwise retribution!
- The House system and rivalry in sports, although I was never any good at them
- Audley End train station going home for the holidays
- Morning roll call in the big room around which our trunks were located
- "Words" for misdemeanours and heavier "detention" for more serious offences
- My first visit to an opera – the Barber of Seville, in Cambridge
- Walking "The Avenue" as a "couple" if one was successful with a fair young lady
- Late night swims in the pool
- The boys' 'Bogs' and woe betide anyone who locked themselves in the toilet.

Martin Michaelis
by his sister, Ruth

My brother, Martin Michaelis, and I talk of 'old times' every time we meet, which is several times a year in Germany or England, or sometimes halfway between. He has given me permission to write about his memories of the Friends' School.

Unlike me, Martin had already started school in Germany but had been taken away when it got dangerous (Jewish children were ridiculed and attacked) and had private lessons in English and about England. He had no difficulty in settling down at the Friends' School – it felt like a big family to him. He remembers coming to Junior House and fiddling with the radio to get it going – that was a knack he developed early! He was impressed by the lack of segregation and the encouragement of boys and girls working, eating and playing together.

He appreciated, particularly, that nobody forced him to do anything. The teachers were kindly and took trouble to explain and persuade. But he did find the punishments strange – if you gathered too many of a certain kind of 'mark' you had to sit in the classroom after class or were barred from games and treats like a fête.

Whereas the other children were eager for the holidays, he became depressed at the thought of leaving Friends' School for the holidays which neither of us relished at our foster-parents' home. We were both eager to come back at the beginnings of terms. He missed it so much when we left abruptly at the end of the summer term in 1943.

Out of curiosity, Martin attended the Reunion of the Wartime Generation in 1995. He enjoyed it and was moved beyond his expectations.

FSSW and the Friends' Ambulance Unit

Roger Bush

The Friends Ambulance Unit was founded during World War One, revived for World War Two and succeeded, in 1946, by the FAU Post-War Service, and in 1950 by the FAU International Service. At no time was it an official agency of the Society of Friends, though the young men and women who served in it shared the Quaker attitude to peace and war and sought to follow Quaker traditions of service. They were unpaid, receiving only their maintenance and a nominal pocket-money allowance. Among over 1000 members of the Unit in World War I, more than 1300 in World War II and a smaller number in the peacetime services, it is not surprising that there were many Old Scholars of Friends' Schools, including Saffron Walden. It's hard to trace them all today, forty-three years after the Unit ceased its activities, but in these pages are a few of the recollections of Walden Old Scholars who took up the challenge offered by this alternative to military service.

World War One

Sadly, the last FAU veteran of the First World War died in 1997, having reached the age of 101. He was Harold Holttum, who was at Walden from 1907 to 1911, as was his brother, Richard Eric, who also served in the FAU. The Holttums are, of course, a Walden family; both brothers were later Presidents of CSWOSA, and Harold's son John was at FSSW from 1941-43.

Other well-remembered names from that first flowering of the FAU are Gerald Littleboy and George Stanley Pumphrey, headmaster and science master respectively at the School during World War Two.

GSP is recorded in the 1914 OSA Report as one of a number of Old Scholars in the FAU who were at Dunkirk or are expecting to go shortly. Their names are listed beneath a longer list of those On His Majesty's Service, but in the following year the order was reversed. In wartime it was by no means easy to get this information together. Although the 1915 Report gave names and regiments for many of those in the Forces and listed others serving in the FAU and Friends War Victims' Relief Committee separately, by 1916 these distinctions had been dropped (and the order had been reversed again!). A more chatty 'Personalia' in the 1917 Report lists the Carrodus brothers (FSSW 1910-12) in France with the FAU and Kenneth Green (FSSW 1909-12), also in France "Driving a GMC British Car" for the Unit.

Another connection with the First World War emerges in the pages of Hunter Davies's book, *Born in 1900*, which includes a whole chapter on Dorothy Ellis. As Dorothy Robson she was at FSSW from 1912-15, returning as an assistant teacher three years later, before becoming one of the earliest women to study for a degree at Birmingham University. It was in Birmingham that she met and married Tom Ellis, who had served in the FAU. Their son, Michael Ellis, was in at the start of FAU International Service in 1950.

World War Two

A third pair of brothers from FSSW were in the revived FAU of the Second World War – John Harper (FSSW 1925-29) and Eric Robert (Bob) Harper (FSSW 1928-32). Bob Harper, who served in the Middle East, North Africa, Italy and France, was attached to the famous Hadfield Spears Unit, working with the Free French Forces in North Africa. He was part of a Poste Avancé at Bir Hacheim, site of a fierce siege, and was among those in the FAU awarded the Croix de Guerre. During his hot, dirty, dusty and dangerous duties in the desert, Bob, a keen mountain climber, cherished one unlikely ambition – to climb the Matterhorn. And, after the War, he did just that!

Roger Stanger's father, Percy Stanger, had served in the FAU during the First World War, and Roger (FSSW 1935-41) joined the Unit in 1943. He found himself part of one of the FAU teams that followed the Allied advance into Germany in 1945. At Bedburg, near the Dutch border, he was not far from the German lines and was nearly blown off his feet by a shell that landed nearby. He also recalls the alarming experience of crossing the Rhine on a Bailey bridge, trying desperately to keep his truck on the narrow tracks while shells were flying overhead. In North Germany his section of the FAU was later engaged in the clearing up of the concentration camp at Sandbostel, northeast of Bremen, where, besides some fifteen thousand prisoners of war, there were eight thousand political prisoners who were starving in appalling conditions. It was one of the grimmest jobs ever undertaken by the Unit.

Godric Bader (FSSW 1935-41) was an influence in Procter Le Mare's (FSSW 1934-41) decision to join the FAU, for they were great friends at School. After learning how to look after motor vehicles as well as hospital patients, Procter went on to serve in Egypt, Italy and Yugoslavia, where he was with UNRRA in Sarajevo and Belgrade.

The contribution made by those whose FAU service did not take them to the battle zones was no less valuable. Hospital work occupied most of the home Sections, and Godric himself, for instance, spent all his time working in this country. David Mattingly (FSSW 1930-38) joined the FAU in 1940 and found himself helping to provide first aid at air-raid shelters on the Isle of Dogs. While such shelters did save many from the effects of blast, they were by no means proof against direct hits, as David records. "One moonlit night a colleague and I were making our rounds when a bomb exploded nearby. We escaped injury but 350 people died in the shelter we were about to visit." Shortly afterwards, Poplar Hospital, where he was based, was also hit, the bomb destroying the main staircase. He spent the rest of the night evacuating patients down the fire escapes to buses waiting to take them out of London.

Felix Hull (FSSW 1926-31) must surely be the greatest surviving authority on men and movements in the war-time FAU, having served in their Personnel Office from 1941 to 1945. He had been working in the Essex Record Office in Chelmsford before joining the Unit in September 1940, and comments that his "rather curious and meagre career" in the FAU is explained by a 1941 visit to his Selly Oak Hospital section by Peter Hume, from Headquarters. "You were an archivist, weren't you?" said Peter, "Come and sort out the Personnel Office files at Gordon Square". As Felix says, his past decided his future, and though ideas of Ethiopia and a projected Burma section were discussed, he was clearly too valuable at HQ for them to release him.

In the autumn of 1940, Tessa Rowntree had been asked to form a 'women's section' of the FAU. The idea was that it would assist the work that was developing in London, mainly in shelters and rest centres for those bombed out of their homes. With Gwendy Knight she organised training camps at Barmoor, in the Yorkshire Moors, and it was through one of these that Eileen Pim (FSSW staff 1958-62) joined the FAU. Eileen's rest centre work involved a stay at Canonbury Place, used by Friends War Victims Relief Service as well as the FAU. Here she met Alan Thompson (FSSW 1930-37), whom she married in 1943. She and Alan worked together for a time in a bombed-out workhouse in Petersfield, Hants., not far from the home of FAU International Service (1948-51) and quite close to where they live today.

When the war broke out, John O Burtt (FSSW 1922-27 and student master 1929-30) and Mary Close (FSSW 1922-27), both of them prefects at school, had been married for three years. Dismissed from his teaching post, and directed by his tribunal into ambulance or land work, John joined the FAU in October 1940. At this time women had not yet been admitted to the FAU, and Mary set to work on her own with a rest centre scheme at Cotebrook, Cheshire for Liverpool invalids who could not get down into shelters during air raids. The Friends Relief Service adopted it and Mary became one of their staff.

In May 1942 the FAU had sent a small group of older members out to India to help organise air raid relief schemes. Although only one raid occurred, the section found themselves heavily involved in cyclone relief work, more members, men and women, were sent out, and it was decided that a married couple should go out to act as wardens for the central headquarters in Calcutta. John and Mary were asked to take this on, and went out to India in 1943. Their arrival coincided with a disastrous famine in Bengal, and their work included milk distribution schemes, as well as the setting up of four orphanages in different parts of the province. The Bengali names of these homes, in translation, were: Children's Garden, Garden of Love, Garden of Peace, and Garden of Joy. Mary and John returned to England in June 1946.

Post-War Service

When the FAU Post-War Service started in 1946, a number of war-time members of the Unit transferred into it. One of them was Geoff Soar (FSSW 1938-44), who went out to Finnmark, the northernmost part of Norway to help with reconstruction work in this remote province which had been laid waste when the occupying German army retreated. It was a return to an area that had figured in one of the first FAU expeditions overseas in 1940.

Conscription was still in force after the war, and conscientious objectors to military service still had to appear before tribunals, which could grant them conditional or unconditional exemption. Mark Chamberlain (FSSW 1939-42), in preparation for his tribunal at Fulham, wrote to Arnold Brereton asking for a letter to confirm that he had attended FSSW for three years. This was supplied, duly signed, but A.B., quite typically, attached a note saying "I fail to understand the point of this!" He was probably right to do so, says Mark, who nevertheless found his request for conditional registration to serve in the FAU readily accepted by the tribunal under Justice Hargreaves. Quakers and sympathisers, he adds, got more generous treatment than, for instance, Jehovah's Witnesses, who were given a hard time and were continually asked to speak for themselves and not to rely on comments from their elders. As an ironic postscript, Mark was asked by a waggish member of the Bench, intrigued by all this talk of 'Friends', "Are you a friend of the previous applicant?". He was able to reply yes quite truthfully: he had been at FSSW with Bill Lipscombe.

Not all of those who appeared before tribunals during the war or afterwards sought or were given exemption conditional on service in the FAU. Procter Le Mare's brother, Peter (FSSW 1934-39), was sent to work on the land and finished up at Rothamsted Experimental Station. Ken Francis (FSSW 1936-40) was another registered to do agricultural work in 1943; he followed this by three years in the Friends Relief Service, mostly in Poland. Alan Sillitoe (FSSW 1947-55) worked as a hospital porter at Guy's, David Tregear (FSSW 1945-50) worked on farms in Hampshire and at St Peter's Hospital, Chertsey (where the FAU also had a team working), and Nigel Watt (FSSW 1946-52) on a farm, in work camps and a hospital.

International Service

One of the early ventures by the new FAU International Service, which took over from the Post-War Service towards the end of 1948, was at Rösrath, near Cologne, where barracks that had been successively home to POWs and then displaced persons were being converted into a Pestalozzi home for orphaned children. Gerard Wakeman (FSSW 1939-45) and Mark Chamberlain (FSSW 1939-42) went there in March 1949, when the very hard work of breaking up concrete pavements and digging cess pits was taking place.

Donn Webb's (FSSW 1942-49) fluency in German led to him taking charge of FAUIS sections at Köln-Bruck, a suburb of Cologne, and at Plön, in Schleswig-Holstein, where Gerard Wakeman had preceded him in the work on a hostel for homeless and workless young people, mostly refugees. Some five years later, in 1955, Graeme Johnston (YG53) and Roger Bush (FSSW 1942-48) were in Germany, also involved with accommodation for refugees, this time in Hanover. They both went on to work in France, at the Chateau d'Avaray, which was home to an international community founded by Henri Schulz, a French Quaker. Kaye Whiteman (1941-49) was another member of International Service who worked at Avaray, in the following year.

Forestry and hospital work were two staple ingredients of FAUIS service. Both provided income for the Unit, enabling it to undertake unpaid work in its overseas sections. David Gray (FSSW Staff 1960-70) was an early section leader at Southwater Forest, near Horsham, and also worked at Bradford Royal Infirmary. Roger Bush was at a more remote forestry section, Kershopefoot, on the Scottish border. Graeme Johnston, Kaye Whiteman and John Veit Wilson served at Brook General Hospital in South-East London. A tuberculosis hospital near Malvern, St Wulstan's, was another long-term commitment. At various times David Fairbanks, Michael Frizzell, Roger Bush, John Veit Wilson and Kaye Whiteman all worked there.

Two natural disasters in 1953, the devastating floods in East Anglia and in the Netherlands and the violent earthquake in the Ionian Islands of Greece, had provided further opportunities for the combination of unskilled labour and enthusiasm that the International Service could supply. David Fairbanks (FSSW 1945-49), who lived in Southend-on-Sea, was among those working first on Canvey Island and subsequently in Holland, And after the work in Greece and Holland came to an end, the 1957 Hungarian uprising became a focus for the last eighteen months of the Unit's existence. With the ending of conscription there was no longer the likelihood of a regular flow of new members. The Friends Ambulance Unit's Council decided, in 1957, that the Unit would have to cease its activities in June 1959. Just forty years later the FAU Management Committee, which had looked after the residual affairs and assets of the Unit, wound itself up and handed over its remaining funds to Quaker Peace Service.

How far did their schooldays encourage Walden old scholars first to register as conscientious objectors and secondly to join the Friends Ambulance Unit? Hard to say, but to John Veit Wilson "the progression to conscientious objection to military service and to the Friends Ambulance Unit (1954-55) seemed like a natural and unquestionable development from my years at Saffron Walden....The twelve years I spent there (an almost unparalleled duration) were not an indoctrination into Quaker thought in any oppressive sense, but they were thoroughly permeated in an almost taken-for-granted manner by Friends' non-violent response to conflict." He also mentions school support for the involvement of sixth-formers in Quaker work camps. And Roger Bush, in an interview recorded for the Imperial War Museum's Sound Archive, recalled first contact with the ideas of non-violence and pacifism in the 1940s through FSSW interest in the figure of Gandhi as conveyed by the talks and writings of Reg Reynolds, a friend of the Mahatma. But it's most unlikely that there is any common pattern to the stance taken by FSSW scholars who joined the FAU, either in wartime or peacetime. In the end you have to think out your own attitude. Perhaps what the School should really take credit for is the encouragement it gave us all to think for ourselves.

Crime and Punishment at Walden in the 1930s

Patrick (Jim) Campbell

For most Old Scholars, our main contact with the school is the *Old Scholars' Magazine*, a fine little publication that keeps us informed of what is going on, where the Old Scholars are now, and a selection of memoires of those of us who have been fortunate enough to survive. The magazine generally does not report much of what is going on at the School today, so we must assume that all is well, and that an exemplary group of scholars are being effectively educated by a dedicated staff who have everything under perfect control.

However, if my memory serves me, it was not always thus. A recent article by Henry Rowntree (*OS Magazine* for the 130th year, pp 32-35) boldly reported various "pranks and pieces of nonsense," with scholars climbing on roofs and others making apple-pie beds. There was also talk of the search for miscreants and the throwing of small boys from the diving board, and I recall an earlier article that mentioned midnight feasts over on the girls' side.

Perhaps all was not sweetness and light then, our dark deeds to be remembered but not reported to present a somewhat sanitized picture of times long gone, but fondly remembered. Such thoughts took me back to those days before Word War Two, and yes, I began to remember events, and the consequences of those events, that had indeed been long forgotten.

As memory serves me, there was no written code of behaviour at Walden, but there certainly were unwritten rules, well understood by staff and students. For the breaking of these rules there was also an ascending scale of consequences. Perhaps my title of *Crime and Punishment* should better be described as *Misdemeanours and Consequences*, but the title will serve.

Taking the consequences first, there was a clear understanding that there would be the following consequences, not of the breaking of a rule, but of being caught breaking a rule. Looking back, it seems to me that many of these consequences were effective, and none were especially resented or considered unfair.

The lowest level was called Standing. The guilty scholar had to stand quite still for a certain period of time, fifteen minutes, or half an hour, depending on the severity of the offence, and after classes when all the others were outside enjoying the sunshine or otherwise pleasantly engaged; perhaps enjoying games of terza, puddox or hicockalorum, from Mark Bertram's list in the same issue of the magazine. To this I can add Monkey-House, played in the gymnasium on rainy days.

The next level of penalty was Words. The condemned scholar had to copy fifty or a hundred words correctly from a small, very narrow book containing five hundred or perhaps a thousand *Words Most Commonly Misspelled*. I am quite sure that scores of mischievous Old Scholars can spell 'manoeuvre' correctly, even to this day.

Misdemeanours on the sports field were punished by Changing Practices, where the guilty had to appear before the staff member on duty, fully dressed in soccer or cricket garb, then reappear properly dressed in street clothes after a visit to the changing room. A sentence of five or ten changing practices could easily waste a beautiful afternoon, particularly when the master on duty could not be readily found. Any attempt to wear the street clothes underneath the sporting gear would be instantly detected.

Going up the scale, one came to Gating. This meant that the scholar could not leave the school grounds, not even to go the local sweet shop (Tintacks) or elsewhere. This was generally set for a Saturday to give the maximum effect.

Corporal punishment was, of course, not permitted at Walden, although there were unreported cases where a slipper was forcefully applied to the appropriate place when a series of events pushed a staff member to the limit.

Finally there was always the ultimate weapon of Dismissal, or being 'sent-down,' but I can recall no such case in my time at Walden, and I am sure that we would have been aware if someone disappeared from our midst.

Now as to the crimes, or misdemeanours, there was a wide choice available to the imaginative scholar. The object would be not so much to break the rules as to determine just how far the rules could be bent without incurring the heavy hand of authority. Such bending of the rules also called for careful assessment of which particular member of the staff was on duty. What could be done successfully with one staff member could not be attempted with another. Certainly useful training of the powers of discrimination of those involved.

The scholars, for their part, had their own unwritten code of behaviour and misbehaviour. Breaking bounds, baiting new members of the staff, midnight feasts, climbing drainpipes and reading in bed after lights-out were all generally accepted, but there were some things that were not even contemplated. For instance, there was an invisible line separating the boy's side from the girl's side, and neither group crossed that line, although I recall an occasion when a group of us, on a midnight ramble, encountered a small group from the girl's side near the Cricket Pavilion, purely by chance. There was also a general agreement that certain recreation rooms, such as the Photography Room or the Music Room were privileges not to be endangered, so these were never used as safe havens for midnight feasts of sardines or cold baked beans washed down with Tizer or ginger beer. Raiding the kitchens or scrumping apples in local orchards were permissable, but we steered clear of the sanatorium and Mrs. Sparkes's garden.

    We usually considered the baiting of new masters was good clean fun, and an essential part of their training. I clearly remember a group of us lying in wait outside the Biology Lab, snowballs at the ready, to pelt a newly-recruited staff member. He, for his part, stood his ground under our barrage, fighting back gamely until some of our side went over to his support. Then, when the battle reached its height, we discovered that our quarry had sensibly slipped away. I suppose we all learned something from that incident.

    One of the most daring of all challenges was to strike the dinner gong several times in the still of the night. This called for the most impeccable timing, and a single individual of great courage. It seemed impossibly difficult to accomplish as the gong was situated in a long corridor, making escape almost impossible. Yet it was done on more than one occasion, but I have no memory of the name of the perpetrator.

    Searching for some new rule to bend, a small group of us discovered a brick-lined tunnel near the Battle Ditches, and it seemed worth exploring. Armed with candles and electric torches, we travelled the length of the malodorous passage, to emerge close to the maze and the castle, having passed under the centre of the town. Shades of Les Misérables!

    One other item to add to the list of punishments for a group of miscreants was to have them line up separately in the Box Room, and all march together into the Dining Room to be seated at a separate table close to the Top Table! Here the supper would consist only of bread and butter and milk, eaten in silence. I have no memory of what necessitated such unusual treatment, but it seems to show that all the imagination was not on one side.

This then was the pre-war system as I remember it, and I am sure there were other misdemeanours and other consequences that could be brought to mind. All in all, the system seems to have been fair and reasonable, accepted by both sides, and about as good a preparation for real life as one could devise. At least we learned how to spell "manoeuvre," as well as how to swim very quietly in the swimming bath somewhat after midnight!

Henry Rowntree

For most of my days at Walden (1916-24) John Edward Walker was Headmaster. He had reigned from 1890, and he retired in 1922. He was a solid, quiet, dignified man, a firm disciplinarian, an effective teacher of perspective drawing, and a good slow bowler at cricket. From time to time he found it necessary to gather all the boys together for a straight talking-to. On one occasion there had been an outbreak of petty thieving, and we were all herded into the big Fourth Form room (the room directly over the Boys' Playroom) while (it was rumoured) some masters made some investigations into the contents of certain boys' boxes. Strange it is how some masters seem to know, almost for certain, who are the miscreants. In particular, Arnold Brereton seemed to know upon whom to pounce. (AB once told a group of us recent OS that "he flattered himself that he could see through the back of a boy's head"). On another occasion JEW had us boys into the Lecture Hall (now the Library) to chide us gravely on bullying, with particular reference to a pastime, favoured over the years by certain larger boys, of throwing some small boy into the Swimming Bath, off the top board. This general bullying seems to have been of long standing, because when my father was appointed Senior Assistant Master, back in 1901, some other teachers sympathised with him going to 'that rough place'. I myself noticed that the rough element, very prominent in 1916, had appreciably diminished eight years later. Perhaps the 1914-18 War had in some way aggravated matters, and perhaps the advent in 1918 of the saintly Stanley King Beer had ameliorated matters: he was a very significant influence for good.

The Deluge

As a postscript to Patrick Campbell's article, **Maurice Allward** tells the following story

Like the majority of pupils, I had a good share of lines for minor breaches of rules. I often speeded up the time taken writing these by tying three pens together so that, when writing one line, three were produced. Surprisingly, no master ever commented on these, although the method of preparation must have been apparent.

As Jim Campbell comments, meals at the Top Table were reserved for major crimes. I served two or three weeks at this table for a prank which went wrong – although the final result was as intended.

A popular pastime among the Juniors during breaks, in the winter terms, was skating on slides of water made by emptying buckets along a line in the quadrangle in the evening. This froze overnight to make a slide. However, even the best of these was only a few yards long. I decided to make the Juniors a really great slide.

Accordingly, one cold night, I got up around 1.00 am and, accompanied by my young brother, James, Jimmy Campbell and Philip Holmes, went up to the top floor dormitory for junior boys which overlooked the quadrangle. On the nearby landing, we connected the fire hose to the wall hydrant and pulled the hose across the beds of sleeping boys to the window. Poking the nozzle out of the window, I called for the hydrant to be turned on. Several things then started to happen :

- The canvas fire hose started to leak as it filled, with water (as such hoses do for a few minutes) wetting the beds over which it passed, waking up the boys, some of whom started crying.
- When the full force of the water reached the nozzle, the reaction forced the hose back into the room, spraying the nearby beds with even more water.
- With help, I finally managed to direct the water out of the window, on to the darkened quadrangle, three floors below. The splashing noise was deafening. Lights came on, and we heard the Night Duty Master coming up the stairs.
- At the hydrant, Philip Holmes (or was it Jimmy Campbell?) tried to turn the water off. In his haste (and fright) he turned the wrong lever and instead of stopping the water, undid the hose. The full force of the mains water then flooded the corridor and cascaded down the stairs, meeting the Duty Master who was on his way up at the run.

Conclusion:
1 The Juniors had the best slide ever.
2 We all got several weeks at the Top Table – bread and water only for tea.

Anna Sargant

What I most liked about Saffron Walden was being taught by men, especially by my favourites – AB (Arnold Brereton) whose maths lessons I loved, Cyril Mummery and Campbell Stewart. Perhaps this was because my parents had separated when I was six years old and I had not had the chance to learn from a father at home. I am sure, now that I look back on my time at School, that this was the reason why I was often disobedient and, at times, even led fellow pupils into rebellion.

One particularly disgraceful episode took place up in the bedrooms one evening when Mary Fulford was on duty. We kept on talking after lights out, bringing Mary up more than once to try to quieten us down. Finally, at my suggestion, we balanced a tin mug, full of water, on one of the connecting doors as a booby trap. To our horror, the member of staff who appeared this time, and whose face and hair were well soaked by the water, was none other than the Headmistress herself, Sylvia Clark. Like Queen Victoria, she was "not amused". All three dorms were ordered to get up, dress and go downstairs to the Classroom where we were asked who was responsible for this disgraceful behaviour. And now I can't for the life of me remember if I owned up or not – or how I, or we, were punished.

Richard M Best

In 1938, there were two things that happened in Bedroom Seven: tossing the potty and midnight feasts. Generally there was a continual mild battle amongst the bedrooms. The gold-rimmed potty was always being stolen so, when it became the possession of Bedroom Seven, the ceremony was attended by all. In the ceiling of this bedroom there was an opening through to a loft which could be closed by sliding a simple lid back into the loft. When open, the skills of all were combined to toss the potty through the opening in the ceiling, into the loft, using a sheet or bedcover. It may still be there.

The midnight feasts were easily arranged because Bedroom Seven was over the Workshop where there were gas rings on which food could be heated up or cooked. It was then hauled up by rope, through the windows, into the bedroom. A great event but, oh, we were so tired the next day! It all stopped after September 1939.

First Impressions in the 1920s

In the nineteen-twenties the School was very much a *Friends' school.* The governors were all Quakers, the staff nearly all Quakers and most of the children came from Quaker homes. Many were 'birthright members' of the Society and children of Old Scholars. We were much more enclosed, isolated from the activities of the town and from the presence of our families. In a sense, the School was a protective community, almost monastic in its seclusion.

But Quakerism was never preached or taught or even explained and no one told us what was supposed to happen in a Meeting for Worship. It was assumed we had imbibed the atmosphere from early childhood and that the School was an extension of the Quaker family.

What influenced us most was the quality and dedication of our teachers.. They exemplified Quakerism better than any books or precepts. ...

The School seemed to attract unusual characters, most of whom shared with us their special interests and enthusiasms. They stayed at the School for decades: perhaps because they were happy and not over ambitious: perhaps because headships were scarce. Whatever the reasons, staying-put gave the School stability. ...

Charles Kohler
From *Unwillingly to School*

Nineteen thirty-five, *eleven years old, and FSSW was not what Angela Brazil and my other school stories had led me to expect.*

The girls' playroom, with its two-tier lining of trunks, the age-order queue before meals, the pinafores for under-twelves.

No Upper Fourth, but groups A, B and C, prep done in Group B en-masse.

The expectation of letters, laid out on a shelf at the foot of the girls' staircase (100 girls can't have that much post!) and anxiously looking down over the stairwell to see if they had come.

Pig drives and the Bumble Dinkies, and Audley End Mansion Bridge, oranges from Ma Warings' 'order' to be eaten outside on a cold winter's exercise.

Gas lights in girls' 10A and 10B.

Laundry – was it really pyjamas once a fortnight?

'Words' – writing out five, ten or twenty words as punishment, being able to take a book into tea – wonderful.

The great joy is the friendships that have endured 65 years.

Audrey Booth

The Road to War

We were much involved in trying to prevent a Second World War, the late John Fleming and I starting up the Inter-Schools Peace Federation", contacting peace groups in other Quaker and progressive schools. We actually held a conference in the summer holidays at Friends House, Euston Road. One of our contacts was Patrick Heron, the artist, who became a Conscientious Objector (serving, I believe, in the London Fire Service) and never lost his interest in international affairs whilst making his distinguished career in St Ives. Unfortunately, he has forgotten about our juvenile correspondence.

I remember Gerald Littleboy announcing the death of King George V and almost bursting into tears. This surprised me, as the event did not move me unduly at the time. I also recall Arnold Brereton pronouncing the folly of the new King expecting to marry the twice-divorced Wallis Simpson and make her Queen of Great Britain, Northern Ireland and the British Dominions beyond the seas, as proclaimed by the Town Crier in the market square of Saffron Walden at the time of his accession.

Alan Carlton Smith

Whatever Happened to the Taper Holders?

I was interested to notice, on a fairly recent visit to the School, that electric lighting has been installed. In my days (1927-30), we had gas lighting. This required the appointment of Taper Monitors whose duty it was, on winter afternoons, to light the gas mantles in the classrooms and adjoining corridors.

The wax tapers were mounted in long, brass, tubular holders which had a hook in the end with which to turn on the gas supply.

The much sought after appointment of Taper Monitor was ranked far ahead of such offices as Blackboard Monitor or Inkwell Monitor. Perhaps even these no longer exist.

If the brass taper holders could be found lurking in the Water Tower or elsewhere, their sale, as collectors' items, might pay for the Swimming Pool improvements.

John Bolton

A Boys' Dormitory in 1938

A Good Idea?

Well, it seemed like it at the time

Maurice and James Allward tell of a School visit to Germany in 1938. This included visits to palaces, various natural features and a Hitler Youth Camp. James says, *"I do not know why the 'Powers that be' organised the event . . All I can assume is that it was considered a good idea at the time, for a cultural visit to Germany. It was, after all, the period of appeasement, under Chamberlain, when most countries were trying to appease Germany in the interests of peace. (However, there are some who think Chamberlain was trying to buy more time in order that England could rearm)."*

It must be remembered that, at this same time, the Friends were setting the standard for giving practical help to those experiencing problems in Nazi Germany and their record in this regard is exemplary – among other things, they provided safe houses, helped to get people out of the country, raised money to bring Jewish children to England on the Kindertransport and many people owe their lives to them. James Allward continues:

"With regard to the reaction experienced when meeting the Hitler Youth (I was only thirteen at the time), I was impressed by the orderliness, although I did not note their military organisation. I thought their living quarters were spartan, with little thought for comfort. The girls' Hitler Youth appeared to be well organised and entertained us with some German folk dancing. I remember walking through the Black Forest with some of the Hitler Youth singing Nazi songs, which were very militaristic in tone. We also went to Berlin and I remember standing in a crowd watching some parade or other. Out of politeness to our hosts, we were advised to give the Hitler salute when the local populace demonstrated their subservience to Hitler. We were not politically motivated at the time, so we remember the trip as an adventure into the world, and did not take note of the increasing militarism in Germany. The Hitler Youth was Germany's idea of the Scouts – but was developed as a cadre for the expansion of the Wehrmacht. . . . . "My later visits to Germany were much later, in 1945 and 1946, under much different circumstances – I was a Flight Engineer, 61 Squadron, in RAF Bomber Command.

"Sadly, we do not seem to have found ways and means of resolving political differences without the use of violence and mayhem. Let us hope that, somehow, some measure of peace can be maintained in the trouble spots of the world."

The School party outside the Sans, Souci Palace. Maurice Allward is third from the right in the front and James, wearing shorts, in the centre.

Maurice, two years older than James, still has a souvenir of the trip – a dagger, inscribed "Blut und Uhre" (Blood and Honour), a gift from the nearby Herman Goering Factory.

In 1938, we were far less politically aware than are young people of the 21st century. Today, news and comment spills into our living rooms 24 hours a day and we watch wars as they happen. In 1938, newsreaders still dressed in dinner jacket and black tie to read news bulletins for the wireless. It was a different world.

German 'girl guides'

The Staff

20th Century Memories

The Staff in 1935 . . .

Back Row: Rhoda Jones, Albert Lindley, Badger, Norma Wright, Mr Skurr,
l-r David Pearson
Second Row: Stanley Pumphrey, Sally Waites, Helen Radley, Annie Murray,
 D Y Pugh, Edna Clark, Gladys Bird
Third Row: Mrs Graham, R P Smith, Florence Priestman,
 Gerald Littleboy, Elizabeth (Leila) Sparkes, Arnold Brereton,
 Margaret Yapp
Front: Mr Heap, Jenny Waites, Walter Baldwin, Dorothea Waring,
 Henrietta Beecham, Stanley King Beer, San Nurse

C BRIGHTWEN ROWNTREE

CBR is spoken of with great affection; he was rarely known to administer punishment at all, let alone of any severity, and his system of punishment by 'words' was mild in the extreme, but on the whole extremely effective except for those bordering on the what we call maladjustment. I remember one occasion when he was really rattled by someone and rapped out the extraordinary punishment of 40 words. For some reason, the standard punishment measures were 30 words for pretty bad behaviour and 60 if really mad with a boy. Never more than 60, as 65 meant he could be gated. It would be fitting to quote a former President's tribute to him, given in his address at A.G.M. "I would like here to pay a tribute to CBR for whom I have a great affection. He taught me such a lot about relationships with people in his quiet way, and I think that much of my own attitude has probably been coloured by his, and by the way he dealt with us, his much younger and less experienced staff. It could not have been easy for him to have such a young and lively crowd of teachers round him in a boarding school, but he managed us with infinite tact and pleasantness. In the olden days at meal times, the Staff always waited in the Old Lecture Hall, now the Library, until the most of the School had entered. One Sunday I spent this short period playing the piano. While I was sitting there at the piano, CBR opened the door, merely looked round at me and went out immediately. I never played the piano there again on a Sunday. I have been 'told off' by more than one Headmaster, mostly when they have been irate and louder in their anger, but never more effectively than on this one occasion by this gentle man in his kind and gentle manner. It is a lesson I try not to forget – a lesson that has stood me in good stead over the years, both as assistant and as a Head". Another OS. says, "he was not an imposing Head. He was of modest demeanour, not at all the high headed foreheaded type which was supposed to be the one which captured the attention of a class. His "Tramps" were models of good planning, and he went on them all himself, shielding his pate from the sun with an old hat. And you knew that the administration was impeccable".

Unless otherwise specified, the appreciations in this section come from Annual Reports of the Old Scholars' Association

GERALD LITTLEBOY

When I joined the Staff in 1944 Gerald Littleboy had just completed his first ten years as Headmaster. When he came in 1934 the Sixth Form was beginning to develop. Two years afterwards the first link was made with the Essex Education Committee and some day scholars were admitted on their recommendation. A new building programme began, specialist rooms for the teaching of biology and geography were provided, the Assembly Hall was built, and the Library was made. Then came the war, and with it a long period when further developments were impossible.

When I first got to know Gerald Littleboy I was amazed at the multiplicity of duties that fell to his lot. There was no bursar, so much of the details of estate management and office administration had to be dealt with by him. He had a heavy teaching programme. At the same time he managed to be to be readily available to those of his colleagues who needed his wisdom and advice and he managed, too, to maintain a warm interest in the progress and development of individual boys and girls. War-time problems included the frustration of being unable even to attempt the essential maintenance and re-decoration of buildings, much less to improve them, and the strain of many nights when air-raid alerts brought the Headmaster at once from his home to be on duty at the School. In the first conversation I had with Gerald Littleboy before taking up my appointment, I discovered how eagerly he was looking forward to the time when progress could once again be made. Already he was anxious to discuss the foundation of a Parent Teacher Association and probable development of the Sixth Form.

The end of the war brought, gradually, the opportunity to develop the School along the lines he had hoped. There was a rapid expansion in numbers, making necessary the restriction of the age range and the closing of the Junior School, so that adequate provision could be made for the growing Sixth Form.

By 1951, when the School celebrated its 250th birthday, the first State scholarship had been won, there was a Sixth Form of about 40 and the total number of scholars in the School had just exceeded 300.

By the time Gerald Littleboy retired in 1955 the School had become a full two-stream Grammar School and the successes achieved by young Old Scholars at Universities were providing encouraging proof that the work of the Sixth Form was providing an adequate basis for their studies.

Shortly before he retired Gerald Littleboy was President of the Old Scholars' Association. He ended his presidential address with these words: "Walden's life is based on a very sure foundation – mutual respect for one another, young and old, and a conception of life that is religious in the truest sense." His comments in Staff meetings, his day to day dealings with his colleagues and the boys and girls, were continual witness to the reality of this belief. He had a kindly and shrewd eye for the possibilities for good in the law-breaking challenging adolescent who, though a disruptive influence in the middle school, might yet be a loyal and helpful member of the Sixth Form. He was quick to sense that when the unexpected comes, a gentler approach could win where sternness could fail. He lived out his Christianity in the practical details of his daily life, and his great wish for the boys and girls in his care was, in the words of Bristol Yearly Meeting of 1695, which he loved to quote, that they "shall not only learn to be Scholars, but Christians also".

I count it as a very great privilege to have worked with Gerald Littleboy in my early years in the School. He was generous and encouraging, good-humoured and far-sighted. His faith in the future of Walden was a continuing one, and I am glad that he lived long enough to see the work that had been his joy and care for so long so ably continued by his successor.

Jennie Ellinor

" . . . Perhaps his greatest assets as a Headmaster were his executive ability, his belief in the worth of the individual, his accessibility, and the patience, forbearance and wisdom he showed in dealing with the more unruly members of his flock. It may not be generally known that, towards the end of term each form-master had a session with GL when he listened to the reports suggested for each boy in the form. Time and again, in my younger days as a form-master, he suggested some change, not that he usually objected to the content of my report, but his apt word of differing phrase made criticism that was largely destructive become constructive, and he was always anxious to avoid anything that would be unnecessarily hurting to a parent: "Remember, Stanley, that even . . . , strange as it may seem, is somebody's darling".

G Stanley Pumphrey

These were obituary tributes, 1962

SYLVIA CLARK

Sylvia Clark was the third of the five children of James and Wilhelmina Clark; he was the Headmaster of Newtown School, a Quaker School at Waterford in Ireland. Sylvia was educated at Newtown and the Mount School, York, followed by an honours degree in Mathematics at Westfield College, London, her mathematical talent being a cause of amazement many years after in Palestine, not being expected of a woman.

Her time at Walden from 1937 to 1944 was over the difficult period of the Second World War. Both in her teaching and her other relations with scholars she was intensely practical and understanding. "It is inevitable that her chickens and her mathematical instruction should remain inseparably connected in my mind as she so intimately intermingled the two. Less distinct are memories of her digressions from a study of Quakerism in a Lower Five Scripture class to tell you of her life on the Yorkshire farm which occupies so soft a spot in her heart." (*The Avenue* Dec. 1944).

Mary Fulford, a younger colleague of those years, writes, "The youthful Headmistress faced with wartime conditions set a lead in sharing with and organising the helping of menial tasks. When the domestic staff situation was strained she took a full part down to the least pleasant jobs. When it was murmured that she should not be doing these unpleasant jobs she merely paused to say that she believed there was a dignity in labour and perhaps the senior girls might catch the concept. Her help to the nursing staff with two children who contracted cerebro-spinal meningitis needing constant nursing in the San illustrated how when she saw a need she stepped straight in and in a quiet way projected strength to others. Her patience with difficult children was immense and there were many such in wartime, as was her tender understanding of children from broken homes, or refugees from wartime Europe. Balancing this was her appreciation of beauty in nature – the nightingales noted singing during fire-watching whilst the guns and searchlights at Debden blazed away. She delighted in being someone else, not labelled Head-mistress, in a play and encouraged the voluntary listening to broadcast classical music in the Assembly Hall after Prep – seniors and juniors alike with rapt expressions held by the spell of good music."

Sally Jacob who, with Barney, knew Sylvia all her years at Walden comments on the rare Irish Yorkshire Quaker who had great dignity, integrity and sense of duty, combined with modesty and a real care for children and adults in distress. She was full of unobtrusive acts of kindness and support, witness the arranging of German tutorials for a colleague or the sharing of wartime coals with the Intermediate Common Room. Her sympathy, sense of fun and warmth of character all helped to convey her sense of Quaker values to old and young around her.

Obituary 1983

Sylvia Clark *was Head Mistress during my three years in the Senior School. I remember her as a quietly spoken, very controlled person for whom I had great respect. She had the ability to make you feel a valued individual, when you were a very young nobody!*

On Saturday evenings during the summer term we used to have 'lengths bathes' in an attempt to see how far we could swim, starting with a small number of lengths and increasing the distance each week. On the last Saturday of Summer Term 1943, I was ready to attempt a mile, but I had no one to count the lengths. Miss Clark offered and patiently spent the evening counting as I swam up and down,

JENNIE ELLINOR

Jennie Ellinor came from a Quaker family in which her mother and maternal grandparents were members of the Society of Friends, her father joining soon after his marriage. At her parents' request Jennie was admitted to membership as an infant and thus was brought up as a Friend in South Shields Meeting. Education at Ackworth was followed by a History Degree, Diploma of Theology and MA at Durham University. Five years teaching at Wigton School led to a year studying at Woodbrooke and then nine years on the staff of Gainsborough Girls High School under a Quaker Headmistress, an experience she valued and enjoyed. So to Saffron Walden in 1944.

John Woods wrote in *The Friend* in July 1983: "Jennie Ellinor came to Friends' School Saffron Walden as a Headmistress, as a historian steeped in Quaker traditions. She formed a working association with Gerald

up and down.

On another occasion, I had been thoughtless (in other words very naughty) and caused her considerable anxiety. Eventually I went to see her and apologise. Instead of telling me what a horrible child I was, she told me she was very glad that I had come. She said I had faced up to my behaviour, decided what to do about it and then acted on my decision. She explained that if I continued to face up to problems in that way I would be all right in the future.

I had gone into her room feeling horrible about myself but came out feeling good.

Time and time again, as a teacher myself, I remembered Sylvia Clark. There is no doubt that I was better able to help other children because of the ways in which she had helped me when I was a child.

Julia Dyer

Littleboy which gave a rock-like quality to the School after the war. Their partnership gave to the School an unshakeable spiritual depth and to Jennie the happiest years of her career.

"She provided, rather than independent initiative, the encouragement to corporate wisdom as it arose. So the relationship with Essex Education Committee, the Sixth Form academic standards, the quality of the staff and the (mercifully abortive!) 1947 building plans grew with Jennie's unobtrusive guidance. She helped Kenneth Nicholson to become a headmaster of vision. She shared the pioneering of the Reginald Reynolds Memorial Scheme to support Old Scholars serving in developing countries. Jennie met the upheaval to values in the 1960s, which were so taxing for teachers concerned for the welfare of the whole child.

"As headmistress, Jennie was a formidable figure. A colleague, before whom generations quailed, admitted that the only person she feared was Jennie! Grasp of wide issues went with close attention to detail. Some found her fussy or interfering. But Jennie was always there, available to deal with a crisis. Those who turned to her in distress discovered infinite care based on loving concern and prayer. Jennie overcame considerable reserve to undertake much of her work, and avoided the limelight, happy that others should receive it.

"Jennie, the historian, worked among the archives, developing a sympathy for the eighteenth-century records of the school at Clerkenwell. Her discovery of the Complaints Book of her predecessor, Richard Hutton, provided rich material, and she created the detailed catalogue of the archives, now available to other students."

Obituary 1983

KENNETH NICHOLSON

In his address as President of the Old Scholars' Association in 1968, Cyril Mummery said the following:

"I am sufficiently old-fashioned as a historian to think that people matter and find some modern approaches to historical interpretation nauseatingly 'trendy'. To me the appointment of a Headmaster is a milestone in the history of a school. Kenneth Nicholson's appointment in 1955 coincided with what historians of the future may decide is a bigger historical milestone – the end of wartime in Britain and the real beginning of the concept of the affluent Society. Inflation has been well described as a 'selective weed-killer'. Kenneth Nicholson very quickly recognised the need to keep abreast and ahead of the demands of the new Britain and the imaginative planning of the School – Essex Wing 1961, Crosfield 1967, and the crowning inspiration of Gibson House, under the splendid care of John Gillett – is his lasting monument. I worked very closely under Kenneth Nicholson for thirteen years – for the last four as his Deputy. It would be idle to pretend that we always saw eye to eye during that time: indeed I think it would be a very sad commentary if we had. But ballasting all our relationships has been Kenneth Nicholson's warm capacity for friendship, his willingness to talk out matters at the deepest level, his eternal approachability. Parents who heard Kenneth Nicholson's memorable final address to the PTA – an address I hope he will have the leisure to work into a book – will be aware of his understanding of, and belief in, people: tolerant, believing in the best – and, as a result, getting the best – he has allowed this great School to emerge. It is good to know that his massive wisdom in the field of education is being actively used in his position as Secretary of the Cadbury Trust.

To the great sadness of all, Kenneth Nicholson died suddenly of a heart attack on Friday, 21 March 1969.

The Staff in 1959

Back Row: Unknown, Olga Miller, John Evans, (Sister) Edith Woorral, (Nurse), Anne Morley, Kenneth Whitlow, Miss Kerrison, Ivan Cane
Second Row: Gladys Marshall (Housekeeper), Philip Houlder, Unknown, Mary Mercer, Kenneth Plant, Robert Hudson, Miss Lloyd, Kelvin Osborn
Third Row: David Lewis, Sara Price, Richard Sturge, Jean Thomson, Donald Benson, Mary Cuthbert, Brian Gelsthorpe, Margaret Kenningham
Front Row: Cyril Mummery, Joy Ashford, Richard Wright, Jennie Ellinor, Kenneth Nicholson, Bernard Jacob, Jean Stubbs, Alison Reynolds, Iorwerth John

STANLEY G KING BEER

by Kathleen Robson –
taught by SGKB in the 1920s

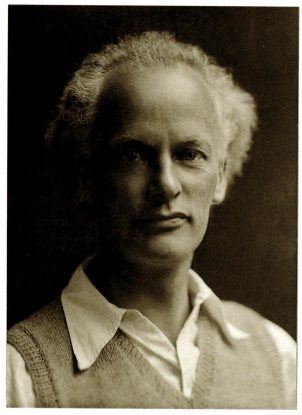

Although I kept in lifelong correspondence with two of my Walden mistresses, the outstanding member of staff in my years was Stanley King Beer, and I would like to add to what Henry Rowntree has written about him. In prison as a pacifist during World War One, he was one of the six British Friends, among others, sent to France so that, under military rule, they could be shot for disobeying orders within hearing of the firing line. Mercifully Friends got word of this in time to lobby their MPs and got the order rescinded and the men returned to England. Prison diet made no allowance for vegetarians such as SGKB was by conviction, and he became so hungry that he ate his bread crumb by crumb to make it last longer. Eventually he became so weakened that he was discharged to prevent the scandal of his dying in prison.

He had a brilliant mind and had chosen history for his degree because it was his weakest subject! This meant that, unlike too many teachers, he understood the difficulties of the slow learners. His methods were unorthodox, with diagrams and concise notes on each lesson given us after we had handed in our own efforts.

Who can forget his 'looking-glass tree' of the Industrial Revolution with labelled twigs merging into branches, finally reaching the trunk rooted in the Reform Act of 1832. Typically, the date came last in importance. SGKB was no disciplinarian, relying on his own enthusiasm for his subject to generate ours. It therefore came as no surprise that nearly half of my Matric year achieved distinction in history.

He married Mabel soon after coming to Walden just after the War, but their happiness was clouded by the difficult birth of their son, Michael. Michael was left profoundly deaf and Mabel was unable to have another child.

Thanks to SGKB's infectious personality, a quarter of the School became vegetarians at a time when this was rare. His love of animals led him to form the Band of Mercy which met weekly, attracting many of the younger children – not surprisingly, he it was who rescued a nestling greenfinch and reared it in his study. His help for fellow staff was obvious when our exam papers in various subjects were cyclostyled in his handwriting.

Henry Rowntree has written of SGKB's acting and production of operas and plays with Penrose Whitlow, but did not mention his priceless caricature of Grand Opera, nor his beautiful whistling which he had taught himself in prison where he was deprived of his precious piano. He improvised his own accompaniments for both. Was that why an Old Scholar, who had forgotten to bring her music, went to him and not to one of the music teachers to ask him to accompany her song?

For many years, Brightwen Rowntree had organised School Tramps – hiking was as yet a word unknown – for school leavers, one or two staff and old scholars to explore the various parts of the country for a week after the summer term. This involved much previous planning of accommodation and routes. SGKB, who had already produced pocket-sized guide books for earlier years, took over the planning and leadership when CBR retired and it was on the 1939 Tramp that SGKB collapsed and died. He was only 48 – had his prison years undermined his health?

It is a Quaker custom to write a Testimony on the grace of God in the life of well known deceased Friends, but SGKB was little known beyond the School and no testimony appeared. Florence Priestman (then Head Mistress) made amends for this omission when she compiled a life of Stanley King Beer, fittingly entitled *A Modern Quaker Saint*.

SGKB – A MEMOIR
by Mabel King Beer

I feel that probably the most lasting remembrances of Stanley are of his overflowing love of life, and how to be with him, even – I suppose – in the classroom was always fun. He, who was so sensitively vulnerable to the unhappiness of others and to tragedy in world affairs, yet radiated an enheartening and infectious joy.

Life with Stanley had "never a dull moment". He described our minor domestic upheavals, such as a flood in the night from a burst cistern, as wildly funny happenings, to the blank incomprehension of our more 'adult' neighbours. The Old Scholars' gatherings were very important to him, and, amid all the many and varied jobs which he cheerfully tackled – rehearsing for a concert, the vegetarian carving great joints of meat, lifting and carrying, and all the rest – he miraculously found time for many precious encounters with his beloved Old Scholars ('Old Collars' in our house, the name due to our son's difficulty with the letter S)

Because he so much enjoyed the company of the very young, Stanley volunteered to teach History in the Junior School. One small girl, having been questioned about the day's lesson with him, replied with a puzzled air: Oh, was that history? I didn't know, but we had a lovely time climbing trees! "Another little lass said to her teacher rather wistfully: " I do like Mr Beer – he is so motherly".

So, dear Old Scholars, when you remember Stanley, think of him with joy. Just listen, and maybe over the years you will hear the sound of his laughter with its overtones of love, joy and peace, which everywhere and always are "the fruits of the Spirit".

Written after Stanley's death in 1939

SARAH DOROTHEA WARING
remembered by Michael How

To the staff she was known as 'Fanny', to the boys as 'The Hag', to anyone who never knew her nicknames that would at least raise an eyebrow. But, to quote her friend, colleague and fellow countrywoman, Annie Murray: "We who came in contact with Dorothea Waring can have nothing but praise and gratitude. She was indeed a good and faithful servant to the highest and the best. Her sense of uprightness was outstanding and she was honest to the core of her being."

Following a short spell teaching infants in her native Ireland, she migrated to London. Obtaining a Diploma in cookery, she took up the post of housekeeper to a private school. Shortages in everything, including pay, determined her early departure, becoming Boys' Matron at Rawdon. In 1916, and then in her late thirties, she arrived at Walden, taking charge of the Sanatorium and morale through the Zeppelin raids.

In 1919, the postwar influenza epidemic swept the country with devastating effect. George Stanley Pumphrey ('Wonkle') writing in the OS Report of 1951: "On arrival at the School, I was met by an Irishwoman who explained, all in one breath, that there was nobody left to teach, there weren't any nurses to be had for love or money, the San was full, that she had an overflow in the boys' bedrooms and ought to be up there now, and could I come and help her as soon as I had had a wash and a cup of tea?"

Records show that, despite an appalling national mortality rate, not one School patient was lost . . . but who, or what, in its right mind would ever have dared defy this formidable Irishwoman. Life, post flu-epidemic, became a little flat for Dorothea and, the post of Boys Matron becoming vacant, she decided to 'have a go'. It is in that capacity that I, and countless generations of Old Scholars, remember her.

As a 'new brat', in 1942, I was required to report every weekday morning, before breakfast, to 'Hag's Nook', her two-roomed bedsit-cum-office, strategically situated on the first floor opposite the boy's washroom. I underwent an inspection of hands, knees and behind the ears. This, however, was only a prelude to the real test.

In that thirty minutes following lunch

and before afternoon lessons some twenty of us lined up in the boys' washroom for what was known as 'Parade'. Again, individual inspection of hands, knees and behind the ears. Then, divided into three groups on the word of command, we collected tooth brush and paste from our cubby holes Following teeth cleaning, and again on the word of command (one, two, three – – – six) we faced the wall mirrors to brush and comb our hair. This completed, the line re-formed, turned left and filed past Miss Waring showing a 'clean' handkerchief to a staccato "Dismiss, dismiss, dismiss . . . ." Even now it echoes down the years.

Any transgression incurred a penalty mark. I no longer remember how many marks were allowed before the final "Dismiss", but freedom from Parade six days a week was not easy to acquire, for some almost impossible. Legend has it that one boy, David Castillejo I believe, made it in one term.

Monday afternoon, Dorothea supervised our weekly bath. The baths, marked with a black painted line at the tap end, were filled to the five inches allowed to comply with wartime regulations. Bodies scrubbed, hair, washed with yellow School soap, was rinsed by Dorothea, using her enamel mug. The use of Silvikrin Shampoo sachets only came much later, when one was old enough for the Group C Dance. Dried, finger and toe-nails scissor-trimmed, inspected, we dressed and, thankfully, made our escape.

Every other Monday, following morning Assembly, we juniors presented ourselves in the boys' bedroom for 'bugraking' – a preventative measure against nits. Our locks were raked forward with a fine tooth comb which was then dropped into an enamel bowl of disinfectant, to be reused six or seven victims later.

Thus did Dorothea Waring ensure the cleanliness of a Godly Quaker education. But this was by no means the end of her duties. She supervised the weekly distribution of clean laundry, the fortnightly distribution of clean sheets and the daily distribution of parcels from home. I say 'supervised', but I never saw or remember an assistant. And, as if this was not enough, she darned our socks – no mean task before the days of synthetic fibres, as the overflowing laundry basket she demolished each week bore witness.

Each week, save Monday evening and she, Annie Murray and Barney Jacob (BBJ) gathered in Hag's Nook for the 'crack' and a game of crib. Our mothers may have grumbled over her darning skills – the wool did not always match the sock – but Dorothea never lost one!

A clipboard, held in the crook of the left arm, was a vital accessory. This being wartime when we were exhorted to waste nothing, her writing paper consisted of the insides of cornflake packets or any piece of cardboard with a plain surface – I am sure Dorothea never used anything else. On this she recorded things to do, Parade marks, lists and her poems. Her poems and random jottings, covering both School and staff, were used to devastating effect on her acclaimed appearances in End of Term or OS Whitsunday Concerts. She never forgot a boy, his misdeeds – or his School number.

Although she was 'of', she was not necessarily 'with' the staff – usually her boys came first. By way of friendship with Alec Clunes, a trombone-playing School Gardener, Peter Bell and I acquired a large quantity of apples. With the help of a book press, 'borrowed' from the Art Room, we filled a Winchester jar with apple juice. Over the next few weeks it was allowed to ferment, moved from one hiding place to another until, to our consternation, one day it vanished. Of course Dorothea had found it and, with unerring accuracy, knew who was responsible. We were summoned to her presence.

"Mr Bell, Mr How, you are wicked animals." Whatever your standing in the School, she always addressed you as 'Mr'. Having found the Winchester, she had placed it, for safe keeping, in her airing cupboard. There was an OS weekend in the offing and they, as 'very wicked animals', might have commandeered it for their own use. The heat of the cupboard accelerated the fermentation, causing an overflow on to the surrounding sheets. Returning the Winchester, she remarked, quite unruffled, "I tort it could be beneficial to the process."

Dorothea Waring retired in 1947 to nearby Rose Cottage. Perhaps in deference to those who tried to succeed her, she seldom came into School. However, her door was always open to visitors, particularly on OS weekends. The prefects in our last term: Owen Edwards, Uwe Gerstl, Michael Comber, Barry Barber and I, were invited to tea. Dressed in black, rather frail now, she proudly showed us round the garden. The lawn hand mown by the wayward 'Pegacious', the edges 'fusselled' and her beloved cherry tree. Enjoying a wonderful tea, regaled by a running commentary on our misdeeds over the years, many of which would have been completely unknown to the School staff, we were probably the last of her 'wicked animals' to enjoy her company. She died in the February of 1951.

I have no photograph of Dorothea, but her image is as fresh in my mind as if it were 1942 – a slim, stooping figure, dressed in a grey house coat, a clipboard under her arm, her hair grey but still naturally curly, lips pursed, eyes twinkling over the top of steel-framed spectacles giving her a quizzical look, a look which needed little prompting to turn to infectious good humour.

These memories and images are very personal to me, but they, and their like, will be echoed by all who ever knew her.

"Well, dat's what I tink, anyway."

SARAH H EVANS *(Head 1989-1996)*

When Sarah took over as Head in the Spring Term of 1989 she began to illuminate us in her own 'tremendous' fashion. She soon embarked on multitudinous changes that were vital at the turn of the decade. Her Head's study immediately became a Friendly place. She placed her desk so that she could look outward to new vistas and we who visited her soon began to do so also.

Educationally great changes were sweeping the nation and Sarah dealt with these in her efficient, organised and intelligent manner. Appraisal of staff, rather feared in many educational circles, took place positively and successfully. Committee after committee met to draw up vital documents on everything from key stages to the philosophy of the School. . . .

She led from the front. If we were going outward so was she. Soon she had infiltrated the Society of Headmasters of Independent Schools, now amended on account of her, to include Headmistresses. . . .

Early on in her time with us, Sarah, along with Jane Laing (recently appointed her successor), Mike Collins and others, gave everyone a practical taste of a spiritual vision with a 'George Fox Day'. The impossible was achieved. Young twentieth-century adolescents became seventeenth-century youths. Colleagues donned the dress of three centuries ago. Mike Collins became Fox himself and rode through Saffers with his retinue. . . .

The spiritual basis of the School was nourished in many other ways. Sarah ensured we kept our young people informed of Quaker ideas and that we regularly worshipped silently. She insisted on handshakes after Meeting, that practical manifestation of Friendship. She also insisted on the best of manners everywhere and from everyone, ensuring doors were held open, visitors looked after, . . . The message, of course, has been to value the dignity of every single member of the community.

From an appreciation by John Dickinson 1996

Probably the most colourful member of staff was **Stanley King Beer**, whose delightful personality and extraordinary versatility and ingenuity made his history lessons into dramatic masterpieces. Then there was **Sally Waites** who on occasions would romanticise about life in Paris, at the expense of half a French period. And I recall the bulky image of **David Pearson** taking his constitutional down The Avenue, after gruelling sessions trying to teach me German, and the precise and pedantic mannerisms of **Arnold Brereton**, who once had me on the carpet in his study to administer a well-deserved dressing down for some misdemeanour I had committed. Another pillar of the School in those days was **Stanley Pumphrey** who reigned supreme in the old Chemi-Lab above the Boys' Playroom. He had already been at the School for 20 years when I arrived, and continued long after I left to complete 45 years before retiring.

. . . I must just mention that legendary institution from the Emerald Isle, **Dorothea Waring**, Boys' Matron. As a day boy, I seldom came into contact with her, which made it all the remarkable when, at Whitsun a couple of years after I left School, she studied me thoughtfully for a few seconds, then wagged a finger at me and said, "Ah, yes – Turnbull, Number 89". **Jack Turnbull**

ERIC BROWN, *appointed School Bursar in 1946, writes:*

Taking over the administrative side of Gerald Littleboy's work in 1946, after the War was over, I can only guess at all that he had to do. True he had a secretary/book-keeper to assist him, but he was ultimately responsible for overseeing everything connected with the running of the School. He worked long hours with only short holidays.

Following on from the above, I am sure it should be noted that, in 1946, the Committee, realising it was asking too much of its Headmaster, decided to relieve him of his non-academic duties by the appointment of a Bursar. He would then be free to give all his time to supervising teaching staff and the needs of children.

One of the first things Gerald said to me on my appointment was, "I am glad you have been appointed, as I can now take a holiday!" After one term of my taking over from him, he went, with the Committee's blessing, for a two-term break in America.

Jennie Ellinor should also be remembered for those War years. She ably assisted Gerald Littleboy wherever she could, especially on the girl's side.

My own experiences over the thirty years I served the School are too many and varied to chronicle in detail. They range from the tornado that swept over the School in 1948, bringing down the heavy chimney stack over the clock bedroom where a dozen boys were sleeping, the rigging of the skylights of the Swimming Bath, the gutting by fire, in 1955, of the newly built Chemistry Lab, rescuing three frightened second form girls from the cells of the Police Station at 2 am and, there being no handyman, replacing tap washers and mending light fuses, blown (twice in succession) by a girl using a faulty iron.

Problems large and problems small came my way. Boilers, coke-fired, broke down with guaranteed regularity – ceilings collapsed and, on one occasion, a heavy angle plate fell from one of the trusses of the Swimming Bath roof into the water. American airmen had used the pool at quite high temperatures during the War and condensing vapour had caused rust to build up between the roof plates. The whole roof had to be stripped off as a consequence.

We had some problems with children. It was the Bursar's duty to arrange for their travel at the end of each term. On one occasion, we lost a girl for two whole days! Her parents, living abroad, cabled that she had not arrived on the specified plane – panic stations. After two days of exhaustive enquiries, it was established that she had left the London terminal office and, presumably, Heathrow. We cabled the parents to this effect and, in reply, heard from them that she had arrived, safely, half an hour after their first cable but that they had overlooked informing us.

I served under three Headmasters, three Chairmen of Governors and five Treasurers, each with their own aims and ideas. Gerald Littleboy established the School, under the 1944 Education Act, as a two-stream grammar school. Kenneth Nicholson consolidated this achievement with the School's population increasing from three hundred to a maximum of 392 with a healthy Sixth Form of over sixty.

John Woods took over a healthy school at the beginning of a difficult time for boarding schools – fewer children were requiring boarding education while, at the same time, other schools were opening their sixth forms, especially to girls.

I very much enjoyed my time at the School.

RICHARD STURGE

Born of a Quaker family, Richard Sturge displayed an early aptitude for music. Besides playing the piano, he received good singing instruction at the Downs School, Colwall, at a time when Friends' Schools were not noted for encouraging music.

Service with the Friends' Unemployment Committee in Whitehaven followed his formal music training and here he met his future wife, Joyce. They married while Richard was serving with the Friends' Ambulance Unit during the War.

He wanted to use his musical ability in the Society of Friends and the opportunity presented itself when he was appointed to teach at FSSW, a post he held for the rest of his teaching career. On his appointment, he persuaded Gerald Littleboy, who was very musical himself, to make provision for every scholar entering the School to learn an instrument. Together, they arranged lessons in violin, viola, cello and recorder as part of the curriculum. Some scholars flourished and went on to become professional musicians. Some were sufficiently accomplished to play in school orchestras and those for whom it proved difficult had, nonetheless, learnt to read and use music.

Joy Ashford (Dupont) joined the staff in 1951. She says, "... there was already a good Choir and a small Choir doing special anthems. We were about to start work on the Rubbra motets which had been composed specially for us to use during the pageant celebrating the School's 250th birthday. They were difficult works and needed meticulous note learning. ... The success of the Rubbra encouraged Richard to think that we might one day manage the large oratorios. We started with cantatas, then the Messiah, then the great day when Richard decided to do the St Matthew Passion. It had been one of his great ambitions and it was unfortunate that on the day of the School performance, he developed mumps; however, he had the great pleasure of conducting the performance at Friends' House."

Out of all this grew Richard's vision of joint choirs from Friends' Schools performing major works. Eventually singers from as many as nine schools took part. The Dream of Gerontius in 1974 was a forerunner of other joint triennial performances.

Besides his work with choirs, Richard was a dedicated teacher of individuals and, more especially with older scholars of musical appreciation. Many had a new enjoyment opened to them, even if they were not performers themselves.

His membership of the Religious Society of Friends was central to his life. He served as an Elder and as the Preparative Meeting Clerk. For many years, with Kenneth Whitlow, he guided Junior Meeting at the school, a demanding service steadily maintained. After Junior Meeting he would walk down to the Meeting House and slip into Meeting with the children for the last fifteen minutes.

Pat Lamond remembers :

Eric Lenz – a wonderful Biology teacher. I don't think anyone gave Biology up for School Certificate – simply because he was such a good teacher and we all enjoyed his lessons. We all had very good results.

Margaret Yapp – Latin teacher – known to all as Fido whose bark was worse than her bite. Geography teacher **Bernard Jacob**. Affectionately known as BBJ. BBJ's top denture fell out during a Geography lesson. Of course we all laughed, but having had to wear a part denture for some years now, I can appreciate how very embarrassing it was for him.

Jeff Follett – PE teacher. If he caught any of the boys smoking he would take them to his study and make them smoke cigarettes one after the other until they were sick and felt really ill. It was a good cure because they were never tempted to smoke again.

CAMPBELL STEWART
(1915-1997)

Campbell Stewart came to a professorship at Keele at the age of 34, having already had considerable educational experience, first as English master and housemaster at Friends' School in Saffron Walden, and then at the progressive Abbotsholme School in Derbyshire, on whose governing body he served between 1950 and 1980. After an assistant lectureship in education at the (then) University College of Nottingham, and a lectureship at the University College of Wales in Cardiff, he was among the first group of professors to be appointed to the North Staffordshire College by Lord Lindsay in 1950.

There he was responsible for setting up the course for the Concurrent Certificate in Education, whereby a Keele undergraduate could qualify for a Bachelor's degree and a teaching certificate on completion of the Keele four-year course. This put Keele graduates on equal terms with their contemporaries from other universities who had taken a three-year course followed by a postgraduate year for the teaching certificate. In the early years this departure from standard academic practice elsewhere attracted a high proportion of intending teachers to Keele.

After the death of the second principal Sir George Barnes, in 1960, Campbell Stewart was acting principal of the University College. He was responsible for hosting the ceremonies associated with the tenth anniversary, which included a visit from the Queen Mother, accompanying Princess Margaret, who was president of the college, in May 1961. His obvious qualities as a leader during those months made such an impression that on the retirement in 1967 of Harold Taylor (Barnes's eventual successor as Principal of the University College and subsequently the first Vice-Chancellor of the new university), Stewart's colleagues were happy to entrust their future to one of their own.

It was a fortunate choice. Keele suffered the common fate of universities in the turbulent years of the student troubles from 1969-1971 – on one occasion a group of students tried to levitate the Vice-Chancellor's residence by humming – but Stewart's calm and firm hand ensured that not a single hour of teaching or examining was lost.

Brought up as a Quaker, he did a great deal to broaden and foster Keele's relations with local and national friends and potential benefactors.

Stewart wrote extensively on progressive education. His first book *The Quakers and Education* (1953) was a reworking of his 1947 PhD thesis, and this was followed by a two-volume study of progressive education, *The Educational Innovators*. He contributed to an understanding of educational theory in his Introduction to the *Sociology of Education*, which he wrote with Karl Mannheim, and his final work, which he published in 1989 – after retirement as Professorial Fellow at the University of Sussex – was *Higher Education in Postwar Britain*.

In 1947 Campbell Stewart married Ella Burnett, of Edinburgh, who survives him with their son and daughter.

Extracted from The Times *Obituary, 22 May 1997*

Naomi Sargant writes: *"When he was at Walden, it was possibly his first job after university, as he got us all to do the equivalent of Eleven-Plus tests, presumably to see how we compared with a selective intake.*

"I met up with him again when I was Pro-Vice-Chancellor at the Open University and he was a member of the OU Council. He recalled, with absolute clarity, the fact that my sister Anna had completed the whole test without a mistake, and that she had completed it twenty minutes before the time was up. As he said her intelligence could not be measured, she was so clever. He was extremely handsome and loved by many, including some lady members of staff . . ."

A First Experience

My first teaching post, first contact with the Society of Friends, first experience of secondary boarding co-education: I expect the novelty showed!

Kaleidoscopic memories include: the wisdom and helpfulness of senior colleagues – and the gale of kind laughter that greeted my appearance at the first staff meeting of September 1962. Kenneth Nicholson had told the staff, correctly, that I had played cricket for my university and would help with games as well as teach English. They were expecting a muscular heavyweight. I was an eight and a half stone blonde.

More Staff Room laughter: David Lewis had turned up a bit late for a French lesson and found young Philip Amis up front taking him off. David slid into Philip's desk and let Philip take the rest of the lesson. He returned to the Staff Room saying how impressed he was! (So was I, at his attitude).

I suffered over-exposure to my Upper Three Tutor Group, teaching them English and Games, putting them to bed (three to four nights a week due to a sick matron). I was doing that the night we learnt that Kennedy had been assassinated – quietest bed-put ever.

Barbara Elaine Mould

CYRIL A MUMMERY

Good Dons perpetual that remain
A landmark, wailing in the plain –
The horizon of my memories –
Like large and comfortable trees.

When Hilaire Belloc wrote those lines he was thinking of the Oxford dons of his youth, but for many of us they sum up perfectly our memory of Cyril Mummery, for few who knew him can recall the School without his figure, and his voice appearing prominently in the picture.

He and I arrived in the Senior School on the same day, and although he was primarily a historian, he was obliged to teach other subjects as well, and the class of that year will still remember the poetry he chose to read to us in English lessons: *Gunga Din*, *The Rolling English Road*, *Kubla Khan* and, for a reading book, an abridgement of *Moby Dick*. We also read *A Midsummer Night's Dream*, but I find it hard to believe that that was Cyril's own choice as a suitable introduction to Shakespeare – except, of course, for the hilarious play within the play at the end. He really enjoyed that.

He introduced us to French too, and by the end of the first year I had realised that my forte was to be in languages, even though

Photo Andrew Mummery

Cyril himself was not a specialist linguist. When it came to starting German, therefore, I was faced with a dilemma because German was an alternative to Latin, and in those days, anyone with any academic pretensions was unwise to abandon the classics before taking School Certificate. With typical care for the problems of all the individuals who came into his care, Cyril solved mine. I started German and he helped me through the second year of a Latin course one evening a week, until I solved the problem myself by moving to another school. There must be scores of others who could tell similar tales of his unending store of personal care for his pupils. I have heard of one who was rather scared by his somewhat forthright manner; when Cyril learnt of this, the young person in question received an invitation to join him and Joan at the ballet.

Few areas of School life were untouched by Cyril's influence; he ran the Library and the Junior Literary Society, he took football, he played cricket, where he and Stanley Pumphrey were the mainstay of the School bowling, and ultimately and quite rightly he became Second Master. In later life, his rural background enabled him to devote time to forestry and the restoration of parts of the landscape.

The irony of it all is that he was not a Quaker; indeed, his sometimes outspoken approach and his discipline could be almost unQuakerly at times, but this was an ingredient the School could accommodate, perhaps even needed, and it was a gracious Providence that sent him to be a gift to the lives of all those whose privilege it has been to have been taught by him.

David Jones
From the *Old Scholars' Magazine*, 2000

Cyril had more effect on my education than any other single person I think, both in teaching detail (how to précis) and in subject (the interest and importance of history if we would understand the present) and perhaps most in attitude (if you put your hand to a job then do it as well as you can). I omit details such as the devastating effects of a fast yorker.

Professor Richard S Clymo

A left handed batsman who could hook the ball – his only forcing shot. When he hit a ball, it stayed hit.

Batting from the Swimming Pool end, he hit the ball for a glorious six – straight through one Biology Lab window and out through another on the opposite side of the room – two windows for one shot.

Chris Wood

VETERAN STAFF ROOM
Richard Wright

Inevitably in a relatively small school, and therefore one with a size of staff which is much more an inclusive body, not departmentalised, it is also a situation where the Head(s), men and women, can have a much more personal link with staff members. FSSW was blessed with having the guidance of Gerald Littleboy through World War Two, supplemented at the end and later by Jennie Ellinor who gave valuable continuity when GL was succeeded by Kenneth Nicholson.

A very important part of staff development in the late 1940s and into the 1950s was the opportunity to have on the staff, whether Quakers or otherwise, those who were not eligible for posts in the State system because of exemption or alternative service orders by war-time tribunals. This gave a rich source of teachers – richer than normal circumstances might have produced. It was a tribute to the School Committee and the Heads at the time that the opportunity was well seized, heralding a period with a more than usual array of born teachers with talents on the Staff.

This period continued into the better provision of buildings in the early 1950s, not least the new Staff Room in the Essex Wing of 1961. These buildings were generously supported by the Essex Education Committee, recognising the place the School played in county education.

The Staff Room had views east across the Playground and south down the 'Mistresses walk', an excellent non-intrusive way of the staff body continually feeling part of the School. 'Quaker plainness' does not necessarily demand spartan conditions and certainly the room became a valuable part of Staff comfort and service. The atmosphere was helped by Kenneth Nicholson getting furnishings rejected by the liner *Oriana*, but highly suitable for dry land. Occasionally, the conditions led to amusement, as when a six-foot member of staff knelt by the side of a woman teacher who was seated in a low chair and was puzzled when the Staff Room gradually took to amused laughter.

I am sure that many others could relate their own Staff Room stories. The School always valued giving teaching practice to those needing a place to gain experience. A Nigerian student teacher, on

The Staff Room in 1961   Photo Michael Gee

practice, taught this writer the lesson "always watch what you say". In a moment of stress, it seemed safe to express a mildish bout of annoyance in Arabic – to the surprise of the student who had done some of his training in Cairo! It is good to remember that the Staff Room atmosphere was happily inclusive; witness the Senior Wrangler (Mathematics) who did teaching practice for one term and, the following year, gave one day a week voluntary support to the Maths Department as he increased his own qualifications.

This reminiscence also gives a chance to pay tribute to Eric Brown who was Bursar through much of this period. His continued personal and professional care for teachers in health and in sickness contributed greatly to the well-being of Staff during his time in office.

One's wishes are that the far-sighted and pleasant surroundings of the Staff Room continue to give support and comfort to Staff in the 21st Century.

It is a particular pleasure to be able to include this piece by Richard. When he originally promised a contribution to this project, his wife, Hildegard, was already terminally ill. After her death, it required much gentle encouragement to persuade him to complete this article which he then proof-read. Sadly, he died on 5 February 2002 before the completion of this publication.

A Day Brat's First Impression in 1943

Ursula Page

"Up the stairs and first door on the left," a tall, red-headed girl, carrying a large pile of books, instructed me.

I had arrived very early that first day, in a taxi to the local station provided by the Essex County Council for Herts & Essex girls, Newport Grammar Boys and "Scholarship Pupils" for Friends' School, the two former having to catch trains. All came from surrounding villages and that first morning I was the sole pupil for Friends' School.

I nervously made my way from the station to the imposing red brick building in Mount Pleasant Road. Coming from a two-roomed village school where even the eight mile journey to Saffron Walden was an adventure, this place seemed enormous. Having rung the MAIN front door bell, I was greeted by a rather surprised but friendly, smiling secretary who ushered me in, summoning a passing senior pupil to escort me. At the end of a dimly lit corridor, she pointed to a flight of stone stairs leading to the Upper Third Form Room. "Wait there until I find someone to show you around," she announced and, with a toss of her pigtails, she disappeared, leaving me to enter the empty classroom from where I could hear distant chattering and clattering of china from the still breakfasting boarders in the Dining Hall.

From this upper window I gazed down upon an asphalt playground with steps leading up to a beautiful avenue of trees, glistening in the September sunshine, a riot of red and gold, complemented by the virginia creeper which clung to the walls of the main building. On the adjacent tennis court, two teachers whizzed a ball over the nets, their laughter filling the air. Below me a group of boys screamed and shouted as they roller-skated. This was a happy school and I was eager to become part of it.

My reverie was broken as a self-assured, bespectacled girl opened the door. "Are you the new day-brat? Elizabeth Bickley at your service."

Crestfallen at being thus addressed, I meekly introduced myself and was then taken on a whirlwind tour, viewing pet sheds, the Rockery, Sanatorium, more Tennis Courts, Hockey, Football and Cricket Pitches, a glimpse into the delightful Swimming Baths, onward to the Gymnasium, Biology Lab, Geography Room, Art Room, numerous shabby boys' classrooms with ancient, carved desks and then on to the more impressive Dining Hall and superb Library.

Next, I explored the girls' dormitories where, Elizabeth informed me, she slept in great discomfort on an iron bedstead with a straw mattress.

Another maze of corridors and we entered a stone-floored playroom where boarders' trunks were kept.

"Here they hand out dry bread and dripping at recess but, to be lucky, you must move fast. It certainly tastes better than the boiled fish and semolina we have to suffer at lunch," said my new companion.

"By the way, do you want to visit fairyland before we go into Assembly?" she enquired, throwing open another door and pointing to a row of lavatories. "The boys call theirs bogs." (These were, indeed, Fairyland to me – my village home in Great Sampford had no running water, no electricity and only a bucket privy at the end of the garden, visited by torchlight or candle if used in the hours of darkness).

Suddenly a bell rang, summoning us to Assembly. My new life was about to commence, one that heralded many lasting friendships and experiences so foreign to those of my isolated village.

Cyril Mummery and Eric Lenz were newcomers on that same day in 1943, both excellent teachers. I owe my love of poetry to the former whose rich voice reciting Tam O'Shanter and many other poems I shall never forget. Perhaps Eric Lenz may remember the day brat who presented him with a live crayfish from her village River Pant, in a milk can, whilst he and his wife, Marie, were still in bed early one morning at Hillcroft. – sorry, Eric.

Happy Days. Thanks for having me.

Who remembers the big freeze of 1947? I remember helping to shovel coke towards the boiler at the back of the old Gym for several days until it was all consumed, and still the freeze went on, with ice-skating on the frozen small lake between the Swimming Pool and the road.

David Tregear

THE GARCIAS
told by Helvecia

On the 23rd May 1937, my brother, sister, myself and over three thousand other children arrived at Southampton in the ship "Habana". There were also some adults–teachers, assistants and priests. There had been a military coup in Spain on the 18th July 1936, which turned into a civil war, and that was the cause of our journey. I was fourteen years old, my brother was ten and my sister eight.

We had been evacuated from Bilbao because the Fascist troops were closing around the Basque country and Bilbao being an industrial city, was being bombed constantly and food was very scarce. The Basque government had appealed to foreign nations to take refugees, and, after pressure from the National Joint Committee for Spanish Relief and much deliberation on the part of the British Government, in April 1937 the Home Secretary gave permission for 4000 Basque children to come to Britain, with some conditions.

It was not until May 18th that the Government's agreement was finally obtained. Leah Manning of Spanish National Aid and Edith Pye of the Society of Friends were sent to Bilbao to make the evacuation arrangements. They arrived on the 24th April, just two days before Guernica was destroyed in an air-raid. This was neither an industrial city nor a military target. The world was shocked by this outrage and there is little doubt that this hastened our evacuation.

From the ship, we were taken in coaches to Stoneham Camp in Eastleigh. A few days later the first 400 children left for the Salvation Army's Training Centre which was to be their

Home for the Homeless

During the 1930s and 1940s, many young people, forced from their homes in Europe, found sanctuary at the School Here are some of their stories

Elvio, Delia and Helvecia Garcia, fugitives from the Spanish Civil War
Photo by Stanley G King Beer

hostel. I left in August in a small group of 22 children and three adults to go to The Oaks in Carshalton, Surrey.

One of the three adults at the Carshalton home was a teacher and the other two assistant helpers. We had lessons every morning. There was a Spanish speaking English matron as well as a cook. Three months before we came to Saffron Walden, it had been arranged for these older children to go, full time, to a local school.

The Committee ran adverts in newspapers asking people to foster a child for a weekly ten shillings towards its maintenance. The response was good. Mr and Mrs Cadbury fostered my sister Delia and also sent her a gift. I wrote to thank them and so they found out Delia had a sister. Shortly afterwards they took us out for the day and I told them about our brother Elvio. From then on we were all in regular touch.

With the end of the Spanish Civil War and Franco's victory, Mr and Mrs Cadbury realised we were terribly upset. They became concerned about our situation wanting to know if we heard anything from our family. I told them that we had received some letters with the news that our eldest brother, the bread winner for the family since the death of my father in 1933, was in prison. He had been fighting for the Republicans and my mother wanted us to remain in England for the time being. The Cadburys told us not to worry, they would see how they could help us. They eventually adopted us, even though they had two lovely daughters of their own.

After all the official papers were signed, we were asked if we would like to go to an English boarding school; we said yes on condition we could spend our holidays with the other children at the Oaks. They readily agreed, being just as anxious as us that we should keep in touch with our friends. And that was how we came to Saffron Walden in March 1939. It had to be a co-educational school and though we saw a few others it was to Saffron Walden that we came.

I stayed at the School until the end of the summer term in 1940, but Elvio and Delia stayed on. Most of our Spanish friends from the Oaks had returned to Spain.

We all survived to see in the new Millennium but, sadly, Delia died in 2001.

IRENE DAVID

As a young child, I used to lean out of my window in Berlin and listen to the Hitler Youth Singing. I thought the Horst Wessel Song, the Nazi Party anthem, was the loveliest and most melodious tune I had ever heard. I saw them as becoming, all these young boys and girls in what I felt was such a super light brown uniform with a red armband, white circle and black swastika.

One could hear the thumping of boots as they marched nearer and nearer, and then you saw the swastika flags, and all I wanted was to join in and march and sing with them. I got the chance to shout 'Sieg Heil' and 'Heil Hitler' when I lay in the bath at night, singing their Horst Wessel Song, and I knew every word but had no idea what it meant. To me it meant togetherness. "Please let me join the Hitler Youth", I begged my parents. They were horrified.

Conditions became increasingly difficult for Jewish people until, eventually, Irene's parents went into hiding.

I wondered where my parents had gone to so suddenly and what friends they could be visiting, and then the most awful day arrived. The Nazis kicked my dog – they kicked my beloved Sherry and laughed at her whimpering. ... Tante Julia (Irene's step-grandmother who was not Jewish) told them that my parents were away; then they looked at me and asked me if I was the daughter. Tante Julia answered for me and said that I was the youngest. They then turned to her and said that if my father did not report to the police within 24 hours, they would come for me. ... My father departed carrying his officer's sword from the First World War. He told us that when they saw that he had been a German officer in the First World War they would surely let him go. But of course they didn't. ...

Irene's father did return home:

An awful, frightening sight greeted me. There was my father, and he was weeping quite uncontrollably, and he had no hair at all. All his black hair had been shaved, his head was bare and he looked so very, very thin and pale and quite dreadfully ill. ...

The reason for his release:

... the Nazis needed him to liquidate the bank in which he and my mother's second brother were equal partners since my grandfather's death.. ... He had to sign endless papers and had been ordered to leave Germany after the business had been sorted out and the bank handed over to the Nazis.

At the earliest opportunity, Irene's parents sent her to England. She made the journey accompanied by Tante Julia. All went well until they reached the Belgian border:

The two men in Nazi uniform, who had entered our compartment, shouted at Tante Julia to show her passport and mine. Mine, of course, had a large J for Jew on it, and I was Sara Irene David. On seeing my passport they seemed to go completely mad. ... They pulled me up, yelled at me and asked if my surname was indeed David. I nodded ... As we pulled into Aachen Station, they ordered Tante Julia and me out of the train and pulled our belongings from the luggage rack and threw them onto the platform. More SA and SS men awaited us on the platform, and with horrified eyes Tante Julia and I saw the train move out of the station ...

They dragged me along the platform between them, and Tante Julia followed as fast as she could. I was taken to some rooms where men were waiting for us and they started to question me about my family, my father, my home. ... And then I was dragged away from Tante Julia and handed over to two huge Nazi-uniformed women. They put me in a room and stripped me naked. What they were looking for I had no idea, but they looked thoroughly and brutally everywhere on my body. Finding nothing, they then abandoned me. ... And then Tante Julia was brought in – she had also been searched ... What I was quite unaware of at the time, but told about much later, was that Tante Julia actually had some of my mother's jewellery on her to take to England, unbeknown to the Nazis, to deposit in a bank until such time as my parents should need it. ... throughout the interrogation Tante Julia had bravely held these precious jewels in her hand.

Irene arrived in Saffron Walden in 1942 and stayed for two years. She did not find it easy. She found that some youngsters did not accept her strong German accent and she had to fight for her place in society.

However, the School must have made a positive impression on her. She sent her son to the Junior House, run by Jeanne Barrie, and he stayed on, through the main Schoool, to become Head Boy.

The quotations are from Irene's book, *Out of Nazi Germany and Trying to Find my Way*, published by Minerva Press, 2000.

PAUL HONIGMANN

I was born in 1933 in a zoo! My father was director of the Breslau Zoo which was then in German Silesia but which, since 1945, has been part of Poland. A few months after my birth, my father was dismissed for being Jewish. It is perhaps surprising that he was not sacked as soon as the Nazis came to power in January 1933. My father had a rather indiscreet sense of humour and, when showing visitors round the Primate House, he was overheard saying that the apes did not have to carry a certificate of racial purity. I am told that he sued for unfair dismissal and actually won his case. We discovered recently that, for this outrage, he was put on a list of those to be liquidated as soon as the Nazi invasion of the UK was successfully completed.

My father did not wish to leave his homeland, believing that this "bunch of crooks" would be kicked out of office within months, but, my (non-Jewish) mother was much more far sighted and insisted that we leave. My father was lucky to have international zoological connections. Julian Huxley, then Superintendent of the Zoological Society of London, found him a post at Regents Park, which enabled my father to obtain, in 1935, Home Office entry permits for himself, my mother and their three sons. We were therefore extremely fortunate and early refugees.

In 1937 my father was appointed Scientific Director of the (about to open) zoo at Dudley in the West Midlands. It was there that my parents first had contact with Friends because, I believe, the Cadbury Family held a garden party at Bournville for all known refugees in the area. My parents became friendly with a number of Quakers, particularly John S. Stephens, a lecturer at Birmingham University (and much later Alice Kendon's father in-law!).

My father died in 1943 in Glasgow, where we had lived since 1940. My mother was left virtually penniless and we moved to London where we had a number of relatives and friends from Germany. She went to work in a rag-factory where children's toys were made from bits of cloth too small to be used for utility clothes. Later she worked as a doctor's receptionist and as a laboratory assistant for a scientist researching the effects of DDT on flies and, finally, at London Zoo until she retired. For about seven years my mother and I lived in a bedsitting room. She cooked on an electric ring balanced on her suitcases. Our water was stored in buckets brought up from the bathroom on the floor below. Not surprisingly, my mother, who looked after her children tenaciously through all adversities, wanted me to be educated in a more congenial environment.

It goes without saying that my years at FSSW were among the most important of my life. I went there as a sickly, nervous and homesick eleven year old. I was fortunate in belonging to a loving and united family but, inevitably, there were fears and insecurities for an impoverished, fatherless child in a foreign country. Friends' School provided a larger family in which one learned equality, regardless of income or background, security, purpose, duty and self-confidence. Put this way, the words may seem trite. But, as I believe I have enjoyed a happy and successful life and, if I have been able to cope with life's more tragic times, it is because FSSW provided me with such a sure and secure foundation.

I would like to emphasise, however, that although my family endured some hardship, the brunt of which was borne by my mother, there were many refugee children, both at Walden and elsewhere, whose problems were immeasurably worse than my own, and who carry the scars to this day. I hope that their stories will also be recorded here. Meanwhile, I shall never forget that I was one of the lucky ones.

Paul practised as a solicitor and is a Governor of the School

CHRISTOPHE GRILLET

Arriving in 1937 feeling very shy and vulnerable with very little French and even less English . . . Finding friendship and curiosity, an unlikely mixture. Also great surprise by helpfulness from everyone, including the prefects (an element and a behaviour I am not used to).

Also lost, being separated from my sister, Elisabeth (now Seale) – another radical difference from the French habits in our previous, Parisian, school life.

I soon connected with some Spanish children and gradually improved my English language and learned the Quaker habits which were very strange to us.

It was not our habit to address teachers so directly and without being spoken to first. Nor were we used to older children (prefects) who behaved with discipline and were helpful to younger pupils.

I have to express my surprise at the hesitations shown in the entry scribbled above. It shows an unexpected emotion which this dive into that piece of my adolescent past has awakened. It is a happy emotion.

MICHAEL ROSSMAN

In the last few years I have had quite a few enquiries about my earlier life which has made me think a little more about these long ago unhappy times. It is of course the pre-WW2 events which eventually brought me to Walden. Thus I could argue how fortunate I was because I doubt that I could have had such a good educational and humane foundation to my adult life in Germany.

I was born in Frankfurt (Main), Germany in 1930. Although at the time the fact that my mother was of Jewish descent was probably not considered relevant, it soon became of utmost importance. My mother's family was of a liberal, middle class background including scholars and business men. She was an artist, having been trained in the politically turbulent Bauhaus in Weimar. She became a journalist for *Die Frankfurter Zeitung*, writing about local history and illustrating her articles with beautiful sketches of old Frankfurt and its surroundings.

I still have a collection of her work. My mother joined the Young Society of Friends in Germany soon after WW1, inspired by the Friends' Service Committee concern about the famine in Germany. There was a small Quaker meeting in Frankfurt. Occasionally my mother took me to meeting and taught me to understand and appreciate the silent "Andacht".

As I approached school years the situation in Germany had become tense. My mother had divorced (although this was not as a consequence of the political situation) and we lived with my grandmother. I was soon recognised as the little Jewish boy by teachers and kids, all of whom enjoyed beating me frequently. The walks to and from school became a daily terror. Fortunately there was one teacher who kindly protected me as far as he could, although I suspect this was rather dangerous for him. Eventually, in early 1939, my mother was able to arrange for me to become a boarder at the international Quaker School "Eerde" in Holland.

Although I could now live without fear, at the age of eight and a half, I missed my home and had learning difficulties. In the summer of 1939 my mother and grandmother immigrated to England and I joined them for the summer holidays. But a few days before I was to travel back to Holland the war broke out and it now became difficult to cross the Channel. I therefore had to stay in England.

Somehow I was able to learn English without noticing it. By my first Christmas I was avidly reading English books (*Dr. Dolittle . . .*). Indeed this was quite a change because with my learning difficulties I had never before enjoyed reading for pleasure. However the environment of being at home and having no fear made learning a pleasure. I soon started to enjoy school. My mother was anxious for me to have a good education and the English Quaker boarding schools were an obvious choice in her mind, although I would have preferred to stay at home. I sat for a bursary test at Friends' House in London. I know I must have done very badly in these tests where we had to decode some secret writing which I completely failed to do. Nevertheless I was awarded a bursary which made it possible for me to go to Walden in the autumn of 1942.

Although I think I did quite well at school even from the beginning, it took me perhaps a year or so to think of school as a place I liked to be. But as you know, with the

passage of time, the experience and opportunities provided were of incredible importance to me.

In the early years we took the "squash" from Liverpool Street Station every beginning of term. By the time I was a sixth former the war had ended and I was cycling from London to school. The end of the war also brought an end to some of the more dreary aspects of school. I remember the taking down of the special bomb-blast protection wall outside the boys fourth form room (see page 65). Gerald Littleboy was a great person with the sledge hammer. This wall had made the inside rooms dark and dingy over the war period. I also remember having to crawl under our beds when there was a "doodlebug" alert. One of these blew out a whole lot of windows, fortunately during a holiday period.

Michael went on to a distinguished scientific career – see page 85

FULVIO CASSUTO

I arrived in England in September 1939 from Trieste in Italy together with my mother, one brother and sister. My father was already in London working for the Italian service of the BBC. He had to leave Italy in a hurry because he was of Jewish extraction and an anti-fascist journalist and considered *persona non grata* in his homeland. I could not speak a word of English and attended a local primary school in Wembley, Middlesex.

In 1941, at the time of the heavy bombing of London, my parents wanted to put me in a school outside the danger area and the Friends' School in Saffron Walden was chosen because a colleague of my father at the BBC had his son, Anthony Marus, already there. Also, another colleague who lived next door to us in Wembley was prepared to put his son, John Plank, in the same school at the same time. And so the two of us went there to join Marus.

We were all about the same age and with the same backgrounds. We were all Catholic and, as Italians, we were considered by many as foreigners from a country that was a fascist regime and allied to Hitler's Germany in World War II. We managed to survive the initial 'rejection' and were eventually accepted as loyal brothers and supporters to the allied cause. We were not brilliant scholars but we all became popular, particularly in sporting activities. Marus was a good swimmer and John Plank and myself were in the first team for both cricket and soccer. Marus left the school after two or three years and John and I stayed on for Matric. I eventually left in 1948 after unsuccessfully trying for Higher School Certificate.

I worked for Lloyds Bank for three years and played in their first team at soccer, but then left to enter the publishing world as an advertising salesman which appealed to me more than journalism which was my father's career. I travelled extensively for my work as Advertising Manager of *The Statist*, a weekly financial magazine and, after two visits to South Africa, I was offered a job as Advertisement Manager of the *Financial Mail* the leading financial and business weekly in South Africa. I arrived in South Africa in 1966 together with my wife Clara and two daughters Paola and Daniela age seven and five (I was married in 1958 and Donn Webb was my best man).

I eventually became General Manager of advertising, the *Financial Mail* until I retired in 1995. I was, however, kept on as a consultant and now at the age of 70 am still working for the same publication and I am very happy. I was divorced from Clara in 1983 and re-married, in 1990, with Carol de Leef, a South African lady from whom I was divorced in 1993.

I am now married for the third time to another South African lady, Roslyn Cathro – it happened on the last day of the century 31 December 1999 in Cape Town. I now have four grandchildren. I last visited Saffron Walden in 1995 for the 50th Anniversary of the end of the War and was very pleased to recognise so many of my fellow scholars whom I remembered so well.

JOHN PLANK

I was born in Rome in 1929. My father was an Englishman, my mother Italian by birth, but on marrying my father, she automatically became a British citizen.

We lived in Italy through the Mussolini years until 1940, when Italy declared war on Britain and we had to leave. If we had stayed on, we would all have been interned for the duration of the war. Fortunately, we were able to board the last diplomatic ship to leave Italy for England. On our arrival in England I attended various schools in the London suburb of Wembley, and at the same time learnt to speak English.

Once we had settled down, my parents were anxious for me to have a good education. They somehow got to hear of a certain Friends' School in Saffron Walden. Though a Roman Catholic, I was accepted by the school in 1942. Fulvio Cassuto and myself were possibly the first Roman Catholics to be accepted by, and to attend, FSSW.

I owe so much to the School. It taught me to be tolerant of, and understand, other people's points of view and opinions. The School was instrumental in helping me to settle down after the traumatic ordeal and upheaval I had experienced on leaving Italy. It gave me the chance of learning, thoroughly, a new language and culture and thus be able to start a new life here. I will always be grateful to the School for the way it helped me to cope with post-school life and the later considerable success of my business career.

ANNA & NAOMI SARGANT

Naomi writes:

Anna (top) and Naomi in their navy Sunday dresses

Saffron Walden (for that is what I still always call the school) was exceptionally important to me. Our parents had separated before the war, and our mother had misguidedly attempted to take us back in Spring 1938 to live in her home country, Czechoslovakia. We returned to England in September 1938, not technically as refugees or aliens, but definitely 'displaced' when Hitler invaded the Sudetenland, and Chamberlain referred notoriously to 'that small country, rather far away, about which we know little'. The journey was not without incident. The guards at the border banged on the door, but they had been bribed to say that my mother was an English lady!'

She was to start to work for Jan Masaryk, then Foreign Minister in the Czech Government-in-exile, and the Friends School was suggested to her by a lovely Harpenden Quaker, Christabel Mennell, as she was going to have to travel a lot for her job. The war had hotted up, and dog-fights with German planes had already reached us. I started (age seven) as a boarder in the Junior House, while Anna (at eleven) was in Big School. We had already been boarders at St George's Harpenden in 1938, when I was four!

MARTIN & RUTH MICHAELIS

The Reunion in 1995 of all the Friends' Schools pupils of the war years was a very moving experience for me. It was of course, enhanced by my husband, my brother and his wife being there with me. I remember talking and talking, listening to and sharing experiences of our times at the School and life's vicissitudes since. It was an enlightening experience to learn how many other children the School had rescued from difficulties, apart from myself and my brother. My memories of Junior House in 1941 to 1943 were always exceptionally good ones in what for me was an exceptionally difficult childhood, and these memories were enriched by the reunion which made me realise that these two years had had a lifetime effect on me.

I came to England with my brother, Martin, three years older than me, in 1939 as part of the Kindertransport which brought about 10,000 mainly Jewish children away from Nazi persecution in continental Europe between Kristallnacht, 9 November 1938 and the outbreak of war on 1 September 1939.

At the time of my coming to England my only thoughts were about how to survive after my parents, home, language and everything familiar had disappeared – except my brother upon whom I relied as a substitute mother. The world had suddenly gone mad. Nothing made sense any more, but my brother had answers to all my questions. My main desire was to keep up with everything he did. Learning to read and write English, memorise poems etc. were all easy compared with my constantly failing attempts to fathom what the grown-ups wanted of me. Our first foster parents (we were fost-

ered by three families) had no children of their own and in retrospect, I think were ignorant rather than cruel in their management of us. My biggest problem was bed-wetting. I knew what to do, but all my efforts failed. I still remember vivid dreams of walking along the corridor in my bare feet on the cold floor and sitting on the cold rim of the toilet only to be awoken by the warm wet flow in my bed! Nothing helped and certainly not the beatings meted out to me by my foster-mother with a leather strap.

When I arrived at the Friends' School and was taken into the dormitory to choose my bed, I broke down in tears, unable to talk for sobbing. A kindly person, Mrs Stubbs, calmed me and when I was able to tell her my fear of wetting the bed, she told me that most children did so to start with and she showed me how every bed had a rubber mattress cover so that it did not matter. As far as my memory goes, my anxiety vanished and I was cured. I don't know now whether or not I wet my bed in Junior House but no-one said anything about it. It was no longer a problem.

I couldn't have been an easy child. With the lifting of the harshness that had made me so fearful, I became a very energetic lively person. I remember racing round and round the garden and orchard out of sheer high spirits. I was forever being told to be quieter, but never harshly and always with explanations I could understand.

To my chagrin, because I was the youngest, I found myself the last in the line of children when we formed a line. But, to my surprise I was the only one who could read fluently. I proudly disdained the class reading books, but this proved no problem. The teacher carefully explained that I should not make the others feel bad by boasting and she found me an endless supply of really interesting story books which I devoured avidly and took no more attention away from the needy ones. Most importantly, the Junior House staff arranged for me to meet my brother, who was in the main school, regularly and spend time with him. We had a secret language, which I have sadly forgotten, just in case anyone overheard and reported us to our harsh foster-parents.

My teachers at the Friends' School did so much for me, more than I realised at the time, and so I was not able to thank them. I was lucky to have mostly very understanding teachers in all the other three schools I went on to. It was inevitable that, in due course, I would become a teacher myself to express my thanks to all the teachers who had given me so much when I was most in need of it. I taught in five secondary schools for nineteen years, each with greater problems than the last. The first was a grammar school and the other four were comprehensive schools under crippling stress from inter-racial hostilities and too high a proportion of children from non-coping families. My interest was always mainly in the most disturbed and disturbing children as I knew with certainty that if I had been sent to those schools, instead of the Friends' School followed by small country schools, I would have been one of the disturbed and disruptive ones. My greatest achievement in schools was a GCSE course in Child Development, for which I wrote a text book and I became chief examiner for the SW CSE Board.

I am now nineteen years into my second career as a psychotherapist. Again it was inevitable that I would need to resolve my inability to understand what my foster-parents wanted of me, and understand myself, through studying human behaviour and unconscious functioning. Since 1989, when I attended the first Kindertransport Reunion, I began to realise just how much I had kept myself unaware of knowledge about the Holocaust and WWII. To repossess it I had to come to terms with the guilt of having survived – the feeling that one of those millions of murdered children would have made better use of life than I did. Since then I have been working increasingly with people affected by the Holocaust – in individual therapy, in groups and, recently, in dialogues between the generations and between Jews and Germans. I work in projects with teachers and schools to develop Holocaust Education. In my opinion, the only possibility to reduce hostile prejudice and envy that lead to violence, murder and 'ethnic cleansing' is through education of the sort that provides opportunities for the young to listen to real experiences of the Holocaust – ' live witnesses' or 'Zeitzeuge'.

Another memory of the Friends' School was of going in a school group to the weekly Meetings, a very different experience from going to church every Sunday with our foster-parents. That first experience of worship had made no sense to me: people had sung beautiful hymns and made good-sounding speeches about good deeds; but as soon as we had got home our foster-mother was as harsh and angry as ever. In comparison, Meetings were quiet and serene and there were restful silences. I have often wondered why it was so easy for me to sit silently in those meetings when most of the time I couldn't sit still or be quiet. I don't suppose, at age six to eight, I could have understood much of what was said but I experienced them as genuine and purposeful. I have always admired the Quakers for their respect for and acceptance of other people's views and beliefs different from their own and have made this my own aim.

My one complaint about the Quakers is their policy of destroying the documentation of their projects and 'good deeds' after completion. This is a sad loss to researchers and archivists and through them to posterity. Due to this, I have not been able to establish whether it was the Quakers who sponsored my brother and me coming to England with the Kindertransport. I imagine it must have been so, otherwise why would we have been sent to the Friends' School?

and Finally . . .

I have my own story which goes back to 1898. My grandparents were on the boat from Russia and it stopped in Hamburg. My grandfather went ashore on his own to explore the town. In the evening, he returned to the boat and told my grandmother: "The Germans are not nice people." Perhaps not politically correct and not Quakerly, but they were simple people and they continued on their journey to London from where, eventually, my sister, Muriel, and I found our way to Saffron Walden.   Hilary Hockley

Unorganised Games

Unorganised, or 'disorganised' games, as one OS describes them "were the best fun". On Saturday evenings there was Terza and Hicockalorum. First man stands against a wall as post". Numbers two, three and four scrum down in line against him. The rest of the team take a running jump on to the backs of the scrummers, one after the other; the maximum number to stay up represents the target for the other team. (A better version for this was the whole of one team to scrum down and it remained for the opposing team to see for how soon and for how few jumpers the first team could be made to collapse, a real tussle of strength and toughness, accompanied by general groans of strain). There was also Puddox, a cross between rounders and cricket, a game taken over from Free Church Camps. There was, too, golf on the field consisting of hitting the ball as far as possible; tennis on grass courts, occasional paper chases, and treasure hunts, especially on the occasion of House Socials. There were enormous teas provided on these occasions, followed by bathes, mixed in the 30s. Farrand remembers the fantastic display of self–sacrifice, when the largest girl in the School, Honor Liddle, was persuaded to do a Honeypot from the top board amid enormous cheers. The whole surrounds were swamped for minutes, it seemed.

Many of these unorganised games disappeared, but others spontaneously sprang up in their places. Skating in the playground was indulged in from time to time – even by younger members of Staff – on borrowed skates.

Bad Eggs – *Chris Timms on the receiving end of a Bung*

My Skates

When I first joined the 'family' in the Junior House, I was very envious of the other juniors – they had roller skates and I pestered my parents to buy me a pair (at Godfrey's – are they still there?). The skates were part of my life for most of the next ten years. I can still picture myself racing down the boys' playground and jumping the steps down to the girls' for a glide and twirl at the other end. I wonder how many of you remember the old hockey sticks especially kept for the games of hockey we played on skates on those playgrounds – great fun.

And guess what . . . I have, in one of our cupboards, my pair of roller skates, now approaching their diamond jubilee.

Judith Layng

Bad Eggs

The sunken area of the boys' asphalt will live in most memories as the venue for *Bad Eggs*, a game probably exclusive to Walden. The only organised game permitted before the end of Evening Meeting on Sunday. It was played between lunch and pig drive. Each player was numbered and the game commenced with number one throwing the ball against the angle made by the Library wall and the School building, calling out a number. Once the designated player had the ball in his grasp, other players stood rooted to the spot. The object was for the designateed player to hit one of his opponents with the ball, to which end he was allowed to take three paces.

Successful, and a Bad Egg was scored – a miss and the Bad Egg went the other way. Three Bad Eggs you ran the gauntlet; six meant a Bung bent double against the Library wall, your fellow players having a free throw against your unprotected backside. It was a game inviting subterfuge, cunning and some indignity.

Other Activities included:
Skating
Table Tennis
Five-a-side Football
Keep-ups – hitting a tennis ball against the end wall of the classroom block at the boys'end, the ground floor window having been bricked over for the duration of the war as a precaution.
Monkey House – a game of tag played in the Gymnasium with every piece of apparatus available. This was supervised by BBJ (Geography) although, if memory serves, there were no accidents.

Michael How

FOOD
Drawings by Marygold Lansdell

The Bill of Fare in Clerkenwell
Standing Minutes (1701-1792) Food as follows:

	Breakfast	Dinner	Supper
Day 1	Butter, Beer, Bread	Bread, Mutton	Cheese, Bread
Day 2	Mutton Pottage, Bread	Pease either as Pudding or Pottage	Cheese, Bread Butter
Day 3	Bread, Butter	Bread, Beef Pottage	as Day 2
Day 4	as Day 3	Furmity and Bread	as Day 3
Day 5	as Day 3	as Day 3	as Day 3
Day 6	as Day 3	Pudding Pies	as Day 3
Day 7	Water, Gruel and Bread	Tripe as Before	

Cicely Rawlings – 1920s
At 7.15 am we had fifteen minutes of Bible reading and then down to breakfast. At the beginning and end of meals we always observed a silence and Mr Rowntree read a passage from the Bible at the end of breakfast. There was then a short time before lessons at 9 am when we could either prepare our lessons or have music practice. Recess was at 11 am when two baskets of crusty bread were put in the playroom. There was always a rush to get a piece, as by that time we were hungry. At this time we could also walk in the Avenue so brothers, sisters and friends could meet.

Robert Dunstan – 1940s
In 1945 I spent a short spell in Junior School literally just after WWII and can still remember the arrival of the first post-war bananas.

I was playing innocently at the time (probably not where I was supposed to be) when everyone but me was issued with a banana. I can remember my distress when I discovered there was no banana for me, and to be honest I have never really come to terms with that loss and the unfairness of it all so many years ago!

Godfrey Pratt – 1930s
As a very small scholar I was impressed by the sight, on Top Table for staff breakfast, of a ham, splendidly displayed on a china pedestal. It may have been only on Sundays or other special occasions, as I doubt if even the staff ate very extravagantly in pre-war days. On Fridays, in those days, the main course at lunch was soup accompanied by mashed potato and a chunk of cheese which, if cut into pieces and immersed in the hot soup, developed a delightfully rubbery texture.

Glossary – 1940s
Dishwater	Tea
Chaff	Bread
Tack	Butter or margarine
Frogspawn	Sago pudding
Accident in the Alps	Rice pudding with red jam
Stodge	Steamed pudding
Flat Meat	Cold roast meat reheated in gravy
Begging	Searching for second helpings from other tables

Pat & Donn Webb

Peter Joselin – 1940s
Part of the sugar ration was given out each week for personal use on cereal, in tea, and so on, with the kitchen keeping the rest for cooking. I used to save as much as I could because, with rationing, to take a large tin of sugar home to my mother each holiday was the best present I could give her. To this day I do not use sugar in tea.

Nigel Weaver – 1950s
Memories of FSSW always become more benign with the passage of time, but one of some immediacy for most of my junior years was the importance of food. Sweets were rationed; sugar for cereal and beverages was limited to one small honey pot full per week, meal portions were strictly controlled, pocket money was restricted on the advice of the School and we at the Boys' End always seemed to be hungry! Anybody not using their sweet ration of four ounces per week could trade it at a vast profit.

The Dining Room in 1950

Charles Kohler – 1920s

At breakfast and midday the children mixed up, a boy sitting next to a girl, but at tea time the boys sat together at long tables on one side of the room, the girls on the other side. Top Table stood on a raised platform. Masters and mistresses were already there, each standing behind his or her chair. At the centre of Top Table stood Mr Rowntree, rocking nervously on his toes. When all the children were assembled he sat down. A grating, scraping and coughing as teachers and children pulled out their chairs and followed his lead. Two hundred heads were lowered, a moment of silence and then a tumult of talk, laughter and clatter of crockery.

In front of each child lay a bowl, a plate, a spoon and a knife. The meal was the same as breakfast: baskets with chunks of bread – 'bricks' – huge jugs of cold milk, slabs of margarine. It was the last meal of the day and we made the most of it. As it was the beginning of term, nearly everyone had brought in 'extras' such as a pot of jam, marmite or fish paste. A few boys were flavouring their milk with Camp Coffee essence. Most children brought with them a story book. We were encouraged at breakfast and tea – but not at midday dinner – to read after finishing our meal.   from *Unwillingly to School*.

Glynn Abrey 1940s tells of a farmer's son who was not keen on sports and would therefore volunteer to do the Saturday run to Bacon's Fish Shop in Station Street. You will remember that there was generally chips at Saturday supper – and these Richard collected, in steel containers, on a two-wheel hand cart and, of course, he had various people to assist him. Collection time was supposed to be 4.30 pm but Richard used to take his cart to Bacons about 2.00 pm and then slide into the Ritz Cinema to catch the afternoon show.   After the film show, he always came out by the side door to avoid being seen by a teacher. He visited the Ritz Cinema 13 times in a 12 week term – not a bad record!

Susan Fry – 1940s

The food at Saffron Walden was pretty poor during the time I was there (1942-49). I dare say that others may have different memories but this is what I remember.:

Breakfast consisted of cereals or porridge followed by something cooked on four days of the week. There was unlimited bread but only one small pat of butter (or margarine). I can't remember what we had to drink but I am inclined to think it was tea. On three days (Tuesday, Thursday and Sunday) we had no cooked breakfast but I think that we had a roll each and there was a dish of Jam or marmalade or a strange sort of dark orange jelly.

Lunch was a reasonable meal except for the awful milk puddings that they sometimes made with sweet macaroni and, worse still, pearl barley. I clearly remember the jam roly-poly that oozed with red hot jam and was smothered in custard. There were some who didn't like the custard skin – tant mieux for those who did!

Sunday lunch was particularly gruesome. Cold meat, potatoes that had been 'roasted' without any fat, sliced beetroot in vinegar. This was followed, in summer, by stewed rhubarb. It took many years before I got to like rhubarb and I have never come to terms with beetroot in vinegar.

For tea we had a cooked meal on four days. Or it might have been a slice of spam, which everyone seemed to like. On Saturday we always had baked beans or tinned spaghetti and, I think I remember that we had chips. These were fetched, by some of the boys, from the town. On the other days we had jam and a small piece of cake of some kind. We had milk to drink at tea time. On Sunday evenings, after Meeting, we had a couple of biscuits each.

I don't think there was a day when we weren't hungry. I know that we broke bounds, regularly, if there were Lyons fruit pies to be had at Housdens.

Pat & Donn Webb 1940s

Food was minimal and presumably the catering staff were urged to be frugal and manage with very little equipment. We had to take our turn washing up on Sunday mornings. We had currant buns on Sundays – quite a treat. Bread formed a large part of the diet. At recess baskets of dry bread were eagerly grabbed, sometimes with a special treat of dripping. Breakfast and high tea also consisted largely of bread. Each person had one small pat of butter which had to be divided by the desired number of pieces of bread. Jam and marmalade were only included twice a week, Wednesdays and Sundays, but you could bring your own with you. This was kept in tuck boxes in the Playroom. Likewise, we all had tins marked marked with our name and number. These contained our sugar ration for use with porridge, tea etc. or sprinkled on dry bread if nothing else was available.

Julia Dyer – 1940s

The School Council consisted of a boy and girl from each age group, some members of staff, the Head Master and Head Mistress.

Anything could be discussed at Council Meetings. We had to report back all that happened and we had to ask permission to discuss anything that I group asked us to - a terrifying, almost paralysing experience! I had to ask whether we could start a Girl Guide group in the School. Even worse, I had to enquire whether the porridge at breakfast could possibly be less lumpy.

Diana Jones – 1950s

In 1952, my second year in the Sixth Form, I decided to make cream cheese. I got the idea partly from the amount of leftover milk and partly from a book (I got most of my bad ideas from books). For a couple of weeks I was very busy letting milk go sour and then carefully decanting it into drawstring bags, three of them in the end, which I then hung in a bundle outside the window of the Girls Sixth Form Room. They dripped busily. The alcove of playground outside shortly became a no go area. Soon after that, girls in the first year Sixth took to hauling the bags up, going 'Yeurk!' and hastily letting them go again. People seriously wanted to know how long it took to make cream cheese. I had no idea. I said airily that I thought a month would do it. Everyone agreed to keep the windows closed until it was ready.

After three weeks, even with the windows closed, the Girls' Sixth Form Room smelt worse than the Boys', where a mouse had been accidentally built into the wall. The mouse was a smell you could get used to: the cheese, somehow, was not. All the same – and looking back on it, I think the rest of the Sixth Form must have been saints – we carried on in spite of warmer weather, until the fateful day when a history lesson was moved to the Sixth Form Room and the Headmistress, Jennie Ellinor, came to take the lesson.

"It's awfully stuffy in here," said she and made for the window.

We had no time for more than croaks of protest before she flung both windows wide. She recoiled. The smell was hideous.

She began hauling in the bags. They were by this time all sorts of interesting colours, green, yellow, brown and a curious red and still weakly dripping. "What is this?" asked Miss Ellinor. "Er," I said. "I was making cream cheese." And waited for the sky to fall. She merely shot me a terrible look and raced out of the room with the bags dangling at arm's length. What she did with them I never knew. It was some time before she came back, looking a little grey, and all she said then was, "*Never* do that again."

Though I was sad to lose my cheese, I secretly agreed with a friend who remarked that she thought it might not have been very nice anyway.

NEVER do that again!

John Robertson – 1950s

Breakfast was cereal or porridge, dispensed from a bowl on each table, followed by a cooked breakfast handed out from a trolley for the head of the table to serve. Toast, butter and marmalade followed, although I must admit that I am finding it difficult to remember the exact details. Did we have tea to drink, or was it just water?

Diane Hollingbery – 1950s

- Have you ever tried to cook tomato soup in the middle of the night over the gas light in the toilet in Hillcroft? We did and yes we did spill some and so got caught by 'Fido' (Miss Yapp). Got sent to the San to do the washing up as a punishment. We also tried to fry mashed potato in a tin lid over the same gas light!
- Wednesday and Sunday mornings some of the older boys went into the town to get rolls for our breakfast – we had marmalade on those days as well – it was gorgeous.
- Saving sugar for my Mum so she could make jam. We all had our own sugar tins so I suppose that sugar was still rationed.

Naomi Sargant – 1940s

Of course, food was more limited, and rationing continued even into the fifties. We had two ounces of butter and four of margarine each week, which we had to make last in individual butter dishes, and by the end of the week had got pretty rancid. I couldn't stand marge and traded my four ounces for somebody else's two ounces of butter. I still spread butter pretty thinly as a result! Sweets were of course rationed, soon eaten, often stolen from unlocked trunks. Substitutes for sweets from the town were lemonade crystals, Ovaltine tablets and Horlicks tablets. The nearest sweet shop was just down by the railway bridge, technically out of bounds on ordinary days but near enough to risk running to. The treat for tea on Saturday was beans and chips, usually fetched back on a trolley, by senior boys from a fish and chip shop in the town. Baked beans are still one of my favourites as a result and much frowned upon by my continental mother!

Ruth Colbeck – 1970s

I shared a room with two other girls and at the time we were inseparable. Looking back I think we provided security for each other in the place of parents although as we were seventeen I don't think we would have admitted it. I had asked my parents if I could board at Friends' after they separated and I don't think I missed home much because home was not the complete unit it had been.

With these three pals my most vivid memories were of our dormitory life. Our dorm was right at the top of the house under the eaves. We used to giggle for what seemed like ages after lights out about nothing in particular. Maybe because we were so far away from the housemistress's rooms we got away with more than those directly above her. Sometimes we had midnight feasts. These were much tamer than they sounded as we had to book them with Mrs Goldspink (our housemistress) so she would not come in and stop them. We never waited beyond about 9.30 pm I remember but we did plan what we would eat in advance by making cheesecakes in the sixth form common room earlier in the day. So at 9.30 pm we would hop out of bed and sit cross-legged on the dark wooden floorboards and dish out all the goodies. Sometimes we would invite girls from another dormitory but on the whole it was just us – a little clique.

Jan Willson – 1960s

While I was in in the first form – I think it was 1961 – we had the bright idea of using the bunsen burners above the toilet cubicles in the girls' cloakroom, intended to keep the water tanks from freezing, for cooking !

We started slowly, heating baked beans, and we cooked every day for a week, mainly using ingredients that we could bring out of the dining room or get with our fruit allowances in town, until, on the Sunday afternoon, we managed the three course feast. It was magnificent, with all sorts of fry up, including chips (I think probably not normally on the school menu), finishing with tinned fruit and custard, the latter made by boiling milk and adding custard powder and sugar.

We had climbed down from the roof and were just serving it all up in the cloakroom, when Jennie Ellinor walked in. We tried to stand in front of the food to hide it, but you could certainly smell it and our Headmistress was a clever lady. One by one she found us each a job to do, like opening the window,

Julia Dyer – 1940s

The prefects were extremely kind. They made delicious fudge for us on the gas ring in their room. We each had our own sugar tin into which was put our weekly ration. This we saved.

The margarine and/or butter ration was put out in little squares on a plate in the middle of each dining table at breakfast time. We were allowed to take a tin into the dining hall to save this – or were we allowed? I'm not sure – either way we saved our fat ration.

When we had enough ingredients, we took them to the prefects who kindly made them into sweet, sticky squares of fudge – delicious.

Sometimes we made our own sweets out of condensed milk, dried milk, cocoa powder, colouring – in fact anything we could buy.

We were allowed sixpence pocket money a week to be collected on Saturday or in two threepenny instalments on Wednesday and Saturday. We were allowed into the town in groups of three or four.

We mixed our ingredients together and made the mixture into sweets by rolling it into little balls in the palms of our hands. The 'sweets' were then carefully placed along the hot water pipes (behind the coats) in the changing room. They were supposed to harden. We were allotted particular days for hair washing and dried our hair in front of two gas fires fixed at head height in the changing room.

One day our sweet making attempts were discovered. Not only were we given the almost impossible task of cleaning the pipes, we were banned from drying our hair by the changing room fires. Life could be very unfair.

so that soon there became too few of us to hide the spread! Then she made us take our plates and walk with them down the Centre Corridor and into the Dining Room where we had to scrape the uneaten meal into the pig bin. I do not remember anything else by way of a punishment, except that we learned later that Jennie and our parents had a good laugh about it at Parents' Evening, Jennie saying that she had found it very difficult to keep a straight face and would have liked to have commended our ingenuity!

That would still seem to be in keeping with the philosophy of the School, but I am not sure that today's students need to find amusement in that way.

Marygold's Diary

On VE Day, 8 May 1945, Marygold Lansdell began to keep a diary in pictures, covering notable events during that Summer Term. Here are a few pages, starting with the victory celebrations

Official VE Day Programme

Programme for today, 8 May 1945

- 9.30 am School Service
- 10.15 am Boys & girls collects for announcements
- 10.30 am Mixed Hockey. All group bathes (details of times later) Refreshments
- 11.45 am Mock Sports
- 2.00 pm Mixed Cricket Match Junior Treasure Hunt
- 3.00 pm Broadcast by Prime Minister
- 3.30 pm Interval for Refreshments
- 4.15 pm Senior Treasure Hunt (won by Katy & Peanut) Junior 'Sardines'
- 5.30 pm Tea outside
- 6.30 pm Games – Terza, Rounders, Puddocks, short dip
- 8.15 pm Lighting of Bonfire & Fireworks
- 9.00 pm King's Speech
- 9.30 pm Refreshments Bedtime

Sports Programme

1) Tug of War Enemy v The Allies ie Masters & 6th form girls v Mistresses & 6th form boys
2) The "Boy Friend" Obstical (sic) Race
   (We will provide a really pre-war line in boy friends for them. Some may be 2nd hand, we fear)
3) 6th Form Blind Obstical Race (All 6th form should attend!) . . . .

On VE day, Fido and Pumps organized a great school treasure hunt. Katy Procter and I reached the treasure (Fido) at exactly the same time.

Michael Rossman (Peanut)

Valuable prizes may be offered, if the organisers have not already scoffed the lot in celebrating VE Night

Marygold's Diary

Election Day

Thursday, 5 July 1945

Those who remember the General Election of 1945 will recall the exploits of one Anthony Brooks who made an unscheduled visit to the Chemi Lab where he mixed a potion into a test-tube. He then invited Michael Stoner to accompany him to R A Butler's election meeting in town where he dropped the said test-tube behind a radiator and emptied the hall.

Both Tony and Mike were sent home for the rest of term – Butler was a highly esteemed Minister of Education and Gerald Littleboy had never been seen so angry.

However, in line with the spirit of forgiveness, Tony returned to the School and, later, became a Prefect. The story has passed into FSSW folklore – all thanks to Tony for allowing it to be recounted here.

The Yanks

During the War, the Americans from the Air Force Base at Debden used to come to use the School's facilities for recreation. They used the Swimming Pool at such high temperatures that, after a while, pieces of girder began to fall down into the water. A baseball diamond appeared on the Field, near the Mount Pleasant Road boundary, and crowds would gather there to watch the strange goings-on

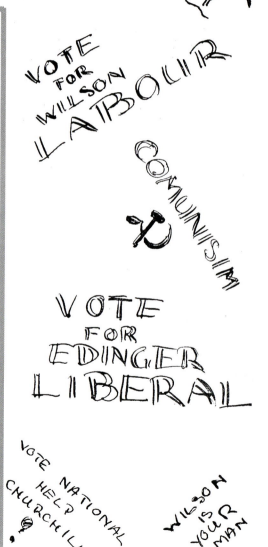

Marygold's Diary

... And the Walls came tumbling down ...

During the War years, blast walls were constructed in front of the most vulnerable windows to protect them from bomb blast. These made the clasrooms very dark. With the war over, the walls could come down.
Story by Glynn Abrey

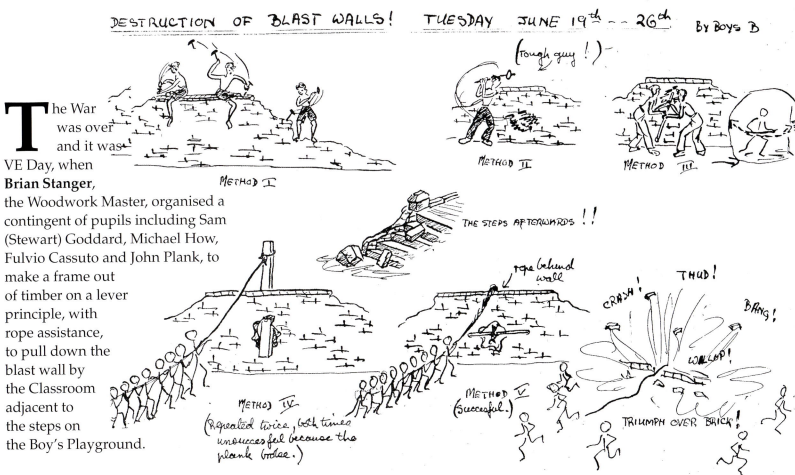

The War was over and it was VE Day, when **Brian Stanger**, the Woodwork Master, organised a contingent of pupils including Sam (Stewart) Goddard, Michael How, Fulvio Cassuto and John Plank, to make a frame out of timber on a lever principle, with rope assistance, to pull down the blast wall by the Classroom adjacent to the steps on the Boy's Playground.

Sam Goddard took one look at this and thought, "I know an easier way". He disappeared to his father's haulage and tar spraying premises in the town and returned with a long jack which he placed between the School Building and the blast wall. Of course, down it came in a hurry, causing considerable damage to the steps. The local builders were then called in to repair probably the only war damage the School suffered.

Marygold's Diary

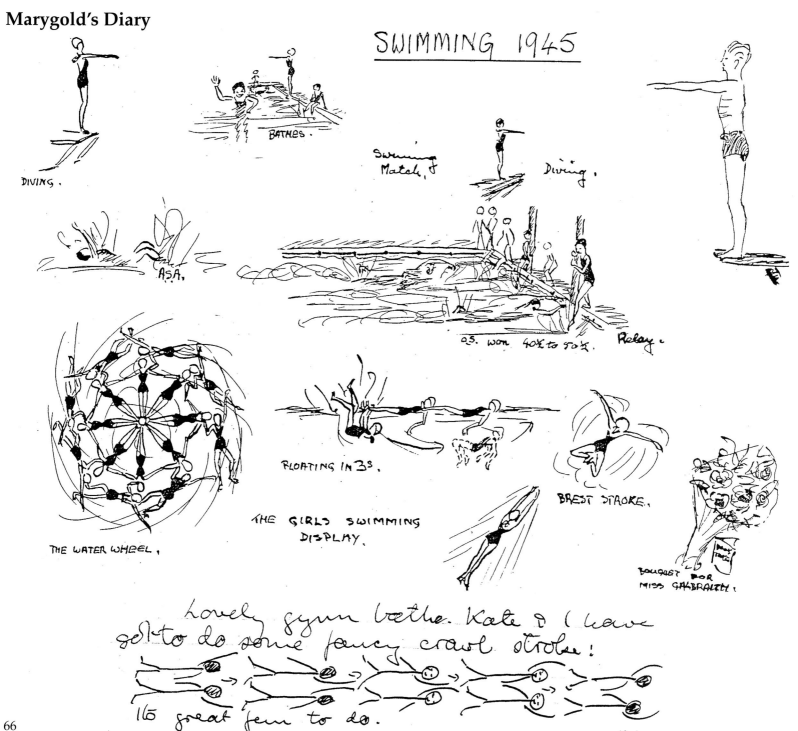

Gillian Hopwood remembers September 1939

I was on holiday with my parents in Woolacombe, the days were hot and sunny and the long stretch of golden sand was occupied by groups of people huddled round portable wirelesses listening to every news bulletin.

We made our way back to London on Saturday, 2 September, stopping in Exeter to buy yards of black fabric to make into blackout curtains. When we got home, there was a letter from FSSW to say that the School would be open the following day so that children could be evacuated from potentially dangerous areas. My father read the letter first and handed it over to my mother. Without a word being said, they agreed that I should return to School the following day. Frenzied activity followed, holiday clothes were sorted and anything for school washed, ironed and packed, along with school uniform and all the other clutter for an autumn term.

Sunday morning, Mr Chamberlain's announcement that Britain was at war with Germany, the first siren sounded, a snack lunch followed by the 40 mile journey to Walden to be greeted by Gerald Littleboy, Mrs Sparkes and various other members of staff who were living close by.

I cannot remember how many of us there were, but it was a strange and somewhat eerie atmosphere, very few in such a large building with seniors and juniors all together.

● We had meals in the staff room at the bottom of the girls' stairs.

● We played tip and run on the field with the school's foremost cricketers bowling (very gently) at one undersized twelve year old girl – unforgettable!

● Stories read in the evening by Mrs Sparkes, then Mistress of the Family, who lived in the rooms over the entrance hall.

● Helping put up the blackout shutters and curtains.

● Gerald Littleboy coming in wearing a white warden's helmet after a stint of fire-watching on the roof.

● Arnold Brereton, who hitherto had seemed to be a distant figure, became someone with whom one could talk.

The school gave temporary refuge to evacuees from London – who stayed in the gym and left behind them a legacy of head lice.

The term began and friends one expected to greet did not return, their parents deciding to place them elsewhere, closer to home, or perhaps in safer areas. Girls from Tottenham High School joined us as day girls together with girls from another school whose uniform was so much nicer than ours! Refugees from other countries came, one by one.

On the girls' side, bedrooms were created out of classrooms, leaving the top floor empty. A ground floor room turned into a shelter with stout pine poles wedged between floor and ceiling and mattresses stacked ready to be laid on the floor during raids. A strange time but somehow, as children do, we adapted to the new circumstances.

Winter Scene, c1949

The Cricket Team 1949: l-r
Back row: Geoffrey Pilliner, Paul Honigmann, Roger Bennett, David Matthews
Bobby Dutton, Tommy Gutwein, Jeff Follett
Middle row: Robin Webb, Jimmy Dutton, Richard Clymo, John Skelton, Michael Comber
In front: Thomas Marriage, Arthur Chalk

Tennis c1950: l-r Pat Chuter, Jean Strachan, Jennifer Rose,
Susan Whiteman, Naomi Sargant and Jennifer Edwards

Naomi Sargant and Lindy Rumsey in 1950

The Hockey First Eleven c1950

One Family's Sporting Links with Walden

recounted by
John Cadman

My family's connection with sports at Walden covered the years 1921 to 1985. How, you might ask.

My parents, Frank Cadman and Lucy Soar, were at Walden from around 1921 to 1928. I joined the Junior School in 1944 and was followed by my sister, Pat, and brother, David, who was still at the School when I joined the staff in 1959.

I remained on the staff until 1964. My niece, Sophie, and nephew, Sam, followed on later and I have kept in contact with the School, if somewhat intermittently, on Old Scholars' occasions over the years.

The range of Physical Training (PT) and games while my parents were at the School, was very different from the Physical Education (PE) on offer today.

The boys played cricket in the summer and football in the winter, while the girls played tennis in the summer and hockey in the winter. There was some social interaction in tennis but, certainly, there was no girls' football or boys' hockey. Sports Day for boys and girls took place in the summer.

The Gymnasium, with its ropes, boxes and wall bars provided an opportunity for some gymnastics but much more emphasis was placed on physical training through a set exercise programme, often performed in rows and to time.

My father spoke fondly of his experiences in the cricket and football teams at Saffron Walden. He never competed in leagues or knock-out competitions but his enthusiasm for school matches, particularly those against Newport Grammar School, came through in our conversations – experiences to be enjoyed by me, in later years, when competing for the School, and, later still, when coaching school teams to play against Newport and Soham Grammar Schools as well as other schools in the area.

I first visited Walden at the age of three when accompanying my parents to Old Scholars' Weekends in 1936 and 1937. It was then that I was introduced to cricket while watching the OS v Boys' First XI. Whitsun became an annual visit for the family and I would follow the OS v School cricket match with interest, never imagining that I would experience some of my worst and best memories during that particular fixture later in my life.

When I arrived at the Friends' School in the summer term of 1944, the programme of sport and physical education was very much as it had been during my parents' time at school. The war years had influenced education and the physical education programme was still based around the concepts of PT and games.

While the range of sports on offer was more limited during my years at School than is the case today, this meant that we were able to spend more time developing the basics of the games we played, developing the techniques and skills more thoroughly.

An activity not pursued by many schools, but strong at Walden, was the participation in the examinations of the Royal Life Saving Society (RLSS) – diving for bricks, swimming fully clothed, dragging others for widths and lengths of the pool (an activity more likely to result in them being drowned than saved). While, hopefully, few had to use these skills in later life, the experience was very valuable.

During my time at Saffron Walden I did not realise how important this part of my education was going to be to me in later life when I was fortunate to be able to compete and coach hockey at the very highest levels, an activity in which I did not participate seriously at Saffron Walden, occasional mixed hockey being our only opportunity to play the game. Richard Wright will remember keeping goal in an anniversary match in 1947, with the circle protected by firecrackers – hardly the ideal preparation for a future international, avoiding explosions when entering the circle. However some future tackling to be experienced felt somewhat similar.

School sport and the success of any particular year's team is, of course, dependent on the quality of that year's intake. We were fortunate in our year, and the years above and below us, to have a number of good individuals who were able to blend in together and create successful teams. Memories of that time for me are not so much about results but more the enjoyment that I got from the excellent coaching and the relationships with the people in the teams. Names which come to mind, include Jimmy Dutton, Michael Atkins, Richard Clymo, Donn Webb and David Fairbanks, as well as Michael How, my first First Team Football Captain.

The Swimming Team c1950. Wearing blazer, Bernard Jacob (BBJ), Geography Master

But looking back now, I have to express my most sincere gratitude to those who taught me and encouraged me to participate in the various sporting activities – Jeff Follett, in charge of physical education, Cyril Mummery, who helped with the cricket coaching, Barney Jacob (BBJ) who took us for some football and particularly swimming, Stanley Pumphrey and Kenneth Whitlow – all of them helped me to enjoy sport as a boy, as I am sure they did many others. Jeff Follett, with his minute attention to detail, and Cyril Mummery, with his great enthusiasm for cricket, both gave me enormous encouragement which was essential to my ultimate success in a sport – and they were not even my designated teachers.

I was a member of Lister House and it was House Matches which provided real competition – they were always exciting. Friend competing against friend. People with whom one played in the First XI or the Under-14 teams, setting out their stall against fellow team members. There was enormous enthusiasm from those watching on Sports Day when the houses fought hard against each other for the coveted athletics title.

In the swimming pool, one tried hard to beat the person who you knew was a better swimmer than you – oh the joy or disappointment when the results went for or against you. Many people who were not involved, could not understand the enthusiasm aroused by House or School Matches at Walden. But the School provided positive experiences for everybody and, for me, it was sport and its competition.

After leaving school and switching professions, within two years I found myself doing National Service, something fairly unusual for boys from the School at that time. However, the seed sown at Saffron Walden proved to be an enormous advantage for me and enabled me to participate in some quite high level cricket, football, cross country and athletics during my time in the army. In fact, there was little time left to be a soldier.

Following National Service, I went to Loughborough to study physical education which I did for three years prior to taking up my first teaching post at Kent College, Canterbury. During the period between leaving school to the end of my post at Kent College, and returning to Walden to take charge of physical education, following in the footsteps of Jeff Follett, I had returned to School regularly for Old Scholars' matches and had watched those who had been junior members of School when I was a pupil develop to be extremely skilful sportsmen. As in previous years, members of staff joined the boys in the combined staff and boys eleven to play the Old Scholars, alongside Kenneth Whitlow and Cyril Mummery.

On my return to Saffron Walden I had, through my education, widened my ideas of what physical education meant and I was keen to develop those ideas through my PE teaching. I had, by then, been introduced to hockey and was determined that the sport should be introduced to boys at the School. I had also developed a belief that winning was more enjoyable than losing. Something

Boys' Hockey, 1961

John Cadman welcomes the winner of Cross Country, 1961

I had, in retrospect, believed at School as a boy but not so intensely as I had by the time I returned to the staff.

My training at Loughborough had also given me a far broader understanding of the development of team games and team skills, something I wanted to pass on to the pupils I was teaching. During my first year on the staff in 1959-1960, hockey was introduced as a boys' game and, in the winter of 1960-61, the games pattern changed to one term soccer, one term hockey, a change apparently accepted by the School. Eventually a Hockey Association (HA) fixture against the School became a regular part of the programme and John Pilgrim proved to be one of our outstanding players who later distinguished himself as an umpire, gaining the International Umpiring Badge in Canada. We met in the early 1980s in Toronto when I was conducting an IOC coaches' course in Canada. It was good to share a common interest and talk over old times.

During my time on the staff, the tradition of cricket continued with the Master's XI a combination of boys and staff playing the odd fixture. However the big development, which was to have a lasting influence on school cricket, was the birth of the Bats XI and the cricket week. The contribution to the Bats XI of 'Danny' Hills, Graeme Johnston and others has been outstanding.

Athletics always formed an important part of the Summer Term, both during my stay as a pupil and my time on the staff. The latter being the more enjoyable when my wife, Val Cadman, joined us and became head of Girls' PE. The organisation of Sports Day was a military operation. Plans and papers were scattered all over our flat in Hillcroft for days beforehand, fitting winners of heats into their rightful slots, ensuring people did not compete too close in time when in a number of activities. A fond memory was of Cyril Mummery mastering the score tent and Richard Wright marshalling the judges. Without the help of many members of staff, Sports Day would never have been so successful.

One particular occasion comes to mind when the Mid-Essex Cross-Country Championships were held at the Friends' School in the snow of 1963. Graham Errington had a good win and, on another occasion, David Wicksteed collected the team trophy from Kenneth Nicholson. Many people will remember, with differing sentiments, the cross-country course. In my opinion one of the best school courses I knew.

Soccer continued to be a major part of the winter programme and I recall sides with Michael Duffill, Malcolm Pim, Arnold Wilson, David Hills and many others being part of enthusiastic teams who performed with great credit.

To see in the Annual Reports that rugby is now also included in the PE programme, shows that development continues. What those of us who have been deeply involved with sport and Walden must always remember is that sport is not for everybody and that it is only a part of life. I hope the pupils and staff who participate in sport at the Friends' School over the years to come get as much fun and enjoyment as I did. The Playing Field has played an important part in my life.

More Wartime memories:

We had a wonderful choir created and directed by music teacher, Richard Sturge. Being a co-educational school with male and female staff, we were able to have a mixed choir with a full range of voices from bass to soprano. We gave many concerts around the country. One day, we went to a German Prisoner of War camp near Saffron Walden and sang for the prisoners there. Afterwards they provided refreshments for us. Knowing we were coming, and with their own sparse rations, they had made some strudel cakes, a German speciality. They were delicious – it's a memory I shall always treasure.

American soldiers (GIs) were billeted next door to Hillcroft House. They made doughnuts for us and handed them round to pupils on the school field. It was my first taste of American doughnuts.

When the sirens went we hid under the beds and heard the V2 rockets come over, hoping and praying they wouldn't drop on us. Fortunately they didn't, and we lived to tell the tale.

For the Old Scholars' Reunion one year, I was made official choreographer for a display of Polish country dancing which was performed on the tennis court by the Avenue. We wore white blouses and long black skirts made of blackout material. (ie the black cotton material used for curtains throughout WWII to ensure no light could be seen from the windows).

After the School Certificate exams we would cycle around nine miles to pick fruit eg strawberries and plums, for Hartleys, the jam producers. It was hard work and back breaking – then we cycled back to School.

Pat Lamond

Theatre at Friends' School, 1977-2002

John Dickinson

"Only memories and love remain"
(Paul Miller, Old Scholar, *A Walk with my Family*)

I have chosen these twenty five years because for almost twenty of them I was directly involved with Theatre at FSSW. This can only be a personal reflection as I am not one for collecting a vast hoard of objective memorabilia. I hope to say something about the place of Theatre in our Friends' School and, for any old scholars and staff who were part of the Theatre scene and might look back on what on earth it was all for, something about the philosophy that lay behind our theatre work. Please would Drama aficionados note that space doesn't allow for Drama, which is not necessarily the same as Theatre, here. Improvised creative work and writing were ever going on in the Studio and during productions, not to mention the academic study of our subject for examinations, a rich source of resource and research for what went on on stage.

In 1977, when I arrived at the School, Michael Collins and Mark Miller were directing plays. I didn't see Mark's *Zigger Zagger* but heard very good reports of it. I did catch Mike's *Caucasian Chalk Circle* and have an abiding memory of the tug of love and Caroline Jones feeding her young baby with such naturalness and sensitivity. This was my first glimpse of how Friends' pupils embrace the 'dance of thought and feeling' that makes good theatre. Schools which think about colourful blazers, super accents and academic results but have not feeling know education to the very letter but not the 'spirit', rather like misinterpreted Brecht without Stanislavski. Ex-students, I'll leave that one open to all your numerous interpretations!

Directing the pre-play for *The Circle* was the brand new Head of English, Brian Gatward, who, soon after this, began to put his distinctive mark on Friends' School Theatre. He began with *The Beaux Stratagem* closely followed by a ground breaking *Oh What a Lovely War*, a perfect choice for the family of this school which set the tone and standards for many musicals to come. With the Juniors he directed a splendidly funny *Hobson's Choice* which Form Eight (then Two) and I backed up with some scenes from *Pygmalion*. He also led one of the oldest societies in the school – The Senior Literary Society – to new heights. In one terrifying Pinter evening, he and Mike Collins (in character) snatched my specs and, having forced me to the floor, interrogated me (trying to be in character). Every time I take my glasses off I still remember it.

Brian died tragically early, in 1997. He left behind a rich legacy in many areas of school life. How he would love to have seen his daughter Rebecca directing at the RSC. Rebecca Gatward and her brothers, world traveller/journalist Matthew and Dr. Jonathan, have recently donated a bursary in memory of their father, for a young Theatre student to have a residency at the Gate Theatre in London, where Rebecca has already directed to much acclaim. All of us who knew Nina, Brian and family will never forget evenings at their home after Senior Lit, when school merged into a wider context and the spirit of true Friendship united pupils, teachers and visitors from the outside world.

The first full length play at the School in which I was involved was *Kes* in which Year Nine (then Three) took part in abundance and for which Phill procured a real live kestrel. This gave the lie to

l-r Rajan Chetsingh, Olga Sheeran, John Skelton, Judith Foster and Susan Whiteman (far r) in A Midsummer Night's Dream, *1950*

Some of the cast of The Comedy of Errors, *1980s*

the maxim 'Never act with children or animals.' Our fear that 'Kes' would leave the auditorium ("Kes has left the building!") never materialised. I hadn't really learned enough about directing in schools (still haven't) but the scholars made sure I didn't make too many mistakes and I learnt always to listen carefully to their views and appreciated their special brand of kindness and sensitivity.

Meanwhile senior members of staff gave endless encouragement. Richard Sturge did so during one Sports' Day which led to him opining on everything from the Proms to classical theatre which made us forget our stop watches during the 400 metres to the chagrin of more fanatical sportsmen. One day when I was co-editing *The Avenue* (with the marvellous scholar half of the partnership, Julian Black) in London, umpiring cricket at Fyfield, rehearsing and on duty in Walden all at the same time and before the age of the mobile, Richard Wright showed the essence of our School. Saying nothing about those who had allowed such a jam or my wretched inability to say 'no', he quietly picked up the pieces and helped in every unknown way he could. And all this despite overwhelming Senior Master and Head of Department duties.

The challenge of all this probably led to the first Senior Scholar production in which I got involved, *Tom Jones*, which proved controversial even before it hit the boards. One Governor declared it inappropriate, a parent refused to come on the grounds it was obscene. Further, the Head, coming round with prospective parents, witnessed a rehearsal of one of the 'Molly' love scenes taking place on the floor of a Leicester classroom and all this after the swearing in the text of *Kes* which, of course, we had to include in truth in some measure, since Yorkshire children of that day did not say 'scones' when upset. The Tom Jones company's reply to the critics (before they had even seen the show, incidentally) was G K Chesterton's maxim, "If the book isn't wicked the author is!" What few adults knew until the actual performances was that Toby Haggith, our Tom, was too nice a guy to take advantage of maidens in the cast and that a meeting of the latter was hastily arranged for them to grab hold of him and make sure he was kissed. I will never forget his face after the first night – something between pleasure and disbelief. Dr. Haggith currently does famous things in the National War Museum.

Although these facts are true, some readers may have realised an underlying lightness which, of course, is a part of the necessary 'letting go' in any worthwhile production. At Friends', tolerance and forgiveness, in the air generally as well as in the studio and on stage, were essential ingredients of the mega team/family efforts required.

The Women of Canterbury – who were they? Where are they now?

In 1942, they formed the Chorus of T. S. Eliot's, 'Murder in the Cathedral'. The Chorus meticulously trained and rehearsed, spoke in harmony. as one voice. They were so good that the BBC (with whom FSSW had some connection through the Bower family, then at the School) sent someone to record the rendering of the Chorus, but it did not get onto the radio. I remember Muriel Hockley, Pauline Milford, Ann Ryan, Sylvia Blake, perhaps Pat Jeffery. I was one of them. Who else? Two more I think.

Then there were the knights, baying for "Thomas à Beckett, the Cheapside brat", the timid priests, the worldly Templers. And Thomas himself, humble and resolute – "Unbar the doors, I say, unbar the doors. I will not have the House of Prayer turned into a fortress!"

And, after the murder, the Chorus, as commentators, "Clear the air, clear the sky, wash the wind, take stone from stone and wash them. wash them".

The production, inspired by and led by Campbell Stewart, took place in 1942 in Thaxted Church.

I think it had a deep and moving effect on the School, and the audience. There are people in Thaxted, (where I now live) who recall it to this day.
                                    Mary Fulford

The Murder in the Cathedral performance turned out to be one of the most memorable and formative episodes of my life. This was partly because it made me realise that School had become a substitute for family – perhaps because of difficulties in my own family.

After the last performance, the School gave us a treat in the form of as many kippers and tinned sliced peaches as we could consume – delicious! *Professor Paul Fordham*

And what huge family enterprises indeed these were. The dance of thought and feeling went on and on through the eighties and nineties. Scholars romped through, in round, square, oblong and on proscenium, The *Dream*, twice with a punk, once with a Puck, *Godspell* in the Hall and in Thaxted Church, *Murder in the Cathedral* in St Mary's Walden and the Richardson Hall/Cathedral, the entire *Lark Rise to Candleford*, *The Comedy of Errors*, *Grease* (plus *Grease Lightning* which really did 'go'), *Zigger Zagger*, *Animal Farm*, *Gregory's Girl*, *The Crucible*, *Romeo and Juliet* and *West Side Story* with Jenny Woolgar, who recently administrated the National Youth Choir of Great Britain, as Maria. And more: the staff in a subversive *Plunder*, Jenny See's *Much Ado*, Pat Lawson's *Little Shop of Horrors* and a *Wilde Evening* with all the professionalism and talent of Amanda MacDonald and Tom Marty. And that hasn't yet included the Junior School's recent special contribution, under the expert baton of Martin Wilson, from *The Wizard of Oz* to *The House of Frankenstein*, from *Asp* to *Smike*.

What joy it was to be alive, let alone doing a 'job', for what wondrous designers, craftspeople and musicians were gathered here! Phillip Rich's phalanx of scholar and 'student in residence' artists; Mike Collins' craftspeople and his and Tessa Brown's choreography; Ann Foxley, Dot Free and their pupils' splendidly imaginative costumes. Then there were Mark Wilsher (later to join his brother Toby at Trestle Theatre and now gone freelance), James Hawkes and Sam Marriage, scholar stage managers, lighting and sound engineers extraordinaire.They saved all the shows with which they were associated by their mature skill at their craft and keeping people like me away from all technical switches and hitches. If my own children bear grandchildren, they will hear the story of the Wilsher/Richardson secret midnight transfer of a forbidden piano from Music School to Hall. "Listen my children and you shall hear of the midnight ride of ..." but shh ... even now the then management know not the full story ...

And who will ever forget Edward (Dodge) and his students' music making. To my meagre book for *Star*, Edward wrote a most beautiful score which enabled us to be given special mention in the National Theatre's School Challenge. His student Suzie Naylor

This was the set for the 1991 production of **Animal Farm**. *It was designed by Artist-in-Residence, Paul Lillie. The play was produced by James Hawkes and Arthur Saunders and instigated and directed by John Dickinson, Head of Drama.*

Paul and Arthur built the set. The white screen, lit from behind, would change colour – the effect of this was quite menacing. Arthur also painted the portrait of Lenin. James extended the stage forward to halfway up the hall and constructed some temporary tiered seating.

Ten minutes into each performance he drove the drunken farmer in through the front door and out of the fire door opposite, using the Groundsman's petrol powered garden tractor, ensuring the audience stayed awake!

A truly ambitious production.

then wrote the music for *Fox* which we took on a Northern tour. In the intervals of plays we would all gather round the Music School Grand, say "Play it again, Ed" and revisit *Casablanca*. Friends' pupils have an astonishing capacity to be involved in all sorts of things at once like any young family.

They even found time in one of these to honour Chris Smith, for being most positive audience participant of the last quarter of the twentieth century. Also Sarah Evans, a Head whose sensitivity to and understanding of the needs of young people involved in Drama and Theatre was so special. Sarah understood that rehearsals do not belong only to time left over at the end of school when staff and scholars are already worn out. Nor can really good Theatre simply arise from prospectus platitudes like "first rate at drama" followed by hope or a sort of "we're in a Friends' School so we ought to be excellent at it!". Most of all, she saw the educational vision of pupils involved in crafts, art, music, acting and, yes, the science of lighting and technology combining in deep and worthwhile Theatre experiences. It takes time to rehearse singers, dancers and actors and for the crew to do their business, and she began to give scholars the time they needed, wanted and deserved. I expect Jane continued this although I departed the FSSW stage just as she was taking over.

So what are we left with? Well, as usual it's impossible to define the Friends' School experience or the full role of Theatre in it. But perhaps a few pointers: the dance of reason and emotion involving 'whole' young people, the realisation that what is essential is invisible to the eye, and the Friendship that binds scholars, teachers and parents in the understanding that it is Love that can bind us in great endeavours and Love, enveloping memories, is what remains in the end.

Half a Century of Music Making at Walden

by Mary Mileson

I had not heard of the Friends' School, nor did I know anything about the Quakers in 1951, but, on leaving the Royal Academy of Music in the summer of 1952, I became a 'cello and piano teacher at FSSW under the guidance of Richard Sturge.

I lived in Hillcroft, across the road, with a bedroom on the second floor, complete with lino and a gas fire, and taught the 'cello and piano in the front room downstairs. This also had a gas fire and a gas ring for a kettle.

'Cello classes took place in the Assembly Hall, and all the First Years (now Year Seven) had to learn either the violin, 'cello or recorder. This enabled the music staff to discover any able musicians and thus keep an already excellent orchestra well supplied with instrumentalists through the years. I enjoyed my 'cello and piano pupils very much. Some were quite promising musicians. Margaret Shepherd went on to study at the Royal Academy of Music. We had a school string quartet, a wind quartet and two orchestras; Barbara Comber conducting the 1st and myself the 2nd.

Bernard Jacob and I were Form Teachers of 3b in the room now the Junior Science Laboratory. It was fun being a resident member of staff, even if it involved things like duties. Joy (Dupont) Ashford as she then was, and I used to cook on the gas ring in my room. Barbara Comber, Agnes Horlick and myself used to squeeze into Barbara's car plus 'cello, once a week, to go and play in the Dunmow Orchestra. When the Saffron Walden Operatic Society were performing (often Gilbert and Sullivan), we would play in the orchestra, and be joined by a gifted violin pupil, Malcolm Harvey. Malcolm was also an excellent footballer and Barbara, his violin teacher, would worry when there was a football match and a concert or music exam on consecutive days in case he broke an arm or finger. I think she and Jeff Follett (PE) often had a few words. Malcolm of course went on to study at the Royal College of Music. He would come back on Old Scholars' weekends when we always had an entertainment and would play pieces like *The Flight of the Bumble Bee* at an amazing speed. Those entertainments were great fun and many will remember Tubby Bennett and excerpts from Gilbert and Sullivan Operas.

The end of the Christmas Term was always an exciting musical time with Richard Sturge's small choir singing carols in local churches and at School. This small choir sang beautifully at my wedding to Geoffrey Mileson in August 1955 at Loughton, Essex. Having left FSSW, I was asked to come back one day a week to teach the 'cello for two terms as they were without a teacher. Every Tuesday I got up early and chugged over to Saffron Walden in a Hillman 10 (built in 1934) at 35 mph.

The Choir in 1952 with Richard L Sturge (l)

We moved to a farm at Little Walden in 1958 and in 1962 Richard Sturge asked me to come back and teach the piano part time. I was delighted, and this then led to a full time music post in 1968 with cello, piano, and class music.

Here are some of the interesting happenings of the next twenty years. My younger son, Timothy joined the School, his elder brother having gone to Newport Grammar. King Edward Grammar School in Chelmsford held a one-day Music Festival every May, which included individual items, ensembles and school orchestras. We took part in this for many years with a coach load of musicians. No prizes were given but a helpful criticism was issued to each competitor. One year our Second Orchestra numbered about 50 and our French teacher David Pope, composed us a special piece under the pen name of Osric Fairweather. This was great fun – the highlight of the day was everyone playing in the enormous orchestra in the evening – quite an experience for some of our instrumentalists.

We had some wonderful musical experiences in the seventies with

RLS, when all the Quaker Schools joined forces and performed a big musical work near the host school. This tradition still continues. In 1970 it was the first time that all eight of the schools had come together, and Bach's *B Minor Mass* was performed in Thaxted Church and at Friends' House. Then in 1975 we again hosted the joint choirs for Elgar's *Dream of Gerontius* in the same venues.

In 1977 our Choir numbered over a hundred, and two coach loads, plus many cars, arrived at Bootham to rehearse Verdi's *Requiem*, and then to perform it in York Minster. I enjoyed playing my 'cello on these occasions as the orchestra comprised musicians and teachers from all the Quaker schools and we got to know each other and look forward to the next 'do' three years later. My husband Geoffrey enjoyed singing bass on these occasions. In 1979 we said a fond farewell to Richard Sturge by giving him a concert which included both past and present pupils, and even a small choir, singing one of the Rubbra Motets written especially for the school's 250th celebrations in 1952. Usually the senior scholars produced a play every November, but in 1979 we performed *O What a Lovely War*, produced by Brian Gatward. I enjoyed producing the music which consisted of a piano, double bass and percussion. Brian was a meticulous producer and many will remember the very successful performances.

Olga Peters, Stalin's granddaughter, joined the Schoool in 1982. She was a musical girl and learnt both the piano and the 'cello with me. Two years later, her mother whisked her back to Russia for 18 months, but she was delighted to return and to be with her friends and teachers again. Her friends at the School sent her letters, which she received, while she was in Russia, but none of her replies found their way back to them.

Friends' School was asked to join in a Concert for Peace in 1985 when Paul Tortelier, the famous 'cellist, and his daughter, Maria de la Pau came to Cambridge. Tortelier had composed a song called *May Music Save Peace*, and our choir, with two choirs from Cambridge, joined forces to perform this at the concert in the Guildhall with Tortelier conducting. I had the honour of accompanying the song.

Sue Hembry (piano teacher) and I took the First Years to see Andrew Lloyd Webber's *Cats* when it was first staged. Sue had procured the tickets for one of the preview performances, so we arrived by coach at the theatre only to find that there was some mistake—on their part—and the cast were still rehearsing. The coach had gone by then and so we were allowed to stay and watch the rehearsal. Apparently Judi Dench, who was meant to be Griselda, had broken her ankle, and so the opening was postponed – Sue had telephoned that morning and the box office had told her all was well. However, the First Years did not mind as they were later invited to a proper performance, with upgraded seats, a visit behind the scenes to meet the cast, a poster and all costs covered!

In the Orchestra in the forties Naomi Sargant (double bass), Gwyneth Jackson ('cello)

The senior scholars did a production of *Godspell* in 1985. It was performed in the Assembly Hall and later in Thaxted Church. Rehearsing was great fun and the performances were very moving experiences. Two other musical plays were produced later – *Lark Rise to Candleford* and *Grease*.

The last few years have been very exciting with the opening of Gibson House, the Junior School. Starting with fifteen children – some musical – it has gradually become a large establishment, bursting at the seams with musicians. I have taught the piano there since it opened and currently have 24 pianists, which is quite enough to contend with. We now have quite a large orchestra and, last Christmas, made a CD with orchestral pieces and carols. Every child in the school took part.

Recently, the staff and children helped me to celebrate my 70th birthday. Flowers, a cake in the shape of a grand piano, candlesticks and a card signed by all my pupils and Happy Birthday sung to me in Assembly.

I must retire soon.

"... never quite so free again"

Adrian Smith (1952-59)

Many people, I suppose, look back on their days in the Sixth Form as the culmination of their school career – they recall their devoted efforts to achieve "A" Levels, or a hard-won goal in a First Eleven match. My life as a Sixth Former at Walden did have successes and happy times, but it is, above all, my fourth year I recognise as most poignant and formative.

That was a year of change at Walden. Kenneth Nicholson succeeded Gerald Littleboy and, within the first few weeks (30 October 1955), received what was literally a baptism of fire when the new Chemistry Lab, by the Tennis Courts, was gutted. I wrote in my letter home: "All order broke down – Prep was abandoned."

Disorder threatened from another quarter in 1956 when the film Rock Around the Clock coincided with the first appearance of Elvis, he of the subversive pelvis, not that either of these events influenced me.

For my own part, I found a new musical interest by joining the School Choir – not possible until the Fourth Year – where we sang Stanford's lovely anthem Beati Quorum Via and Adoremus Te Christi by Palestrina, with its unearthly upward run for the altos.

I have always liked the contralto voice. How many schools were there, in the year of Elvis, when Fourth Form boys ran upstairs at bedtime singing Stanford and Palestrina? Thanks to the influence of Richard Sturge, Latin remains, for me, not so much an ancient language as the tongue of the medieval church. Part of its effect was the atmosphere of the buildings where the works were performed. On the rood screen of the Parish Church at Saffron Walden stand the figures of St Mary and St John gazing up at the crucified Christ, and the fading dusk of a summer evening seemed to go on for ever. But teenage tenors have a plaintive quality. We were supplemented by men from the town whose full blooded efforts were mercilessly mimicked by Peter Dunstan in the dormitory afterwards.

In the Fourth Year I was at last free to have my bicycle at School and Kenneth Nicholson most generously allowed me to go out for rides by myself, contrary to the usual rule, provided that my parents gave permission (they gladly did). Even when still half-fare, I used to travel to London on the train by myself. I never got into mischief and always returned when I said I would, I see now that I operated quite a successful parent policy. Many teenagers are furtive and this makes parents suspect, maybe quite wrongly, that they are up to no good.

From the autumn of 1955, the whole of the Saffron Walden One Inch Map (Seventh Series) became my province. I always had a passion for maps, exploration and following linear features such as railways and canals. Now I began to track down tumuli, Roman roads and the mysterious earthworks of South Cambridgeshire. Cyril Mummery gave me every encouragement and I see how this year marked the start of my serious interest in the past. I spent much time checking the condition of rights of way and recording the results on a series of parish maps which won me, in July 1956, a Major Leisure Time Award – the only time I achieved this at Walden.

Significantly, 1955 was the year of publication of W G Hoskins' book The Making of the English Landscape. On reading this, I realised that this was what I really wanted to study. I wandered happily in the common ground where history, geography, archaeology and place name study meet and puzzled over just what human experience had given rise to features of the landscape which we see today and, mostly, take for granted. "Some there be that have no memorial, who are perished as though they have never been . . ." But the woodlands and bridleways around Saffron Walden record the lives of innumerable people who created the scenes we know and love, though their names are long since forgotten.

The bicycle changed my view of Walden, making me more solitary and reflective at an age when many boys are unthinkingly sociable. No longer did I experience school life as something isolated from the rest of the world. I am glad there were so many day scholars to link the rest of us to the town and the surrounding countryside, and was impatient with the prejudice some of the boarders showed towards the so-called 'day brats'. Some, such as Oliver Weaver, spent so much of their lives at the School that they were accepted as honorary boarders. To Tom Hopkinson I am specially grateful, as his home in the High Street provided a quiet haven at times when the clamour of school life was just too much.

Once I reached the Fifth Year, the approach of public exams cast a shadow over life and I never felt quite so free again.

Hugh Clarke, Jan Berny and A N Other beneath ladder. Chris Wood retrieves ball, 1950s

Photo John Skelton

Distinguished Old Scholars:

EDWARD BAWDEN
1903-1989

"In an age of specialists I have behaved like an amateur. However, believe me, I don't regard myself as a disappointed man."
Edward Bawden, 10 March 1979

Phillip Richardson (Staff) wrote this obituary:

I arrived at Friends' School some eleven years ago. One of the strongest images that has remained with me from that first tour around the School was of large lino prints hanging along centre corridor and, in the library. I was soon to discover that Edward Bawden not only lived locally in Saffron Walden, but was also an Old Scholar of the School. Since then, I have had a growing admiration for him as an artist, which was fully confirmed when I took a group of Sixth Form students to a retrospective exhibition of his work at the Victoria and Albert Museum this autumn. The work we saw surprised us in its great variety of imagery and media – from witty pen-and-ink sketches to large, patterned, powerful watercolours; from tapestry and poster designs to plate motifs; from strikingly designed linoprints to the grim drawings of an official war artist. His output was prodigious, professional and exciting, always maintaining a strong integrity but never losing sight of the chance for humour.

Edward Bawden was born on 10 March

Puzzled Lion and Startled Unicorn
*appeared on the masthead of the Observer
for some 50 years until 1989*

*An advertisement by Bawden for Shell-BP
in the thirties*
Reproduced from the BP Archive

1903. From the age of seven, he attended Braintree High School. When he was eleven, he strained his heart "by too-zestful swimming" and, in the enforced rest that followed, began to copy Louis Wain's cats from the *Girls' Own Paper* ... "I didn't much care for the *Boys' Own Paper*, which I actually took, but I liked the drawings in the *Girls' Own Paper* ... What lovely cats they were! – and, like a sissy, I resolved to be a book illustrator. From then on I became an indefatigable copier of magazine drawings, not at random, but picking mannered work for choice and that which was reproduced in black and white. Also, I received a few lessons from the daughter of a Congregational minister; she took me out sketching and, by her sensible precepts, laid the foundation of a habit which has persisted intermittently ever since."

By 1918, Edward had amassed so many lines as punishment for his many misdemeanours that he was taken out of the High School and he was given a fresh start at the Friends' School, Saffron Walden. Here he "went full out to get my need of recognition. I did unkind caricatures of the staff; also wore a silk handkerchief and would have sported a beard if I could have grown it – for I was a budding exhibitionist." Edward thought the Headmaster, John Edward Walker, "was a man of great character" and "a sensible man being a Quaker" and indeed was a fair draftsman himself. He must have viewed Edward's enthusiasms sympathetically for, in the first summer, he set Edward a task – "He asked me to enlarge a Seventeenth Century engraving of the Mermaid Theatre and Old London Bridge and St Paul's – I think it was by Wenceslaus Hollar. I did it with the greatest of pleasure. I did not know how to scale things up, but I managed it. It was a lovely thing to do, kept me busy every day of the summer holiday."

During Edward's final year at the School, he was allowed to attend the Cambridge and County School of Art for one day a week. "This weekly jaunt diverted my attention from working for mischievous ends, and I fully expressed my horrid little nature in designing large, elaborately enamelled plates."

Edward spent two years at Cambridge Art School and then went to sit an examination at Camberwell School of Art on the same day as Eric Ravilious who was going to become a close friend until his death in the War (1942). Other students, already installed, were Barbara Hepworth and Henry Moore. Paul Nash was teaching there in the Design School and his encouragement, friendliness and natural dignity had a profound effect on the young Edward Bawden.

He left the Royal College of Art in 1925 with a diploma in book illustration. Then, in 1926, he won a Travelling Scholarship and went to Italy. "The Italian buildings were very important to me. Sacherevell Sitwell had just brought out a book on southern baroque art, so naturally, being perverse, I looked at it as much as I could in Naples and elsewhere. It wasn't fashionable. I didn't like it much, but I imagined I did. I don't think one Italian painter was more important to me than another. It might have been the Italian food as much as the painting that mattered."

In 1928, Edward, with Eric Ravilious, was commissioned to paint a mural for Morley College. It took two years to complete, but the publicity attending the opening ceremony by the Prime Minister, Stanley Baldwin, did much to establish Edward in the commercial world. Unfortunately, this mural was destroyed in the Blitz; however, thirty years later, he painted a second mural which still survives. In 1930, Edward left London and moved to rural Essex, renting a house with Ravilious in Great Bardfield. He married Charlotte Epton in 1932 and took over the whole house. His happiness over the next few years is reflected in much of the vast amount of witty and inventive work he produced. He did a great deal for the Curwen Press and his popularity grew with posters for banks, hotels and railways and, perhaps most memorable, his brilliant Shellmex advertisements.

In 1940, Edward was appointed Official War Artist and his war was certainly

A Pontoon Bailey Bridge over the River Po near Ferrara
1945 watercolour 812mm x 1041mm
Reproduced by kind permission of the Imperial War Museum

eventful. Being sent to join the British Expeditionary Force he soon found himself at Dunkirk. He was then sent to the Middle East for two years. On his return voyage to Britain in 1942, his ship was torpedoed off the coast of West Africa. "I spent five days in a lifeboat but there was quite a lot to watch: sharks nosing round all the time, plenty of dead bodies floating about in different positions. It's very strange: when one's in danger, one gets excited, one doesn't worry at all."

After the War, Edward found that his quirky humour had become less in demand. However, his work over the next four decades matured and reached new heights, showing his true genius for pattern and design. He had started lino-cutting when still at college, but now he began to use this medium to its full strength, producing some magnificent prints – *The Pagoda* 1954; *Brighton Pier* 1958; *Hares, Foxes and Eagles* 1975. But perhaps his best work came in his linocut book illustrations for *Morte d'Arthur* and *The Hound of the Baskervilles*. Maybe his most familiar work was the *Puzzled Lion and Startled Unicorn* which The Observer newspaper used for their masthead for some thirty years. Sadly, in 1989, a new design was needed but Edward was too frail to redraw it.

During his life, Edward gained many awards. He was appointed CBE in 1946; elected ARA 1947 and RA in 1956; Royal Designer for Industry in 1949; and Trustee of the Tate Gallery 1951-58.

I only met Edward Bawden once, soon after I came to teach at Friends' School. More recently, I met, and briefly worked with, his son, Richard – a lovely man; I really enjoyed hearing the few stories he told of his father. I also enjoyed reading of the involvement of the third generation in Edward's work: " . . . For a week, my grandson, Tom, has been staying here to help with the printing of the large Saffron Walden Church lino block which is more than five feet long. Somewhat to my surprise, Tom called me by my Christian name for which I was grateful because I can't say I enjoy being dubbed Grandpa, though to hear oneself called Gaffer might be worse."

Edward Bawden died on November 21st 1989, aged 86.

RICHARD ERIC HOLTTUM
1895-1990

Henry Rowntree describes Eric Holttum as 'our most distinguished Old Scholar'; Tim Whitmore, as 'one of the greatest botanists of our generation'; while Walter Baldwin, in 1962, said he was 'our most scholarly President'. The obituary writers in the broadsheet press agree with them: "probably the greatest taxonomist of this century" (The Guardian); "Few botanists of our time have left a more enduring and valuable legacy of taxonomic achievement" (William T Stearn of Isleworth Friends' Meeting in The Independent) . . .

Richard Eric Holttum was born at Linton (Cambs) on 20 July 1895. His parents were Nonconformists and his father and uncle kept the village store. Eric attended the local school till the age of eleven when he entered the Friends' School, Saffron Walden, having acquired a knowledge of gardening from the family gardener and an interest in botany from his mother, Florence (Bradley), a self-taught botanist who organised family walks where flowers were meticulously identified. . . . At Bootham (1911-13) he won a leaving scholarship and a place at St John 's College, Cambridge. He returned to Walden as a student teacher for a year and completed Cambridge entry requirements in Latin and Greek. His Cambridge studies were interrupted after Part I of the Natural Sciences Tripos when, in 1916, he joined the Friends' Ambulance Unit and served some time as a cook in a French ambulance convoy. . . . he was one of a team of six whose gallantry under fire was recognised by the French Government, which awarded them all the Croix de Guerre. . . . In the same year, he graduated with first class honours in Botany and was awarded the William Smart Prize for the best student in Botany. He was also awarded a Foundation Scholarship at St John's College and became a Junior Demonstrator in the University School of Botany. . . . in 1922, when he had to choose between a post at the Natural History Museum and the Botanic Gardens at Singapore, he chose the latter.

At Singapore, Eric was plunged in at the deep end. The long-lived Director and only other botanist there, I H Burkill, gave him the task of "putting the fern herbarium in order" and, in the following year, took a long overdue break and left REH in charge. When Burkill retired in 1925, Eric was appointed Director. In 1927, he married Old Scholar and art student, Ursula Massey (1909-15), . . In 1928, H Burgeff of Würzburg, who had published a book on the root fungi of orchids, gave Eric information about the Knudson method of growing orchid seedlings in sterile culture. REH set up the apparatus for doing this and began to raise hybrid seedlings – the beginning of Malaysia's famous orchid industry. . . .

Gathering war-clouds in the Pacific split up the Holttum family and when the Japanese came down the Malay Peninsula, Eric sent Ursula and their two young daughters, Deborah and Catherine, to his half-sister, Olive in Australia. Later they went to Tasmania where Deborah attended the Friends' School, Hobart. Eric stayed in Singapore where the Japanese occupation of 1942-45 played a crucial part in his life: Emperor Hirohito, a keen botanist, ordered that the botanic gardens of conquered territories should be maintained. Professor Hideo Tanadkate, whom Eric had met in a Pan-Pacific Science Congress, arrived to oversee this and, after the appointment of a Japanese Director, REH was ordered to continue his research, though he pleaded with the authorities that he be treated like the other internees. The only option now was to improve the unsmiling hour. Robert John, the recently appointed head of the fern section in the Herbarium at Kew, writes in *The Guardian*: "Thus isolated from the rest of the scientific world and untroubled by administration and the numerous visitors to the famous Botanic Gardens, Holttum was able to prepare drafts

Eric Holttum in 1982

of several first-rate books. *The Ferns of Malaya, The Orchids of Malaya, Plant Life in Malaya* and *Gardening in the Lowlands of Malaya* were later to emerge as publications between 1953 and 1955. Each volume would be considered by a lesser scientist as their life's work." This was, as Eric expressed it in his OSA Presidential Address, "observation of the most rigorous kind . . . necessary to provide the mind with material on which to work."

. . . . Eric's movements were circumscribed and defined by a card he wore round his neck; his rations were the same meagre portion as the rest of Singapore's people and his weight fell to seven stone . . .

When the Japanese regime in the Pacific was obviously cracking, Eric was interned for about a month. He failed to recognise in the emaciated forms men he had known for years, and regretted more than ever that he had not been with them, as he could have told them what to grow to reduce the incidence of dysentery. Soon after hostilities ended, Eric got on a vastly overcrowded ship to England . . . He was met at Cambridge station by Dorothy (his sister) and when she asked what was in the cardboard box he was clutching, he said: "Three and a half years' work – and I'm going back to finish it." Ursula and the girls came later from Australia and, after a brief while with them, Eric returned to the gardens and to his unfinished work. His daughters entered FSSW in January 1946.

In 1949, REH retired from the Directorship of the Botanic Gardens and became the first Professor of Botany at the new University of Malaya in Singapore....When he retired to Kew in 1954, after 32 years in Singapore, Eric had no idea that he had another working life of 36 years in front of him. ...

Eric died on 18 September 1990, just a week after a family reunion in Walden with Harold, Dorothy and two or three others for a delayed celebration of his ninety-fifth birthday. Jean Stubbs recalled to the 1990 AGM of the OSA Eric's words then: "I've finished my scientific work; I've finished my autobiography; what shall I do with the rest of my life?"
Adapted from the obituary by Cyril Mummery in the OSA Annual Report, 1990

In a feature, dated 26 January 2002, *The Daily Telegraph* previewed a forthcoming display of orchids at Kew Royal Botanical Gardens. The exhibition was to include 15,500 cut stems from the Singapore Botanic Gardens. The article, by Jonny Beardsall, ended as follows:
You will find no hint of revisionism at Singapore Botanic Gardens. Holttum is still famously revered and a fine building in the grounds is named in his honour. When I met Phillip Cribb, Kew's foremost orchid expert, who arranged the forthcoming festival, he told me he took Professor Holttum – by then a nonagenarian – to the 130th anniversary of the Singapore gardens. 'People there literally kissed his feet.'

REGINALD REYNOLDS
1905-1958
From : the Croydon & Saffron Walden OSA Annual Report 1959.(Abridged)
Testimony as to the Grace of God in the life of REGINALD ARTHUR REYNOLDS.

Reginald Reynolds was the third child, and the eldest boy, in a Quaker family of five children. Although much of his life was spent in London or near Croydon, at the time of his birth his parents were living at Glastonbury, in Somerset, so he quite rightly regarded himself as a West Countryman.

At the age of eleven he followed his sister to the Friends' School at Saffron Walden, where he remained for five years, entering fully into the academic side of school life, introducing much wit and fun in unaccustomed places to the manifest pleasure of his school fellows, if frequent dismay of the Staff. Perhaps it was indicative of some lack of understanding of him in later years that even at that early stage though he came top of the School he was not made a prefect. Although this was a disappointment to him, it did not disturb the great affection he came to feel for the School, so that throughout his life he was ever ready to help each succeeding generation to share the deep attachment he had for everything associated with it. His frequent visits, both to the School and Saffron Walden Meeting House, gave him a greater sense of renewal and refreshment than almost anything else in life; and his old school fellows, who there met with him, found one of those rare people with whom it was always possible to resume at once all the happiness of old and treasured relationships.

When he left School the way ahead was not clear. so Reginald Reynolds first spent two years at Woodbrooke and later joined the firm of Clark, Son and Morland, at their factory in Somerset. During these formative years the fire which a Quaker upbringing at home and School had kindled within him was fanned by contact with Friends and others with whom he associated in the Birmingham area and at Street, where he met Laurence Housman, whose friendship and guidance came to mean so much to him. With a mind becoming filled with many turbulent thoughts centring round the welfare of his fellow men throughout the world, it was no wonder he had little aptitude for business, so after some four years he resigned and embarked on a journey that was to have a lasting effect on his life. This took him to India where for a period he lived and worked alongside Mahatma Gandhi, experiencing the quiet simplicity and meditation of his life, but in an atmosphere disturbed by the tensions of that country in the late 1920s. In those conditions the sensitive receptive mind of the young man developed, and on his return to this country, work for the cause of peace became his vocation.

This took him into the political field, where he became a left-wing idealist. But at the height of his "political period" he maintained a personal integrity of which some of his new friends disapproved. Often he protested against unscrupulous political opportunism and ruthlessness, until he became violently assailed by the very people with whom he had been collaborating. This did not bring him back to a more moderate standpoint: on the contrary, it drove him further to the left. During the Spanish Civil War, Reg and Ethel Mannin (who was soon to become his wife) devoted themselves to supporting the anti-Fascists. It was certainly not love of war or blindness to its horrors that drove them to support the defence of the Republican Government, but the evils of Fascism and a clearer vision of what lay ahead for Europe that was seen by the three great political parties in Britain at that time.

Commencing in 1932 with his work with the No More Work Movement his connection with War Registers International extended for more than twenty years.

When World War Two began, Reginald Reynolds registered as a conscientious objector and initially trained for work with the Friends Relief Service. An accident prevented his attendance before the Tribunal, which took his case in his absence and gave him a wide form of conditional exemption. He had applied for unconditional exemption and felt quite unable to accept their decision since he regarded the right not to kill as a moral absolute which could not be dependent on the will of any tribunal. He resisted all attempts to coerce him into accepting these conditions, but joined the Chelsea Civil Defence as an ambulance driver, not under any direction but as a volunteer, and later was one of the few people selected to handle tracker-dogs used in searching for victims of heavy bombing. During the hours of waiting he employed himself in much reading and research, which subsequently led to the publication of the first of several brilliantly witty, yet philosophical and learned books. This close association with the misery and suffering brought through War to his fellow human beings rekindled within his supersensitive mind the smouldering embers of his Christian Pacifism and Quaker faith. Then came Hiroshima. Few people in the Western World could have been so deeply affected by the searing flash of the first Atomic Bomb as he was, when he heard the news on his way to a joint meeting of the Peace Pledge Union and the Council of the War Resisters International. Stunned by this new horror of immense man-made human suffering it was quite surely the Grace of God which (to use his own words) prompted Reg quite suddenly to pick up a copy of Woolman's Journal. It had been among his

Reginald Reynolds signing autographs at the 250th Anniversary Reunion in 1952

father's books, retained by himself for sentiment rather than for use; but that day he put it into his pocket with the feeling that with his own new orientation, he might find something of value in John Woolman's writings. That same day he was taken suddenly to hospital. There his study of the Journal filled him with wonder and admiration. Gradually a whole new philosophy of life and conduct unfolded, which was in itself the answer to many queries which had been in his mind. When he had turned the last page his feeling of gratitude to John Woolman was equalled by the imperative need to share what he had found.

We must be forever grateful for the outcome of the loving study which followed, both for the production of the book *The Wisdom of John Woolman*, in which he showed the relevance of these writings of two hundred years ago to our lives today, and for the impetus it gave to Reg to redouble his efforts on behalf of peace and inter-racial brotherhood.

Though his health was always uncertain, the fire which lit his whole life enabled him to embark on some years of travel and service to the Society, both in this country and abroad. As Field Secretary for the Friends Peace Committee he concentrated his endeavours on the rising generation, speaking at schools and colleges and talking with the young people in their free time. It was a natural development from this for him to join the Works Camp Committee, going to camps at widely separated points where for short periods he led these international gatherings in the exercise of worship through work. He neither ennobled nor belittled work – anything that had to be done was just part of the daily task leading to the realisation of the totality of life. It was the warmth, the laughter and love which he generated that gave to all a new security, a security in a simple kind of Kingdom of Heaven, from which no one could be excluded and into all who took a glimpse wanted to enter. His humour, his colourful clothes, his sense of drama, the often unusual presentation of his ideas, all contributed to making his concerns vivid to other people. Because he had deep religious convictions, without being sanctimonious or pompous, he made young people feel they could discuss their problems and beliefs with him – and he was never shocked by what he heard. His interest, affection and belief in what they could do in the world, made them feel they had a significant part to play in the future to which they could go forward, bound together in a deep and permanent fellowship – the fellowship of people who had learned that the love of God leads inevitably to the service of God.

As he travelled around the world he found much that could only cause him sorrow and bitterness. Prisoners at home and abroad, coloured people in foreign lands, victims of inter-racial strife in Africa or America and, finally the problems of the aborigines in Australia, all came within the orbit of this versatile and apparently untiring man. He, who had such rare gifts of loyalty, affection and understanding, chose to battle among crowds, and often against crowds, with only his burning faith in God to sustain him. We may have meant to give him more of our support, but good intentions are not enough. Much more is needed: the wisdom not to mean well, but to do what is right. What is rare is to find a person who cared sufficiently to put intentions into effect. Reginald Reynolds did just that. Well may we echo words spoken of him on the first day of this year: "This was a Man. Thanks be to God."

Signed on behalf of Kingston Monthly Meeting 9.5.1959.
Frederick H. Philips, Clerk
Endorsed in and on behalf of London and Middlesex Quarterly Meeting 27.6.1959.
Anthony Skelton, Clerk

FARRAND RADLEY

In 1965, Kenneth Alexander proposed Farrand as President Elect of the Old Scholars' Association with the following words :

"This fellow I am proposing is a very brainy chap. His progress at School from form 4b to the top was rapid and he has the distinction of being one of the first to study for the Higher School Certificate at Walden. From School, he entered St Edmunds Hall, Oxford, where he took honours degrees in French and German. This probably accounts for his present day globe-trotting.

He was abroad in the Forces during the war, ending up with rank of Major and in the Military Government in Austria engaged on rehabilitation.

He is one of those very rare birds (in fact, he may be a unique bird) viz, he is the progeny of two Walden teachers. One of them even came back for a second teaching spell. His mother, before her marriage, was Miss Helen Howell. Hence the advice given in bygone days to anyone who was searching for a lost article to "go to hell and howl for it."

This character inherited a great love for music and used to play the 'cello in the School Orchestra. After the war, he became Assistant Director of Personnel in the British Council. In 1950, he left and joined the BBC. In 1958 he became Secretary of the London Branch of Office Management and, four years later, Chairman.

In the BBC, he came back to his original interest of music. He is rather a modest type and when I asked him at Television Centre, some four years ago, what his job was, he mumbled something and I was little the wiser. Officially, he was BBC Television Music Organiser. (At the time of this article, he had become Travel and Features Organiser, BBC Television)."

Farrand maintains his love of Walden and still serves as a much loved and valued member of the Old Scholars' Committee. He recently married Laura and they are a familiar sight at Old Scholars' gatherings.

RALPH ERSKINE

Ralph Erskine is one of the best known architects in the world and one of the most respected by his own profession. He was at the School from 1925 to 1931 and then moved to what was then the Regent Street Polytechnic, qualifying in 1936. A couple of years later he qualified also as a town planner. 1939 was perhaps the pivotal year of his life: in that year he both married Ruth Francis, also an OS and, unlike Ralph, a Quaker; and he set up his own architectural practice near Stockholm.

He started out by studying the architecture and building materials of Sweden and became a major authority on building in northern climates. Many of his earlier designs were for houses in Sweden (and one, for his parents, in Lewes in Sussex). He moved on to larger housing schemes, civic buildings and urban planning schemes, developing an organic and expressive architecture that was inspired both by his Swedish studies and by British community planning. He has always avoided monumental designs and sought solutions that respond naturally to the climate (and save energy) and that are built with traditional forms and textures.

In the 1950s he was a member of Team 10, an international grouping of like-minded architects who sought to develop an architecture that fostered a sense of belonging and identity in the machine age, within the context of more humane cities. His largest project in Britain, a major urban redevelopment at Byker in Newcastle from 1968 to 1982, attempted to put all this into practice. He broke new ground, also, here by setting up a consulting surgery so that local residents could come in to discuss and

DAVID C. POWELL

I was frequently in trouble at Friends' School. I considered learning French a waste of time when all I wanted to do was learn about nature and the creatures that live in water.

At one point I was temporarily expelled for blowing up the school's goldfish pond and cooking and eating the fish in the chemi lab.

In 1944 I shipped out to America on a merchant ship and spent the remainder of the war in the Pacific.

Fortunately, an MA degree in marine biology from UCLA led to a career in public aquariums where I shared my passion for aquatic creatures with millions of aquarium visitors.

influence the design as it developed.

From about 1970 his projects, mainly in Scandinavia, grew further in size, encompassing university buildings, offices (including the Ark in Hammersmith), sports facilities, suburban areas (including Eaglestone at Milton Keynes) and town centres. More than 60 years after he started it, the architectural practice still thrives. As recently as 1998 he was involved in the winning design for a huge residential development at the Millennium Village in Greenwich.

Ralph has designed an enormous number of projects, mainly in Scandinavia, and has won innumerable architectural competitions, awards, doctorates and honours in many parts of the world. Perhaps, from the perspective of his British (in fact, Scottish) roots, the crowning glory was the Royal Institute of British Architects' Royal Gold Medal in 1987.

Mark Bertram

I created living exhibits at Marineland, Steinhart Aquarium, Sea World and the Monterey Bay Aquarium. My book, *A Fascination for Fish: Adventures of an Underwater Pioneer* was published in April, 2000 by California Press. Reviews: "This autobiography is a charming and accurate telling by a modest man whose brilliant career has allowed millions to venture into the sea and feel what Dave feels when he's underwater—without getting wet!"—Dr. John McCosker, Steinhart Aquarium, San Francisco.

"Dave Powell is one of the giants in the development of the modern public aquarium. His great talents and skill have come from years of working with the technology of public aquariums, and from a great love of the sea. This book is a wonderful tale of his adventures (and misadventures) as he worked to capture the essence of the ocean and bring it to public view." *Dr. Bruce Carlson, Waikiki Aquarium.*

MARGARET BALL 1933-93

Margaret was at FSSW from 1945 to 1949. She was one of the cleverer girls, and very hard working. However, it was not yet common for girls to go on to higher education and many, including Margaret, learnt office skills instead. After the disappointment of being rejected for university, it soon became apparent that she had exceptional gifts in both Shorthand and Typing, winning the British Championships three years running. Her speeds were incredible – shorthand 220 words, typing 120 words a minute.

After some time spent teaching, she went on to work in publishing. Then she turned to a life of crime – she was the first woman shorthand writer at the Central Criminal Court, the Old Bailey, and was in court for the last hanging sentence in Britain. She found cases of fraud particularly fascinating and was present to record the trials of Emile Savundra. She also worked on the cases of both the Kray and Richardson brothers. This meant that she required police protection and her talks about her experiences were enjoyed by many audiences round the country.

She was appointed Recorder of the Central Criminal Court at the Old Bailey in 1962, the first woman to hold this post, although she reported that, by 1968, there were more women than men. From the Central Criminal Court she moved to the High Court, and later to St Albans Crown Court.

Margaret served on the Old Scholars' Committee from 1953 to 1961 and served as Secretary and Assistant Secretary, as well as a short term later on the Nominations Sub-Committee. She was a Group Secretary for twenty years from 1955 to 1975 and served as OS President in 1980-81.

MICHAEL ROSSMAN

For Michael Rossman, his School years were fundamental to everything he has ever done, from social concerns to scientific investigations. Teachers such as Cyril Mummery, Arnold Brereton, Stanley Pumphrey, Margaret Yapp (Fido), Richard Wright, Eric Lenz and others had an impact on him far beyond anything those hard working, dedicated, extraordinary people could have imagined.

He was not very interested in sports but preferred to read, play with amateur radio equipment, do experiments in the Chemistry Lab and so forth. He mostly enjoyed the pig drive on Sunday afternoons which, for the younger boys, meant taking walks off the premises. He explored every field and spinney from Walden to Debden and in other directions.

His was essentially part of the first, larger Sixth Form which the School had hosted. Much of the teaching was as new to the teachers as it was to the pupils. Although the result was, perhaps, lacking in substance, for him it was an opportunity to learn how to teach himself. Nevertheless he did not do well in the various college entrance exams. Fortunately, Barrington Whitlow, a Friend, – and a friend of the School (later his son became a teacher at Walden) – came to his rescue and introduced him to the Head of the Physics Department at the Regent Street Polytechnic. It was an extraordinary coincidence that BW knew a person who was in charge of exactly the educational opportunities he was seeking!

After graduation with a BSc degree in physics and mathematics, he obtained a job as an assistant lecturer at the Royal Technical College (now the University of Strathclyde) in Glasgow. But he was not finding the intellectual stimulus he desired. In desperation, he wrote to Kathleen Lonsdale, a member of the FSSW Governing Committee. While he had been at the School she had offered five tickets for the annual Christmas Lectures at the Royal Institution in London. He was one of those fortunate enough to be allotted a ticket. Kathleen did a great job, showing him and the others around the Royal Institution and the equipment which Michael Faraday had used. He was in awe. Thus, in his dark days at Glasgow he turned to her. Although she offered him a place in her laboratory at University College, he failed to win a scholarship. However, he had started to read crystallography (the subject of Kathleen's research) on his own. In this way, he discovered that another well known crystallographer was the chemistry professor at Glasgow University. He was equally kind and accepted Michael as one of his students while he was earning his keep at the Tech. Three years later, Michael had qualified for a PhD.

During this time he married Audrey Pearson, an old scholar of Ackworth Friends' School. Audrey was a member of Leeds Young Friends and a friend of Martin Dodsworth who had been one of Michael's closer friends in Walden. Before Audrey and Michael had left for two years of post-doctoral studies in America, Martin (their oldest) and Alice had been born. Their youngest, Heather, was born shortly after they returned to Cambridge. Six years later they emigrated, permanently, to America where Michael had a number of excellent job offers. He and the family have been at Purdue University since 1964.

He was fortunate to have chosen a topic of research (structural biology) which has been at the fore of the biotechnology revolution. As a consequence he has been honoured extensively, including becoming a foreign member of the Royal Society and a member of the US National Academy (the American equivalent of the Royal). It was exciting for him to sign the The Great Book, also signed by Newton, Boyle, Faraday and others of whom he had studied during his School days.

One of the by–products of a scientific life is that he has friends in almost every part of the World. International recognition has brought him in touch with US National policies. If the US Senate confirms his nomination, he will be participating in the formulation of scientific policy for the President during the next few years.

Michael stresses how very important FSSW has been to him and how grateful he is for all the help he received. The School was his home for six years, and remains a very powerful memory for him.

ANNA SARGANT

Anna has had a distinguished career as a lecturer in Burmese at the School of Oriental and African Studies, University of London, which covered some 36 years. On taking early retirement, she was appointed a Senior Research Fellow in Burmese Studies there. She has visited Burma regularly and Daw Aung San Suu Kyi, the well known political activist and Nobel Prize winner, is a student and close friend. She was awarded the OBE for her work linking Burma to this country through the Britain-Burma Society.

Her early interest in, and facility for, languages was helped by the fact that her mother was Czech and taught French and German at Channing School in Highgate. After graduating with a First in Russian Language and Literature (with French) from London University's School of Slavonic and East European Studies (SSEES), her ambition had been to join the Foreign Office. However, her hope of becoming a diplomat were somewhat diminished when, after sitting the examination, she was not selected.

There is, says Anna, a certain irony, an element of surprise, in life. Whatever they say about only having one chance, you can sometimes see the same film twice and it is ironic that, in a lifetime career as a university teacher of Burmese, she has become more and more involved, not only with the British Diplomatic Service, but with the Australian as well, having taught the Burmese language to several future and present British and Australian diplomats posted to Rangoon, with whom she is still closely involved in a number of important projects.

After graduating, she had thought of a teaching post in Russian. However, despite the Cold War (it was 1951), there wasn't one going. On the suggestion, and with the help of, the Secretary of SSEES, she went next door to the Department of Linguistics of the School of Oriental and African Studies to take up a postgraduate studentship which, it was promised, would lead to a lectureship in Chinese at the School of Slavonic and East European Studies. She therefore followed an introductory course in Phonetics and Linguistics, at the same time following an elementary course in spoken Chinese, but, by the time her studies came to an end in 1952, the promised post in Chinese had disappeared. However, the School had a vacancy for a lectureship in Burmese – was she interested?

Anna knew not one word of Burmese and practically nothing about the country or its people... but a job was a job and a challenge a challenge, so she said Yes – a decision she has never regretted and which, she feels, has brought her all she could ask for. It has given her a deep involvement with one of the world's most fascinating countries and cultures, and a people who are both charming, blessed and – these days – oppressed.

And that is not all... the School, and the Burmese post, also brought her a husband, Antony Allott, a young lecturer in African law at SOAS. Actually, he had spent part of the War with the 14th Army in South East Asia Command, preparing to invade Burma. In 1952, they decided to marry. As a weird wedding present, the School authorities decreed that Anna should go out to Burma for the best part of a year to learn Burmese on the spot. This she duly did (1953-4) and it was the start of a lifetime's immersion in things Burmese.

Anna and Tony have four children – now grown up – and live in a converted water mill near the village of Bodicote in North Oxfordshire where they pass the time cultivating the garden, and keeping in touch, by email, with all their international contacts. Their greatest delight is to spend time with their nine grandchildren.

JOHN CADMAN

After leaving the School in 1950, John joined the Army where he was able to join in sports at quite a high level. After completing his National Service, he went to Loughborough College where he obtained a First Class Honours degree in Physical Education and Geography, a qualification he later supplemented by gaining an Intermediate Examination of the Auctioneers and Valuers Association.

From 1954-57, he taught PE and Geography at Kent College. From here he moved on to Saffron Walden, where he taught until 1964 (see page 89) and then on for a spell in property management.

In 1970, he became Director of Coaching to the Hockey Association, including Under 21 Coach in 1974 for five years and England Coach in 1982.

His proudest sporting achievements have been as a member of the England Hockey Team, 1960-65. He gained 27 Great Britain and England Caps, including the 1964 Olympic Games in Tokyo.

He now has his own business dealing with the design and project management of sports facilities.

He holds several offices in the field of sports, has written books, given papers, all too numerous to mention. He is married to Val, who joined him during his time at Walden, as head of Girls' PE. They have two daughters, a grandson and a granddaughter.

NAOMI SARGANT

After leaving FSSW, Naomi studied sociology at Bedford College, London. She married, firstly, Peter Kelly with whom she had a son, David. Her second marriage was to Andrew R McIntosh (now Lord McIntosh of Haringey). He was a GLC Councillor from 1983 to 1993, when Michael Foot asked him if he would be prepared to be a working peer in the Lords. He is currently Deputy Chief Whip in the House of Lords and a Labour Government Minister. They have two sons, Francis and Philip.

She started work as a market and social researcher with the Gallup Poll organisation, but, after twelve years – some of it part-time while the children were small – moved to lecturing in marketing and market research at Enfield College of Technology (now part of Middlesex University).

During this time she was a Councillor on the newly-formed London Borough of Haringey (1964-68), serving on the Education Committee and as Chair of the Children's Committee and Vice-Chair of the London Boroughs Training Committee. Andrew was also a Councillor, particularly involved in Planning, which stood him in good stead when he became the GLC Councillor for Tottenham and Leader of the Greater London Council Labour Group.

Naomi joined the Open University at its inception in 1969, starting up its Survey Research Department to evaluate how the OU was meeting its students' needs. John Sparkes (whose mother had been Mistress of the Family when Naomi arrived at Walden) was Dean of Technology.

She subsequently moved up the ladder, becoming a Reader and then Professor of Applied Social Research and Pro-Vice-Chancellor (Student Affairs) – the first female Pro-Vice-Chancellor in the country. She was Chair of the Advisory Council for Adult and Continuing Education's Planning Committee (1977-83) and responsible, under Richard Hoggart, for its report, Continuing Education: from Policies to Practice (1982).

After eleven years (1981), she left the Open University to become the founding Senior Commissioning Editor for Educational Programming at Channel 4. Here she was involved in setting up both the Open College and the Open Polytechnic. After 1989, she worked mainly as a consultant and writer in the fields of the media, lifelong learning and evaluation and her books have included Learning and Leisure (NIACE, 1991), Adult Learners, Broadcasting and Channel 4 (C4, 1992) and Learning for a Purpose (NIACE, 1993). More recent books are The Learning Divide (1997) and The Learning Divide Revisited (2000).

As if all this was not enough, Naomi has immersed herself in public service. She has been Chairman of the National Gas Consumers' Council, a member of the National Consumer Council and then the Commission on Energy and Environment. She has been Vice-Chair, then Chair, of Governors of the University of East London.

Among her leisure activities, she admits to being a Fellow of the RSA and a Member of the Royal Television Society, BAFTA.. She is an Executive Member of the National Organisation of Adult Learning and Chair of the Open College of the Arts. She was admitted to the Royal Television Society's Hall of Fame for her work in educational television and, last but not least, she is President of the Highgate Horticultural Society.

Naomi is currently a member of the Board of Governors at Saffron Walden

RICHARD CLYMO
Emeritus Professor of Ecology

By the time Richard Clymo, the future Emeritus Professor of Ecology reached Saffron Walden at the age of ten, in 1944, he had already acquired, from both genetic and environmental sources, some useful assets: the fact that he tended to see problems as opportunities for independent purposeful activity must have been an advantage when he was moving through ten different primary schools as a result of his parents' wartime commitments. He says this enabled him to accept conditions of continuing change and innovation as normal, and it must have helped when he was adopting innovative methods of research and pioneering the use of the computer for greater precision in dealing with complex biological problems.

At a personal level, it helped him to succeed in his efforts to find work which was "partly teaching and partly outside" and later on when he was coordinating the redeployment of colleagues to meet changes in academic resources. Typically he included arrangements for his own early retirement "out of fairness to the others".

His interest in botany began at home and was furthered by lively botanical walks during two years at Ackworth before he came to Saffron Walden. In his own words Saffron Walden provided " seven years of stability and some extraordinarily good teaching." Arnold Darlington was one of his teachers, others were Maurice Haselgrove, Stanley Pumphrey, Cyril Mummery and Richard Wright.

There followed three years of Noncombatant National Service in Forestry, which he says were useful because he learnt the skill of carrying out dull routines and doing so efficiently. There was little in the way of a promising future in Forestry and University candidates were entirely responsible for their applications in those days, so he spent his evenings obtaining an extra qualification in Chemistry to widen his choice of University Entrance examinations, only to revert finally to Botany and a place at "the second best Department in the Country":

University College, London.

There the Head of Department, Professor Pearsall, was an ecologist and students were allowed a certain freedom in their choice of study. Richard's degree eventually brought him an offer of the Quain Research Studentship. By 1961 he had moved to Westfield College. Here he ascended the academic ladder to Head of Department in 1983.

During that time he had satisfied his curiosity concerning the factors controlling the exclusiveness of the third of our flora which is confined to chalk habitats. In his experiments he used the resources of field, garden, laboratory, workshop, and, as soon as opportunity arose, set up his own computer programs to produce results of sufficiently satisfactory accuracy.

Westfield had had no science department since the Botany School closed in 1946 so he was able to join in setting up a new science department with a large up-to-date computer and as Chairman of the Computer Users Committee supervised its use in the increasing complexity of biological research.

He had moved on to study, among other interests, the relationship between the growth of Sphagnum moss and the methane and carbon dioxide emissions from peat and this has proved a useful basis for widespread studies by others which are of particular importance in connection with increasing concern about climate change which surfaced in the nineties. He is very highly regarded by fellow scientists and, now semi-retired, he is still pursuing several relevant lines of research.

Joan Mummery

SALLY TUFFIN

Sunflower teatime – a promotional photograph 1996. Sally, pouring tea, with some of the staff

Throughout her childhood and teenage years, Sally Tuffin designed and made clothes, first for her dolls and then for herself. In 1954, she enrolled at the Walthamstow School of Art, intending to be a painter but, at the last moment, she ended up on a fashion course. At the end of her three-year course, she went on to the Fashion School at the Royal College of Art, where she won the Silver Medal. In 1961, immediately after graduating, Sally started a dress company with her friend, Marion Foale, with whom she had studied at Walthamstow and the Royal College of Art. Working from the ultra-fashionable Carnaby Street, they began with two sewing machines and a steam iron making clothes, to order, as fast as they could.

The company Foale and Tuffin was an immediate success and went from strength to strength, finding and filling a gap in the market with individual, fashionable clothes for young people which were otherwise difficult to obtain. Sally and Marion were unusual too – not only did they start their own company, they did not have the customary male backing. Soon they were selling to top stores all over the world and employing two factories of outworkers, although their priority was always to work for enjoyment rather than large profits.

Eventually, both Sally and Marion married and had children and, in 1976, Sally and her husband, Richard Dennis, an expert on pottery, moved to Somerset, where Sally set up a children's mail order clothes company. It was called Tuppence Coloured and, again, Sally designed the clothes herself.

After six years, Sally and Richard decided to start up their own pottery; at the same time, however, they discovered that the well-known Moorcroft Pottery in Stoke-on-Trent was in financial difficulties and about to be wound up. Together, Sally and Richard helped rescue the Pottery, Richard establishing a now thriving collectors' club and Sally developing new designs. Sally found a new kind of freedom in working with ceramics. She says, "I just treated the pot like a body, putting in the tucks and darts to decorate it – and it's much easier to design a pot because a pot keeps still and doesn't tell you it doesn't like it."

Sally was Art Director at Moorcroft from 1986 to 1992, when she and Richard opened the Dennis China Works in Somerset. Since then, she has designed all Richard's pieces which are renowned for their decorative, colourful patterns.

In 1995, Poole Pottery asked Sally to become involved in designing for their studio range, which became famous in the 1960s and was revived in the early 1990s. Sally's work for Poole, which has a strong reputation for innovation and for collaboration with artists and designers, is recognisable for its intricate and graphic qualities, using the traditional Poole technique of brush stroke painting on a matt glaze.

When British Airways revamped their corporate image, they asked her to design a livery for one of the planes. Based on a plate she had created for Poole Pottery, the plane featured Poole Harbour, plus the artist's signature. "Fitting the image to a Boeing 757 the size of a three storey building was quite difficult," she says, "but I enjoyed the challenge."

Sally's work is represented in the collections of several important museums, including the Victoria and Albert in London.

TONY NEWTON (The Rt Hon Lord Newton of Braintree, OBE)

After leaving FSSW in 1955, Tony went on to Trinity College, Oxford, where he graduated with an honours degree in Philosophy, Politics and Economics and was President of the University Conservative Association and of the Oxford Union Society. From 1960 to 1974 he worked in the Conservative Research Department before being elected MP for Braintree in February 1974. He served continuously in the Thatcher and Major governments from 1979-97, first as a government Whip, then as Social Security Minister and Minister for Disabled People. He then served as Minister for Health. In 1988 he joined the Cabinet as Chancellor of the Duchy of Lancaster and Minister for Industry, going on to become Secretary of State for Social Security from 1989-92 and Lord President of the Council and Leader of the House of Commons from 1992-97. Following his defeat at the 1997 General Election, he was made a life peer and has continued with public service, for example as Chairman of an NHS Hospital Trust and of the Council on Tribunals.

TOM ROBINSON

Born in 1950, Tom was a choirboy until his voice broke, and everything else fell to pieces along with it. At a time when homosexuality was still punishable by prison in Britain, he fell hopelessly in (unrequited) love with another boy at FSSW. Racked with shame and self-hatred, he attempted suicide and the then Head, Kenneth Nicholson, managed to get him transferred to a pioneering therapeutic community in Kent.

It was here at Finchden Manor that Tom's life was changed for ever by a visit from old boy, Alexis Korner. This legendary blues singer transfixed a roomful of people singing about love, poverty and racism – about human life in the raw – and Tom was mesmerised. In a moment the whole future direction of his life and career became clear.

His first attempt at producing an album failed, but Tom didn't care too much – he'd discovered London's emerging gay scene, fervently embraced the politics of gay liberation, and soon began questioning the wider issues of equality and justice in society at large.

Aged 26, he formed the Tom Robinson Band (TRB) in 1977. The band had a hit that same year with 2-4-6-8 Motorway, quickly followed into the Top 20 by a live EP, despite a BBC ban on the controversial lead track Glad To Be Gay. Tom's photograph appeared on the front cover of Melody Maker eight times in a single year, TRB's debut album Power in the Darkness won a gold disc and they appeared regularly on the BBC's Top of the Pops. However, the tide soon turned, TRB fell from favour and broke up, demoralised and squabbling, within a year.

In 1984 a radio producer saw Tom in a late night cabaret at the Edinburgh Fringe and, impressed by his communication skills, offered him a series of his own as a presenter on the BBC World Service. He soon moved from this cosy BBC backwater into mainstream radio where he fronted his ground-breaking series of programmes for men, The Locker Room, which ran from 1992-95. There were also documentaries, including his history of gay music You've Got To Hide Your Love Away which won a Sony Radio Award for the BBC. Accepting John Birt's thanks on behalf of the corporation that banned Glad To Be Gay twenty years earlier remains one of Tom's sweetest moments.

The other was becoming a father. In 1982, across a crowded room at a Gay Switchboard benefit, Tom spotted the love of his dreams, Siouxsie. Over the years they became friends, then they married and now have two delightful children.

Tom remains an active supporter of Amnesty International, The National Assembly Against Racism and The Samaritans, as well as gay, lesbian and bisexual rights.

When not writing or performing himself, Tom can be found running creative workshop sessions for adults and teenagers everywhere from the Royal College of Art to the Greek island of Skyros. Since March 2002 he can also be found on Radio Two's new digital music network for the BBC – 6 Music – where he introduces new and interesting artists to a wider audience four nights a week.

A former President of the OSA, Tom has done a terrific job creating the School's excellent website. He is Database Officer for the OSA - as well as one of its most popular members.

The Squash

or how a generation found their way to and from Walden before the ubiquitous motor car

by David Fairbanks

It is the late 1940s and the end of term. The last lesson has been given and the final swim has been taken. The mad rush to get everything ready for the school concert has come and gone. On the blackboard, the last days have been crossed off, one by one 4, 3, 2, 1. Trunks in both the boys' and girls' playrooms have been packed, emptied out, repacked and packed again. Soon they will be collected and sent home by rail.

The morning of departure has finally arrived. Scholars come down to breakfast, a little bleary-eyed having slept little the night before. The excitement grows with the prospect of going home. While most boarders would have seen their parents during a half term visit, no one has been allowed home since the last holiday. Even telephoning home to one's family and friends was not permitted

Eventually, a long crocodile of scholars wends its way down to Saffron Walden station, where many boarders will commence the first stage of their homeward journey by *The Squash*, the scholars' name for the train because it was always very full.

This is the age of steam. An old tank engine (affectionately known as *The Crank*) is waiting on the single-track line ready to take us, bunker first, one stop to Audley End on the LNER main line from Liverpool Street to Cambridge, Ely, Kings Lynn and beyond. Arriving at the branch-line station, everyone alights and walks over to the main-line station. Once on the crowded up-line platform, our group waits for the specially hired non-stop train that will take us to London's Liverpool Street Station.

Suddenly, from a distance, the noise of the steam locomotive can be heard. It arrives in a swirl of steam and smoke. We all climb aboard and the near-panic rush to get a window seat is almost unbelievable. We have all been told, beforehand, to squeeze up to allow others to sit down. From my memory, the carriages were either open with two pairs of seats and a table on each side of a central gangway, or had compartments with seats for six people and a sliding door opening onto a long corridor that would take one the length of the train. I will never forget the unique, smoky smell of those carriages.

The signal clatters to the 'Off' position, the guard's whistle blows and we hear the heavy Chuff...., Chuff..., Chuff.., Chuff, as the train slowly pulls out of Audley End station on its way to London. The train begins to gather speed and, after several minutes, it is travelling quite fast. At first, it passes, at a good speed, through pleasant countryside with small villages, following the course of the River Cam. Then we are running through Bishop's Stortford where we pick up the course of the River Lea, then, passing what was to become Harlow New Town, across the Lea Valley with its string of reservoirs and into the suburban fringes of North East London – Broxbourne, Cheshunt, Enfield, Edmonton, Tottenham . . . The excitement becomes intense – we're nearly there.

As we enter the war-torn East End, more and more scenes of bomb damage and dereliction confront us, we realise that we aren't seeing the worst of it. Many bombed buildings have been, and others have still to be, demolished. Yet, already rebuilding is going on and many people have been rehoused in 'prefabs' – prefabricated buildings made of asbestos. After the first part of the journey we approach the curve at Bethnal Green. The train goes slowly, incredibly slowly it seems. The post-war vistas before us appear to want to stay within sight as a reminder of the suffering that war brings.

Once round the curve, we pick up a little speed again before slowing down to a snail's pace as we, hesitantly, creep through a series of short tunnels and into the station. The platform is full of parents, all eagerly awaiting the arrival of *The Squash* which disgorges equally eager scholars, each searching for a familiar face. There are scenes of happy parents finding their children and the fond farewells of scholars to their friends. "Good-bye, see you next term".

Soon the platform will be empty, as the young people continue their onward journeys to their homes. In a few weeks, the same platform will be full again. The same parents will return, bringing the same offspring, once again, to board *The Squash*, this time back to School for another term.

Footnotes:

LNER: London North Eastern Railway, one of the four pre-nationalisation railway companies (the others were London Midland and Scottish Railway, Great Western Railway and Southern Railway) that had been formed in 1923 by grouping together the operations of the multitude of privately owned companies. These four companies all disappeared in 1948 when the railways were nationalised and became British Railways, later British Rail.

100 Years of the OSA

In his President's Address, 18 September 1999, **Mark Bertram** *took an affectionate meander through the rites and rituals of the Old Scholars' Association. It was thoroughly enjoyable and here is some of it again.*

I have the honour to give the last President's Address of the twentieth century, and I thought that I would use the opportunity to take a brief look back at the Association over the last 100 years. I therefore stand before you as, perhaps, the only person in the world who has read all the Presidential addresses of the last 100 years. The prevalent introduction to most of them was an expression of unworthiness and an uncertainty of what to say. It was elegantly expressed by my predecessor exactly one hundred years ago, Alfred Sawer, who said "I would if I could spare the Meeting the next item on the programme, but I am informed that the rules of our Association require that at least once during his term of office, the President shall submit himself to the more or less kind judgment of his friends and present himself before them in the guise of a public speaker."

Frank Rivers Arundel in 1912 got round the problem in another way. He said, after seven pages in the Proceedings of genial rambling, and one paragraph from the end, "But I haven't yet got to my subject and am afraid it is too late to commence one now, but I would like in conclusion to consider for a moment how the influence of our School should help us to face present day problems."

The rules of the day did indeed require an address. Our rules – though twenty times wordier – are less specific: they only imply that the President's address should be an agenda item at the Annual General Meeting. Our rules, in this age of lawyers, are not easily to be adjusted, and so I have likewise submitted to the requirement.

I must say that our agenda is a less varied one than in 1899. The Meeting then began with a Psalm, and the more bureaucratic items were interspersed with four songs, a recitation, and a flute solo. It was held in the Old Meeting House at Devonshire House in Bishopsgate Street in London, which was then the Society of Friends Headquarters. The Meetings moved to Friends' House in Euston Road when it was built in 1926, and then to Westminster Meeting House in 1958. It was not until 1975 that the AGM was regularly held at the School on the Hill, which is how the Croydon Old Scholars described Saffron Walden. Indeed, quite a number of the early Presidents, who had been schooled at Croydon, apologised for not having visited Saffron Walden in the course of their year.

The first President who attended School in Saffron Walden was James Fairbanks, and he used his Presidential address in 1910 to contrast the two schools and, fortunately, finding Saffron Walden on the whole a Good Thing. Until 1935 there were Officers on the Committee of the Association who had attended the Croydon school.

Our Old Scholars' Association is the oldest of any of the Quaker schools. It was founded through the energies of John Armfield in 1869, as the inside cover of the Yearly Magazine has for long explained. One of the six whom he summoned to discuss his ideas for the Association was Alexander Radley, and the stream of Farrands and Radleys has continued within the Association to this day.

A Constitution was adopted in 1894 and John Armfield was our first formal President. He had attended every AGM for 47 years when he died in 1917. Almost every year it fell to him, though I rather fancy he ensured that it did, to propose the next President. There are contemporary references to his performing each time the guessing game that still characterises this procedure, but I am sad to tell you that the Secretary seems, year after year, to have believed that this would confuse the readership and the annual tease is not apparent from the recorded Minutes of those days.

The meetings tended to become overlong. All the letters from OS were read in full. Then the accounts of Rambles were read. Then accounts of Whit. So long, indeed, that it was recorded of the 1911 AGM that "the evening will be long celebrated for its ideal Presidential address, which was of a powerfully uplifting character. In view of the high tone and priceless value of this address, it was a matter for keen regret, amounting to chagrin, that the unlooked-for protraction of the business items of the agenda so far delayed the President's opportunity, that many expectant members had to leave the meeting without participating in the evening's chief event." The following year, the President was brought higher up the agenda. I am not sure when he or she was put back to the end again.

John Armfield's longevity was matched by that of John Edward Walker, who was Headmaster for 30 years from 1890 until 1920, and President in 1908. Each year he came to the AGM to represent the School, and the meetings evidently forgave him his cultivated inconsequentiality which they knew cloaked a brilliant Headmaster. In his own words, in 1912, "I hardly need say that it gives me very great pleasure (and so on) . . . I am not able, on these occasions, to write out my speech, because I never know what I might have to say. I am allowed, I believe, by your indulgence, to be as irrelevant as I choose, and I shall venture to follow my usual custom." Jane (Laing), you may wish to try this approach some year! But we should not be deceived by this languid style. On the following agenda item, the Headmaster lucidly made the case for instituting the Weekend Lecture Schools, which lasted, on and off, until the mid-1970s.

And there were two women of equal longevity to these two men throughout these years and who helped so much to make the Association really an extraordinary organisation through the first part of this century. One was the Headmaster's wife, Anna Phillis, entitled Mistress of the Family, who worked so closely with him throughout his tenure. And the other was Lucy Fairbrother who was Headmistress for 28 years from 1894 until 1922, and President in 1920. In this office, she was the third lady. Mary Townson was the first in 1905. But I think that John Armfield must have slipped up here because Ackworth beat Saffron Walden to having the first lady President. The second was Ethel Crawshaw Morland, and she was also the first President to serve two consecutive terms, in wartime in 1916 and 1917, because other candidates were called away to other things. The other two Presidents who served two terms were Brightwen Rowntree in 1918 and 1919 and Anthony Skelton in 1944 and 1945.

It was an obvious strength of the Association that it could assimilate women so readily, and to a much greater degree than either the School or the Committee which ran the School. Although the School contained both boys and girls, they were taught entirely separately and they almost never met. Indeed, one of the great draws of the Association to leavers at that time was to meet those of the opposite sex that they had been to school with. It was not until 1910 that the School went properly co-educational. For all those years, too, the men and women of the Committee which ran the School met separately.

So the Association was ahead of its time. In 1934, however, Owen Clover earned few marks for what would now be called political correctness by saying that "while I believe in equality – I may be quite wrong – I have a very strong feeling that men should do the running and that it is for men to make the pace: for I have seen so many tragedies where women have rather set themselves at men and made for trouble sooner or later. Women stand on a higher pedestal than men, but the making of the pace must rest with the men."

He was indeed wrong. I was reminded of a much better formulation the other day when Farrand Radley, on learning of my mother's recent death, sent me a resumé of what she had said at a Lecture weekend on Woman's Place in the World in 1973: the sexes were different but equal: each was like half a pair of scissors, not necessarily the same shape as the other half, but equally indispensable.

Despite the Association's success, collection of subscriptions was a perennial problem. Arnold Green in 1923, in an address mainly dealing with Veneration of the Old, said that "with all the emphasis at my command I urge all our members to be faithful in little things and to regard prompt payment of annual subscriptions as a sacred duty. They say money is the root of all evil,

John and Mary Bolton on Audley Mansion Bridge in 1929

Pat Chuter

- Gas light in the bedrooms – we had to take it in turns to sit under one in order to cut our toe nails.
- The winter of 1946/7 was very cold. We took it in turns to warm up against the radiators.
- One of my first lessons was 'Domsci' with Miss Cottrell. We had to prepare a knicker draft, including the measurement 'waist to knee'. Even in 1946 we thought this somewhat amusing. I don't know what Cotty would make of today's g-strings.
- One memory of Hillcroft is the fun we had sending Morse Code messages to the boys' bathroom opposite, using the electric lights.

Barbara Burtt – 1960s

I remember:

- Iowerth John's rendering of "There's a one-eyed yellow idol to the north of Katmandu" at every (or so it seemed) End-of-Term Concert – and the encore we always yelled for. I think I had only a very sketchy idea at the time what it was all about and only years later looked it up – to find the graphically gory tale of Mad Carew whose lover finds him stretched on his bed and slithers through his blood to find that he has stolen the idol's eye as a gift for her.

- *The last hymn in Sunday evening meeting on parents' weekend which was always the same and always made me cry: "The day Thou gavest Lord, is ended, The darkness falls at Thy behest..". Whenever I come across it today, the memories flood back.*

- *Was it the brainchild of David Gray or David Lewis or both? Over a goodish period of time, no-one was allowed near the place and he would go out each morning and put a fine layer of water over the frozen base, gradually building it up until it was thick enough to skate on. Heavens knows where people got their skates from! The photo is dated 1963.*

but it's nice to have a little root. Certainly, without a root that is continuously fed we cannot function properly as a liberal subscriber to our old school." The Association has a fine record in contributing to the School: the swimming pool in 1902, help with the Sanatorium in 1913, the Pavilion in 1924, which was the same year that the New Avenue was planted, and help with founding the original junior school in 1930.

The 1920s and 1930s were perhaps the height of the Association's success. The programme for 1922, for example, had the Annual Soirée in January – "a riot of innocent folly" a breathless rapporteuse recorded; Lecture weekend in March, attended by about 50, tackling the theme of "Ourselves and Society"; a dance for 120, many in fancy dress, at the Bishopsgate Institute; a games weekend in October; and 300 at Whit weekend. Whit lasted from Saturday morning, or even Friday night for some, until dispersal on the Tuesday morning. Receptions, teas, a play, bonfire and singing, Meeting, At Home, two concerts, an aquatic display, games throughout, men on straw palliasses in bell tents, women quartered in the town. Muriel Rigby described very much the spirit of these occasions in her address on Friendship a generation later in 1964. "And eventually Whitsun drew near, with the longed-for opportunity of returning to Walden. One of the things that I recall most vividly on our first evening was the warmth of the welcome we received from all the staff as we met them again, and how genuinely pleased to see us were all the people we knew. Old Scholars two or three years our senior, who at school had little time for us, greeted us as old friends; present scholars two or three years our junior and now people of importance in the School, whom we had ourselves, I am sure, treated at times with similar indifference, were equally friendly." It was the high point of many an Old Scholar's year. The modern day President can only marvel at the strength of interest.

The Association also had its own colours, and above all its blazers. Indeed the debate about how the Blazer Fund should be treated in the accounts was a hardy perennial. And the Association seems to have played its own games: terza, puddox, and even hicockolorum, are referred to, but their rules are now recalled by only a few.

The abiding spirit of the Association was described in numerous different ways. John Butler in 1900 said: "Knowledge is passing away, and other knowledge is taking its place. It seems to me that kindness and sympathy will never lose their value. The world is longing for this message." James Lidbetter in 1922 said: "Friends' Schools. . . turn out people of more originality and independence, people not all of one type, people not afraid of being thought peculiar. . . . This unity without uniformity is an important trait of our Quaker training." And Gertrude Rowntree in 1932 said: "A call for fellowship leads to a making of friendship." The importance of fellowship has always been at the top of the Association's agenda.

In 1935, 500 attended on Whit Monday. Stanley King Beer was afraid that the OS were taking over and he pleaded for the Old Scholars and Staff to have more contact with each other.

The second half of the century has been, on the whole, less colourful in respect of the Association's activities, but certainly not in respect of its Presidents. Their addresses covered a vast array of subjects close to their hearts and experiences: imagination, friendship – even the Lord Chamberlain's Regulations for the Licensing of Theatres. Many of these Presidents will have been

Chris Timms – 1946:

Austerity, rationing, pinched faces, smoky air, grimy buildings, leaden skies all greeted a very podgy fifteen-year-old returning from six years of state schooling in California.

Speech, not yet tuned to the cockney twang, alerted the sharp tongued who had had years of subservience to the loud-mouthed, over-fed, over-paid, over-sexed over here Yankee servicemen, fighters for the Four Freedoms.

Questions, answered as correctly as possible, were met with replies of "Liar", "Prove it", "Well, who cares, anyway?" Use of words often gave offence, as meanings were different. Remembering what NOT to say was the priority

Joining the Fifth Form in the Winter Term, the greatest 'relief' was stumbling on the boys' loos. Being afraid to use any common term to explain my need, as this might have caused great offence, having been proudly shown the washrooms, bathrooms, the long wait left the memory seared.

In sport, remember not to ask the whereabouts of the bleachers, floodlighting, hand and basketball courts, training courts and loan of equipment. Coach and assistants were on the grounds before, during and after school, supervising, organising and arranging sporting events. Where were the maintenance shops, car parks, as everyone had a car at sixteen (fourteen if you were a one-parent child)? Keds, not clogs, for football, cafeterias, auditoriums.

My parents' optimism for a sudden change of academic record was not well founded – in every class in every school, since the age of five, I failed to get above the bottom three.

Later, there were jobs in estate agency and advertising sales – those the Career Masters chose for dullards. At least when my own offspring reached the stage for careers advice – my eyes were not downcast.

High Spots: Swimming Colours, picked for the First Eleven and staying with class friends during holidays.

Low Spots: Not being able to respond to Richard Wright's positive and caring one-to-one extra help to understand algebra. Getting 'gated' for being caught at the pictures, told off for shouting "come on" at cricket. Having my well made pass key confiscated.

Lowest Getting beaten at tennis, by a girl.

known to us personally. Stanley Pumphrey in 1946 was the first ex-President that I knew. One of the most colourful characters was Reginald Reynolds in 1951, who delightfully described his researching of the School's archives for the Pageant that he wrote for the school's 250th anniversary the following year. This polymath's life was cut tragically short in 1958, but he is remembered of course by the Travelling Scholarship that for the next 25 years carried his name – and by the portrait that hangs in the Library.

In 1953 the Presidential address was re-termed the President's address, though it is far from clear that this made any difference to the scope and variety of what was said. Basil Burton, that splendid bachelor in black suit and wing collar who was for long the Secretary of the Penn Club and whose calm demeanour was brought to bear by Head-masters over many years to invigilate important exams and induce calm in the examinees, including me, gave a fairly full history of the early years of the Association in 1958.

Farrand Radley's masterly illustrated address in 1967 explored the four sites that the school had occupied, and became known, naturally enough, as the Four-Site Saga. Much of its material is in the Old Scholars' Archive, so carefully tended these days by Roger Buss. This Archive is a treasure trove of social history that I very much hope can continue to be given attention, and possibly improved conditions for its storage.

Characteristically for the Association, there have been threads of family continuity through the Presidents. Father and son Lemere; father, wife and son Rowntree; father and son Watts; the brothers Holttum; husband and wife Skelton; uncle and nephew Whitlow; father and son Cadman; father and daughter Watson; and now brothers Bertram. I have warned my other Saffron Walden brother, William, that he could be in the firing line one day.

Perhaps one of the best Presidents that we never had was Kenneth Nicholson, who died in 1969 so soon after retiring from the headmastership. So many of us mourned the loss of someone whom we had counted on as a friend for a much longer life.

The addresses of the last 20 years have tended to be structured more directly autobiographical, with associated and prescient observations. They make very good reading for their variety and insights. None perhaps exceeds in personal depth than that by Tom Robinson in 1996. And one of the best lines, I think, comes from the closing sentence of Iorwerth John's address in 1985: "Your face, I heard recently, shows what you are and up to 50 you can change it. At 70, however, it's no use turning over a new leaf, you only get to the index."

Times and contexts change. The quick and erratic skim that I have been indulging in illustrates that clearly enough. The remarkable pre-war peak of the Association's success reflected the leisure habits of the day, the smaller range of alternative attractions and responsibilities, and friendship patterns that preceded the expansion of tertiary education, during which a greater proportion of friendships are nowadays forged. As Alan Thompson put it in 1974, when introducing proposals for a new and slimmer pattern of Old Scholar Gatherings, "These suggestions accept the fact that though there is loyalty to the School, its methods of education and its community spirit, this loyalty does not now take the form of returning regularly to the school for reunions. (He went on) To our generation, who left School without the complications and diversions of television, university and cars for all, the School became a way of life,

Godric Bader

"A wonderful school!" I told my daughter, Hansi, who followed me to Walden and, in retrospect, she must have felt the same.

There was a swimming pool and teachers to entertain you, a choice of boys or girls for friendship and sports in beautiful grounds   It was a good move to become a veggie in the summer as you could avoid dead baby.

Of course, as a new boy, your elders would see you were deprived of butter for ten days at tea time. There was jam in a few weeks if you were promoted from a brat to a squirt. To become a gent, maybe in your second term, it helped if you did a bit of fagging and did not split on your elders when they poached to tin-tacks or brought chips back to eat in the bogs at night.

Would not have missed it for the world!

Scott Bader, *the company founded by Godric's father, Ernest, has endeavoured to work on Quaker principles – ethics are more important than money. This aspect of the company has had considerable coverage in* The Financial Times *recently. "Blame Walden for getting me high on values," says Godric.*

a social centre, a place where we would return again and again for a weekend of pure enjoyment.   Let us be realists; this does not happen now, nor can we expect it to happen, but we do feel that a major effort every few years, in which we contact non-members as well as members, will bring a reunion on the scale of the pre-war and immediate post-war one, we remember with such pleasure."

The 1974 pattern of gatherings has gradually become further slimmed over the past 25 years. David Hadley in 1993 focused on the way ahead for the Association in the light of weaknesses that were then apparent, but those thoughts were never really followed up.   But the great success of Tom Robinson's Mass Reunion in 1996 well illustrates the sense of the 1974 intent about periodic major efforts.   2002 may well offer the next major opportunity.

On a broader front, I think that the time is coming for the Association to examine whether it needs to adapt further to today's ways of life, in order to fulfil our aims.   As with so much else, we need to manage change rather than be overtaken by it. Our two foundation slabs are the May Reunion and the Annual Magazine. Both have seen us through the Twentieth century and are likely to take us well into the next.   But what we now need to factor in, to harness to the service of our aims, is the potential of information technology.

On this, we have made massive strides, thanks to several of your Officers in particular and thanks to the school, towards computerising the membership database, developing the OS section of the school's website, furthering the class list project, and facilitating email contact between members.   Email is perfect for one OS to make contact with another: it is balanced just where it needs to be between the formality of a letter and the fear of being intrusive through a telephone call.   And I know that a lot of this renewing of contacts is going on.   So much information and so many contacts will be only a few mouse clicks away for those that seek either.

But those are thoughts for the start of a new century.   My enjoyment today has been to review aspects of the Association through the century that is closing.   Our Association has a remarkable record of deep worth, huge friendship and great fun. Arthur Williams in 1907 called it "this delightful body of, what shall I say, hearts that trust one another".   I liked that phrase.

Long may it continue to be true.

Mike Turnbull

Cross-country running was an exciting challenge for the more fit and enthusiastic, but a real drudgery for a feeble few of us! Undeterred by the prospect of the muddy exhaustion awaiting us we would do our limbering up exercises under the encouraging eyes of John Cadman and then jog off down the Avenue. Just out of sight, half way down the Avenue was (and still is) a wooden shed, used at the time to store potatoes, and a few of us found that we could slip unnoticed into it as the main body of runners headed towards the countryside. Safely inside we would laugh, joke, chat and relax sitting on the sacks of potatoes. The group had a hard core of 'day-brats' including myself and s(I seem to remember) Mike Meyer, Mike Housden, and Graham Turvey, plus a few boarders such as Adrian Good, Tom Robinson and Simon Wood (but please don't tell anyone – I wouldn't want them to think I sneaked!).

Thirty minutes or so later we would hear the fastest runners plodding back up the Avenue towards the school. This was our cue to spend a few minutes jumping up and down to generate some bodily heat and sweat, and to smear mud and juice from the potatoes onto our legs and faces so we were not too dissimilar from our mud stained, waterlogged class mates now passing by. After a quick glance to make sure the coast was clear and no teachers were about, we would edge out of the shed, join the slower runners now passing, and run back up to the school under the watchful gaze of Mr Cadman who would be standing warm and dry sipping a cup of coffee at the staff room window. Neither he nor his successor Brian Capell ever seemed to rumble this dodge – or perhaps they were wiser than we thought and just realised that when it came to trying to get this particular group to do cross country running there was little point in flogging a dead horse! (I wonder has anyone else owned up to hiding in the shed?!)

Michael Snellgrove

As a refugee from Germany, my English needed attention when, aged ten, prefect, Michael How, punished me with writing out Psalm 139. I only had my German Bible and, to his shock, he received it written out in German.

When looking round the School prior to coming here, I expressed interest in all the pictures – Gerald Littleboy dutifully took several down to check the details on the back and dust of ages descended.
- Had a ride on EKO tandem, sat at back, sometimes forgot to pedal.
- BBJ frequently combed my hair – loved his Monkeyhouse.
- Was a defenestrated doughnut for Cyril Mummery.
- Wrote secret notes to girls to lure them down the Avenue.
- Was awestruck by Malcolm Harvey's violin playing.
- Was thrilled by Reg Reynolds fantastic revues and seeing masters differently.
- Loved any tea invites offered by Friends after Meeting, particularly those of a large lady, Mrs W . . .
- Loved escaping to local flea pit cinema – often bought 3d piece of Edam Cheese.
- With Film Club, must have seen *Life of Alfred Nobel* a hundred times.
- Loved the smut and smell that came with the *Crank* steam engine at Walden Station.
- Loved my weekly ginger booze from Little Fitch's.
- Loved the bedtime story readings at Richard Wright's – how lucky to have been in such a caring environment.

At the time I was at the School, understandably, food and facilities were lacking, but the dedication of the staff made up for that in abundance – bread and dripping at bedtime.

What days!

The Dinner Gong – now pensioned off and in store

Jane Russell Outlawed

One bright summer's morning in 1949, Assembly was over. All that remained was the reading of the notices.

Arising from his place at the of the top table at the end of the hall, the Head, Gerald Littleboy, stood up with a stern and purposeful look on his face. He announced that the smaller of the two cinemas in Saffron Walden would, the following week, be showing the Howard Hughes film called The Outlaw, starring Jane Russell. A murmur of excitement went round the hall as we considered, with anticipation, the prospect of seeing this 'scorcher' of a film. Then the bombshell dropped. The film was to be out of bounds to all scholars. A deathly silence fell on the hall.

Outside the Assembly Hall and wherever one went in School, everyone was talking about the film. No other film during my time at School was ever banned. The temptation to see it was irresistible.

Soon, the famous photograph, in technicolor, could be seen outside the cinema. It showed Jane Russell, lying on the barn floor, scantily dressed and revealing a deep cleavage, highlighting her well-endowed bosom. Pieces of straw were in her hair and the look she gave was most inviting.

That was enough. With Gerald Littleboy banning the film and a more than explicit (for those times) poster advertising it with the slogan "How would you like to tussle with Russell?" it just had to be good! I decided, there and then, that I would go and take the chance of getting caught.

The following afternoon, I made my way into town, taking a long way round. I planned to arrive a few minutes after the film had started, since I half expected that there would be a teacher on duty turning scholars away, but when I arrived, there was no one.

I hurriedly paid for my ninepenny ticket and slipped into the darkened cinema. The usherette showed me to a seat in the front. After a little while I ventured to turn around and see if there were any other scholars present. To my amazement, all I could see was row upon row of them!

After the film I made my way back to School, again taking the long route. I had not been missed nor was I caught on my way back. I was lucky – a number of other scholars were caught and were gated for many weeks.

David Fairbanks

Footnote: The Outlaw *was originally made in 1938 and initially released in 1941, distributed in 1943 and re-released in a slightly longer version in 1947. Although there is no pornography or profanity in this movie it was, nevertheless, sufficiently risqué for its time to result in its being banned in Finland (1950) and in Sweden (from 1943 to 1964).*

250th Anniversary Cake

It is hard to imagine it is fifty years ago that our domestic science class was given the honour of making the cake for the 250th Anniversary celebrations. Under the guidance of the Domestic Science Teacher, Pauline Goddard, we blocked off sections of three enormous tins to make cakes in the shape of each number. Each tin was carefully lined with greaseproof paper, mitred exactly at the bottom so that the numbers would be perfect. A vast amount of Christmas cake mix was prepared and placed carefully in the tins. As far as I remember, the cooking was done in the Aga which, by the time we had reached the Fifth Form was a cooker we had all mastered, right down to raking out the ashes daily with a long-handled scraper.

Over a period of several weeks, the cakes were iced with almond paste and royal icing. Icing baskets, in a lattice pattern, were created over bun tins and filled with handmade flowers and leaves. I am not sure when the cakes were cut. However, I do remember there was enough for everyone in the School to have a taste.

Another lasting memory of the 250th Anniversary celebrations was singing, in the School Choir, music specially composed by Edmund Rubbra. This was recorded for a BBC religious affairs programme. I can still remember the alto part for "Let us now praise famous men" and I carry, in my mind's eye, a picture of Barbara Comber playing the kettledrums.

Ann Wickenden

Pig Drive

For several years in the 1940s and 50s the School had a policy of chasing the boys off the premises on Sunday afternoons for some (presumed) much-needed exercise, and for the lower years this took the form of a group walk – Pig Drive – led by the master on duty.

There were a number of well-worn routes: Audley End was one of them, though we never visited the House itself. Another was the Beeches, that striking line of beech trees which bordered the stream which flowed under what was then the embankment carrying the branch line from Audley End to Saffron Walden.

Most people's favourite was the Copse, the grassed-over mounds and trees that could be reached by going down the Avenue and carrying on in a straight line along a footpath where I think there is now a housing estate. The Copse was ideal for games of the hiding/finding/tagging variety. It is still there, though now very overgrown.

If it was too wet for walking, and if Barney Jacob was on duty, he would announce (to great excitement) that we would have a Monkeyhouse instead. Every single item of equipment in the gym was brought into use and we played 'he' among the ropes, climbing bars, box and pommel horses, mats – the lot. It must have been quite risky and would probably nowadays be banned on Health and Safety grounds.

What did the girls do on Sunday afternoons?

Alan Sillitoe

Taking a break from Pig Drive: l-r Tony Newton, Chris Wood, Alan Sillitoe, Don Atkinson, Peter Nash

While in their spare time . . .

There was both a Senior and Junior Literary Society with records of a Senior Society from the turn of the century. The junior society probably faded following a Cyril Mummery report in *The Avenue*, "This term the Society has been more junior than literary." Meeting regularly through the School year, the seniors enjoyed a programme of readings, debates, literary criticism and discussion.

A Boys' Reading Club met on the last Sunday of term at Robins Acre (home of Headmaster Gerald Littleboy). Each member was expected to read three or four books, preselected novels or biographies, before the meeting. Discussion was lively, particularly from those who had managed the programme in its entirety.

At one time or another there was a Gardening Club, a Railway Society, a Wireless Club. The most durable was an Air League – this was devoted to aircraft recognition.

Under its Editor, Margaret G Yapp (Fido), assisted by a small band of pupils, *The Avenue* appeared each term. It recorded sporting events, meetings of societies, voluntary service accounts and outings. Further literary pieces, poems and articles were contributed by pupils. The whole was professionally printed and bound by Harts the Printers.

Michael How

The following are a few reports on the activities of the various societies as they appeared in The Avenue :

Report of the Senior Literary Society

The year 1944-45 has certainly not been a dull one for the Senior Literary Society. We have enjoyed several essay evenings, including one on Jane Austen and Thackeray and another on Shaw. A third meeting was devoted to the subject "Pessimism in Literature," while yet a fourth dealt with the subject- "Science in relation to Literature." The essayists on these occasions all produced detailed and interesting papers which aroused lively discussions.

The "high spot" of the year came in the Spring Term when the society paid a visit to Cambridge. This formed the yearly outing, and everyone enjoyed seeing Shaw's "St Joan" at the Arts Theatre.

During the Autumn Term two members produced short plays. This made a welcome change from the usual procedure and was appreciated by both the actors and audience, who afterwards discussed the performance, making useful comments. The plays were Good Beating, *one of the* Little Plays of St. Francis, *by Laurence Housman, and the last Act of Galsworthy's* The Silver Box.

A debate was arranged, the motion being that "Too much is done for us in the modern world." The voting was fairly even and was preceded by interesting arguments put forward by both sides.

As a relaxation during the tense period of examinations, we read Shaw's "Pygmalion." This proved to be the last meeting of the year as the talk promised for the next meeting was not forthcoming.

Muriel D. Hockley (Age 17)

Dramatic Society, 1949

This year the School was invited to enter the Drama Festival and accordingly we selected a cast to present *Elizabeth Refuses*, under the direction of Mrs Whitlow. The later rehearsals were pleasing, and in the actual performance the cast rose to the occasion and received an excellent report from the adjudicator. Alice Kendon, Elisabeth Collinson and Susan Whiteman all gave good performances; Hilary Jackson by no means lowered the general standard, in spite of the short time she had to study the part; while Paul Honigmann, apart from occasional inaudibility, made a satisfactorily smug and pompous Mr Collins. Mrs Whitlow's production was very effective, not only in the mere mechanics of acting, but in the creation of atmosphere. To conclude, we can do no better than quote the closing words of the adjudicator's appreciation: "This production gave us all great pleasure, and we shall look forward to their work in the future."

Another performance was given as part of a Saturday evening's entertainment; Eleanor Marriage, whom illness had prevented from taking part at the Drama Festival, gave a good performance as Jane, and the play was much appreciated by the School.

We owe Mrs Whitlow our thanks for her interest and work in this production.

Outing of the Natural History Society*, 1947 *(*known as NATCH)*

This year the Society decided to have its annual outing at Wicken Sedge Fen, a National Trust property some six miles north-west of Newmarket. On Saturday, 5 July, therefore, having hired a double-decker bus, the members of the Society set forth in high spirits with the prospect of a fine day before them.

Lunch was taken outside Newmarket, at Devils Ditch, opposite the race course. After lunch members were left to their own devices for three quarters of an hour, most exploring the ancient British dyke and ditch, and some studying the flowers of the dyke under the direction of Mr Lenz.

At Wicken Sedge Fen itself we were able to observe at first hand the way in which plants will grow if left entirely untouched by man. We were able to see the black peaty soil of the fens and the sedges of rushes used for basket making.

Unfortunately, the outing came at a time when the first breed of Swallow-tail Butterflies had finished, and the second one had not yet begun. The entomological members of the party who had come equipped with butterfly nets and permits were disappointed.

Perhaps the most amusing event of the day occurred when a plank across a pond, on which members of the Society were swinging, collapsed, precipitating the unfortunates out of their depth in the water. Happily they were retrieved without loss of anything except one gym shoe, and were sent on a cross-country run to help dry them out.

The bus reached home about 7.30 and the outing finished up with a cheer for Mr Lenz who had done so much to ensure the outing's success. **Anthony B Miller (VI)**

Orchestra Report, 1963

Both School Orchestras have grown this year. Under Miss Brown's guidance the Junior Orchestra, about 30 strong, entered the Chelmsford Music Festival in May and did well against strong competition, losing by only a few points to the winner of their class. At the Instrumental Day, Jennie Arman and Margaret Collison gained a Merit Award in the Sonata class.

In November the Senior Orchestra gave a concert in the High Street Baptist Church, Saffron Walden. After intensive effort over an unusually short period of preparation everyone was delighted to learn that nearly £18 was raised at this concert towards the World Hunger Campaign. Following this effort the orchestra was enlarged, by the addition of younger players, to over 50, in readiness for the Spring Concert, eventually to replace the high proportion of sixth formers who must inevitably leave us this year. The woodwind has been exceptionally strong and for the first time the orchestra has undertaken a Rossini overture. **Ivan Cane**

Music 1959-60

The main musical event of the Autumn Term was the customary series of carol concerts given by the small choir at Abbey Lane, Finchingfield, Newport and, of course, at School. In one respect the programme broke new ground in that it included an Annunciation carol for female voices alone. In addition to these local concerts the choir also sang once more in Trafalgar Square on the first evening of the holidays.

Earlier in the term was the Senior Concert. Although this is still described as Senior, it has in fact ceased to be given exclusively by seniors. Performances of a high standard were contributed by several juniors and Margaret Collison gave a very mature account of a Mozart piano sonata.

Thanks largely to Kenneth Plant, an informal recital was given by members of the School one Sunday morning in the Winter Term, the main aim being to encourage individual live music-making. Unfortunately it has not yet been possible to repeat this, although it is hoped to do so this term.

A Natch Outing, 1949

Boys' Reading Club

We have carried on with our usual programme of reading three books a term and having a protracted meeting to discuss them. In the Autumn Term, with many new members, we started with a light assignment: Louis Bromfield's *The Rains Came*, Rowena Farre's *Seal Morning* and John Drinkwater's *Abraham Lincoln*, which last provoked most discussion.

In the Spring Term David Lindsay gave a brilliant introduction to Kafka's *The Trial*. The other books discussed were *The best of Saki* and Lord Birkett's broadcast talks *Six Great Advocates*.

The Summer Term meeting was excellent. Matthew Robinson introduced William Faulkner's *Light in August*, the Headmaster Iris Murdoch's *The Bell* and James Sheehan Hoyle's *The Black Cloud*. James Sheehan's introduction was supplemented by a very scholarly paper from Mr Evans, whom we have been happy to welcome into the Club in place of Mr Gelsthorpe who, we hope, will be introducing yet another educational experiment into the Leicestershire schools.

The Tramp of August 1945

The Centre: Pardshaw - the Young Friends' Hostel, kindly lent by Cumberland and Young Friends through Robert Gillies, The Lea, Pardshaw.

The Tramps: Kathleen Moore, Jean Palmer, Molly (Egg) Eggleton, Pauline Goddard, Jean 'No-brake' Lyell, Judith Layng, Iona Brereton, Pat Jeffery, Dick Palmer, Diffy Butler, Tony Brooks, Marie Lenz, Sheila Galbraith, Bryan Stanger and Eric Lenz.

The following is a truthful account (I hope!) of our amazing adventures in the wilds of the English Lakes, written from day to day by each of our members in turn.

Monday, 13 and Tuesday 14 August

At 4.40 pm on Monday, a strangely bedecked and excited crowd gathered on Walden station. We understand that some hours later this strange phenomenon repeated itself at Euston (our London party).

The Walden group proceeded to Cambridge, and in imposing array we trekked with cycles the whole length of the Cambridge platform to the Bletchley train. Here we changed for Rugby, and there joined our London group. All through the night, we roared north, eating and sleeping, but not much sleeping. At 8.50 am we were thrown out at Cockermouth, and trooped down to the town in search of food and drink. The natives must have seen us coming, for the shutters were all up and no one was about. At 9.30 we stormed the first café to open and before the astonished gaze of the locals disposed of vast quantities of ice-cream and coffee. We then cycled over to Pardshaw and inspected our future abode. We (the boys) found as we expected, that the girls had bagged all the best rooms, beds and clothing and everything else worth having. Having put them in their places and recovered the spoils at the risk of our lives, we then proceeded to eat soss and mash till bedtime which was early – and weren't we tired.

The following were appointed to posts of authority because of their special qualifications: Dick and Diffy as milkmaids. EOL and BS as kitchen maids, EOL as memory-jogger and general-picker up to No-brake Jean (a very busy and difficult job, this!).
Distance: Train 300 miles, Cycle 5 miles.

EOL

Friday, 17 August

It dawned a fine day so today we started off early on our bikes equipped with lunch packages and bathing costumes and in the highest of spirits for Lake Buttermere. The ride was exceedingly pleasant.

Arriving at last at Buttermere, we enjoyed the spectacle of Mr Lenz chaining the whole of our thirteen bikes together. The general opinion was most decidedly in favour of a bathe.

After the bathe and lunch, the party split up, and the boys set their ambition on the highest peak they could see – High Crag (2700 ft). From here they had a very good view of Helvellyn and all around.

The rest of us, however, were not to be outdone. Mr and Mrs Lenz with Judith and Molly, went up Scarth Gap and from there up to Seat Crag, whilst the rest of the girls delighted in following a little stream right up the rocky mountains to its source in a large cavern. Once there the answering echoes of the surrounding rocks well repaid us for our struggles in getting up.

We descended in odd groups from our various heights, and about 5 o'clock, re-assembled at the foot of High Stile for a final bathe at

the edge of the lake, afterwards finishing up the remains of our sandwich lunch.

The ride back was rather a race against the threatening clouds, but as some carefree folk chose to take their chance with the rain, and staunchly stuck to their principle of ambling, there were washbowls vacant for everybody, no queues and all were satisfied. Distance: 16 miles by cycle.

Jean Lyell

Saturday, 18 August 1945
During breakfast, Mr Lenz informed us that we were to have an easy day – doing whatever we liked in the morning, and going out to Ennerdale Water in the afternoon. Most of us spent the morning in Cockermouth – devouring ice-cream, apples and coffee, and doing a little shopping for Mrs Lenz, and on arriving back at Pardshaw, found a delicious meal of stew, vegetables, peaches and blancmange waiting for us.

At 2.30 when we had been presented with our sandwich tea, we all jumped upon our trusty steeds and set forth for Ennerdale. Everyone was told to wait at the first 'Major Road Ahead' sign for the tail-enders of the party, but Bryan, the boys, Jean and Molly forgot the order and raced ahead, and consequently the six of us got hopelessly lost, and had to translate the weird Cumberland dialect before we finally found our way. However, when we did arrive, we found that Mr and Mrs Lenz and Judith were missing. Eventually they turned up, having had to rescue Judith who had lost her way. We then selected a sheltered spot by the Lake edge, and the bathers undressed behind very prickly gorse bushes. Miss Galbraith and Mrs Lenz showed us how swimming should be done, and Bryan Stanger illustrated perfectly how slowly one can make up one's mind before entering a very cold lake. . . .
Distance 18 miles by cycle.

Pauline Goddard

Monday, 20 August
Today, Mr Lenz had planned a long walk round Derwentwater. We cycled to Cockermouth and there caught the 11.30 train to Keswick. We arrived at Keswick without mishap, and after wandering around for a short time, we set off for the lake. After a pleasant walk we arrived at a suitable spot and all sat down and ate our sandwiches (plus custard tart and apples).

When we had finished our dinner, we started the three or four miles walk to the Lodore Falls. After admiring the falls, we climbed up to the top of them. On the way up, No-brake Jean (Lyell) left her shoes under a boulder and when returning to find them, had completely forgotten where she had left them! Mr Lenz valiantly offered to look under the 2000 odd boulders for them! After a very hectic search all over the falls, he eventually found them. We then continued to follow the stream to Watendlath Tarn where we saw the house of Judith Paris.

. . . . At the Bowder Stone, we had a drink from a nearby cottage and refilled our water-bottles in preparation for the six mile walk back to Keswick. This water came in very handy as the walk back had to be done very quickly as we had already missed the 6.30 train and simply had to catch the 7.20, the snag being that very few of us had lights to our cycles. The hurrying proved of no avail as we missed both trains and had to wait till the 8.30. We filled in the time by eating fish and chips and drinking hot tea.

We arrived at Pardshaw however, in pitch dark without any trouble after we lampless ones had been carefully instructed as to the order in which we were to cycle there. Tony led as lookout.

Everybody had a comfortable night after a strenuous day except for Mr Lenz, who paid the penalty for making applepie beds by having to sleep without any blankets!
Distance: 15 miles walk, 10 miles cycle, 20 miles train.

Kathleen Moore

. . . .

Tuesday, 28 August
Up at 5.00, breakfast at 5.30, packing and a hectic ride to catch the 7.10 train at Cockermouth. How we hung out of the train windows as we saw the mountains gradually fade in the distance! Then a long tiring and uneventful journey to Bletchley, where we said goodbye to the Londoners, and on to Walden where we arrived at 8.00 at night.
Distance 5 miles cycle, 300 train.
HOME AT LAST

Total distances travelled: Train 620, cycle 165, walking 31, lake 2.
Total expenses: Fare £2 18s 6d + 6s 5d cycle.
Food, rent etc: £2 10s 0d.

Two Generations as Visiting Students

Eckehard Schöll

At the age of fifteen, I embarked on the adventure of spending three months in a foreign country, this being the first time I had been away from home for such a long time. It was in January 1967 and, after a whole night on the train and rough crossing on the boat from Ostend to Dover, I arrived in the middle of nowhere – Audley End station – from where I was taken to Saffron Walden. That Spring Term of 1967, which I spent as a Visiting Scholar at the Friends' School, turned out to be one of the most influential experiences of my life.

Having been brought up in a caring middle-class home in a small town in South Germany, near Stuttgart, it was not only the change from a public German day school to a private British boarding school, but the experience of a new language, a new culture, a new way of life and religion, and the free spirit and humanity of the Quaker School which formed my views and attitudes and prepared the grounds for my strong feelings of internationalism and open-mindedness which have persisted until today.

In the following years, I returned to Britain many times, and endeavoured also to explore other countries all over the world – from the United States to China and Japan – and make friends with people from other cultures. In fact, after completing my school and university degree in physics in Germany, I decided to take a PhD in Britain. So, in 1978, I graduated from the University of Southampton with a PhD in Applied Mathematics. As well as a year's stay as a Visiting Assistant Professor at Wayne State University, Detroit, in 1983-4 and several shorter research stays in the US, including a recent Sabbatical at Duke University, North Carolina, in 2000, attendance at many Physics Meetings and private travels with my family have complemented and enriched my experience of foreign countries.

Today, I have the privilege of a profession which is truly international: I am a University Professor of Physics in Berlin and,

Eckehard at work on a view of the School in the Art Room

as a member of the international community of scientists, I maintain friendly ties with many colleagues, students and institutions around the world, and my present research group includes a Russian, a Ukrainian, a Malaysian and a Brazilian.

Some of my memories of the Friends' School are very vivid: the history lessons where Cyril Mummery taught me English Seventeenth Century History – from the Stuarts and Oliver Cromwell to the Glorious Revolution – which made such a strong impact upon me that I still remember them in detail after almost 35 years and I can still see him standing behind his desk. I thoroughly enjoyed music and art, and took advantage of painting freely in the art room. Mr Lightfoot taught me Russian, which was quite intricate: translating from English into Russian and vice versa without going via German. I remember the philanthropic Headmaster, Kenneth Nicholson, Kenneth Plant, my House Master, Iorwerth John, from whom I learned much about the Quakers' beliefs, Imogen Rowlands, David Gray, and many others. One evening a drama group performed a play on Cain and Abel – the key sentence "Am I my brother's keeper?" which is characteristic of the Christian humanitarian spirit I felt at the FSSW, is still in my ear.

Many years later my daughter, Claudia, came to the Friends' School as a Visiting Scholar for one term. At the age of fourteen, for her too it was the first time away from home. I accompanied her to School on the first day and took her home on the last day of the Summer Term 1994. The School building still looked the same, although new wings had been erected, and even a few of the teachers I had known were still there. Above all, I could still feel the spirit of internationalism. She shared her room with a girl from Korea and two girls from Hong Kong and made very good friends with a Norwegian girl. Now Claudia studies English and German literature and linguistics, and North American Studies at the Free University of Berlin. We both share our love for foreign cultures and languages. Who knows if this family tradition at FSSW will continue?

Lenon Beeson Remembers

I arrived at Friends' School in the middle of the last century, that is in 1950. A young teacher, in my first permanent job. There were about 300 pupils, mixed in every way – gender, class, background, boarders and day scholars, genteel and deprived. Cooperation with Essex Education Authority meant that we had day pupils from the town and the villages, parents who were shopkeepers, workers and managers from local industry, even some London commuters. Several of the teaching and other staff – gardeners, groundsmen, maintenance – had children in the School so, for most occasions, there were strong town-School links. A few other LEAs sent us pupils from difficult or deprived backgrounds – even a few refugees or other social 'casualties' from the recent war.

One or two memories from Staff Meetings will illustrate our concerns. There was a debate about how many 'problem' children we could take without creating instability. Fortunately, sometimes the 'problems' became the stable influences. On another occasion, a supremely kind colleague described a pupil as 'a bit of a pudding', a remark which led Headmaster, Gerald Littleboy, to say, in a rare fit of anger, "Will you remember that somebody loves these children?"

It was a good school. Of course, not every pupil thought so all the time, and maybe a few never thought so. However, most pupils would only have one school experience, while most teachers are able to make comparisons. One teacher, Kenneth Whitlow, taught all the youngest children as they entered the School. He had wide interests, from drama to sport, and was able to seek out the strengths and capabilities of each pupil, ensuring that children met teachers who could develop their skills, in classes or in clubs. In a small school, it was essential that scholars took part in several activities – sport, music, drama, debates, creative clubs – in addition to classroom work.

It was, in my opinion, a civilised and tolerant school, where pupils seemed able to respect and accept the eccentric. In 1952, we celebrated the 250th Anniversary of the School's foundation, with, among other events, performances of 'The Pageant'. For me, and for many pupils without much previous knowledge of the Quaker 'Unbroken Community', this celebration emphasised the ethos of the School. The tolerance, I noted, relied upon the underlying faith and humanity of staff and pupils who were Friends.

I am sure it was easier, in the less affluent and less worldly 1950s, to run a boarding school than it is today. Though we all had good links with town and Meeting House, there were inevitably times when our community felt a very closed group. There were rare occasions when a pupil ran away – obviously a serious matter. The Head went out in his car in pursuit of one escapee, along a road thought to be a likely escape route. The incident ended, probably happily, when the girl tried to thumb a lift from the Head.

As with all communities, there were local rituals – particularly the promenading down The Avenue in groups or in couples*. It was rumoured that Jennie Ellinor warned the girls about holding hands, "because you don't know what it leads to." I can certainly vouch for the fact that a young Old Scholar married couple met me while wheeling their young child down The Avenue in a pushchair and said, "Look what holding hands led to."

Long lasting friendships of all sorts are the most important achievement of any school, and I am grateful for those that I formed.

I have avoided, for the most part, mentioning names of the Staff. I can say, however, that, as a group, they were the best set of colleagues I ever worked with. As to pupils, teachers are not permitted to have favourites, so I will not refer to any living people. We all accept that for a parent to lose a child is grievous blow, but for a teacher to live longer than his pupils is also painful. So I remember, with much sadness, but some delight, five boys – Tom Marriage, Malcolm Harvey, David Greenland, Chris Eames and Brian Gatward. Girls live longer!

*The Couple System

This is, amazingly, the first mention of the couple system in this book and yet 'being a couple with . . .' was the way in which our personal relationships with individuals of the opposite sex were legitimated. I do not know when the couple system started, but it was in place the whole of my ten years. Its results are clearly recorded in photograph albums. Nowadays, sociologists might recognise it as a form of self-regulation, and it was clearly accepted both by individuals and the wider school society and almost certainly ensured that such relationships were kept within bounds (there were no pregnancies).

Its pattern in my time was that (usually) a boy wrote a letter to a girl, asking her to be a couple with him. If she accepted, they would spend spare time together – walking up and down The Avenue at recess and after meals, sitting together in the Library, using the far side of the playing-field for some privacy in summer or sneaking into the darkened dining-room on winter evenings. Especially, they would enjoy Saturday evening dances.

Some relationships were ephemeral, some longer lasting and some culminated in marriage. Conventional barriers were broken in the sense that a girl in the Lower 5th could be a couple with a boy in the Upper 6th and, more unusually, a boy in the Lower 5th was a couple with a girl in the Upper 6th. Being chucked, the term for ending the relationship, did cause some grief, but mainly my memories of my many partners are very friendly (and it was quite special to meet some of them again at the 1995 reunion).

Naomi Sargant

Stanley Pumphrey & John Skelton, 1947

My father died suddenly and tragically in August 1947. My brother Ted and I had restarted at Walden at the beginning of the following term – he to Junior School and me (I think) to Lower Three. Some time in September, on what must have been one of the first Sunday evening assemblies of term, the school was singing the lovely naval hymn, *Eternal father, strong to save*, and memories came flooding back and the agony and grief over my father's recent death became too hard to bear. I remember Stanley Pumphrey stepping down from the platform, where he had been sitting alongside Gerald Littleboy, Jennie Ellinor and Margaret Yapp (the School's Senior Staff).

He beckoned me outside and I wondered whether I was to be remonstrated for disturbing assembly, but we went up to his study in the Masters Block where he lit his pipe and talked – he talked of my father's school days and of the School itself and of the happy times that might lie ahead for me. Later the same evening, much cheered after my meeting with GSP, and after declaring that I had 'washed and cleaned my teeth, Sir' to the master on duty (probably BBJ), I arrived in Bedroom Six, the largest and most junior of the boys' gas-lit bedrooms. Here I met John Skelton, a year older than me and generally acknowledged to be leader of the junior occupants of that bedroom. He marched purposely up to me clutching a model plane. "You can play with this if you want," he said, handing it to me, and my remaining seven very happy years at Walden had commenced.

Robert Dunstan

The Night the Sky Fell In . . . Or did it?

My first term at FSSW (50s), I shared a small room at the back, right up under the eves. One night I woke in terror at the dreadful noise just over my head. There was quite a storm blowing. In fear and trembling, I went to waken a member of staff, who slept a few doors away. It was not a popular move and I was told "Don't be such a silly girl. Fancy disturbing me in the middle of the night. Go back to bed. There's nothing wrong." With difficulty, I eventually dropped off into a troubled sleep.

The next morning the cause of the noise was all too evident. The bedroom windows were thick with grime and, outside, a huge pile of tiles from the roof above our heads filled the playground below. Elsewhere, pieces of masonry and ceiling had come down. Fortunately no one had been hurt. It was a considerable number of years before I overcame my fears of howling gales at night, when in bed, trying to sleep.

A few years later, something similar happened, but not nearly so frightening. One evening; I think it was in the summer, I was in the assembly hall with many others, listening to one of the many excellent subscription concerts we used to have there. I no longer remember the exact details of ensemble playing or the music. However, when the flautist (if my memory serves me, it was certainly a woodwind) was playing a high note, there was a deafening roar and a thud, followed by a big cloud of dust and a loud bang. The musicians paused in their playing and the entire audience held their breath; a large piece of ceiling had fallen to the floor at the back of the stage, just behind the musicians. When everyone realised what had happened and that no one was hurt, the musicians continued from exactly where they had left off, to finish the piece of music they were playing. As you can imagine, the applause at the end was rapturous. Apparently, when the boarders' trunks had been stored in the loft space overhead, those putting them had been a little rough to say the least and loosened the ceiling.

Gillian Lampard

Do you remember . . .

- Playing 'Tin Can Tommy' in the Bumble Dinkies, there are classrooms there now.
- Playing waves amongst the bushes on the far side of the field.
- Walking up The Avenue and kicking the gate – later replaced by a stone – the New Avenue was not open in those days!
- Sunday afternoon the girls had to rest on their beds while the boys had to go for a walk.
- Later on the older girls were allowed to go for a walk after taking a rest, needless to say we met the boys.
- Merit halves and if you were lucky a Merit whole. A complete day off school!

What fun we had with Kelvin Osborn and Aggie Horlick who were our long suffering form teachers. We went to the 'swing beeches', a toy factory and a farm just to mention a few.

- Birthday parties on the long table under the balcony.
- Lining up to have our hair 'bug-raked' by Miss Hull.
- Is bread and butter still known as 'chaff and tack'?
- Drying our hair in front of the gas fire!
- Bath water up as far as the blue line –five inches.

Diane Hollingbery

Amnesty at FSSW

John Evans

I taught at the school from 1958 to 1965. I was not a Quaker, and did not contribute to the religious life of the School. Towards the end of my stay, the Headmaster, Kenneth Nicholson, told the staff that he had been talking to Peter Benenson (think that was the name) who was in the process of founding a new 'Amnesty' movement, and wondered if someone might like to begin a group in the School. No one else seemed to be interested, and my own friends outside the School were strongly cynical – just pie-in-the-sky idealism of well-meaning but misguided people. However, I expressed a tentative interest, and arranged a first meeting with not the faintest idea of what we would do. Hopefully there would be an informal chat with two or three enthusiasts. To my surprise, almost the whole of the sixth form attended, and the hall had been set out for me like an international conference. The only thing to do was to let as many people as possible have a say, and try to be a little more prepared next time.

In due course, we received three names: one was Helen Joseph, under house arrest in South Africa, another was a Greek political prisoner, and there was some French connection with the third. Helen wrote us charming letters, seemingly more concerned about us than her own condition. The Greek Embassy reasonably asked us why we thought we had a right to question their credentials when they had given civilisation and democracy to the world. The third I remember little about, except for discussions with the language staff about formal French correspondence. Quite naturally, we failed to have any direct impact. Our only achievement was a little local publicity through two musical concerts and a jumble sale.

Soon after these early beginnings, I left teaching, and Amnesty went out of my life. But strangely, bit by bit, year by year, I noticed Amnesty gaining ground in the universities, and becoming steadily more influential. Outraged governments began to feel it necessary to deride its activities, while humanitarian agencies, even the UN, began to take note of their reports. Not that I cared for the international lawyers who came in very much later, and tried to switch the emphasis from releasing prisoners to setting up war crimes tribunals who would dispose a victor's justice - that was never the intention. But attending Cyril Mummery's commemoration service last year, I was greatly heartened when I found myself facing a few of those dedicated pupils who, unlike the quitters like myself, had stayed the course, and helped to develop a truly international organisation.

I hope the School will recognise in some suitable way those sixth formers who persevered against the odds with something that surely goes to the heart of Quaker tradition and its religious values.

The Weather Girls of 1953

Preparing a weather report: l-r Ann Wickenden, Janet Smith, Janet Rice, Jane Goodrich   Photo John Skelton

In 1953/4, Ann Wickenden, Janet Rice, Janet Smith and myself took part in a weather project. We measured the rain, minimum and maximum temperatures etc, etc. For General Meeting 1953, we mounted a display for which we won ten shillings (I can't recall whether this was in total or whether we each received ten shillings).

I think that lasting friendships say much about a school. For ten years, Janet Smith, Ann Wickenden, Patricia Chuter and I, without our men, spent a sunny week's holiday together. We have now known each other for fifty years and it is a very satisfying feeling.   **Jane Goodrich**

Saturday Evening Entertainment

This took the form of talks and slide shows, some very interesting, eg one by the London taxi driver.
Films (about three per term) – no TV then! – School Dances Special occasions like the School Play – Choir and Orchestra End of Term Concerts which were always great fun, including the old School Song, as well as old favourites like *Riding Down from Bangor* and, usually, skits on the staff.   **Pat & Donn Webb**

The Night We Saved the Girls' Honour

as remembered by NIGEL McTEAR

It was a balmy summer's night in 1979. Too warm to sleep comfortably and even with the dormitory windows wide open one could only dream about the benefits of modern air conditioning.

Some time after midnight, still unable to sleep, I heard the noise of people running towards the girl's end of the School along the asphalt between the Avenue and main school building. As my bed was immediately adjacent to the open window I looked outside to see a number of people disappearing out of sight talking in hushed tones. Clearly, they shouldn't have been there and were up to no good. I woke up my friend and dormitory colleague Michael Fenton and he too heard the noises of people outside. By now they were outside the girl's playroom and, although out of sight, could still be heard. Being responsible Sixth Formers, we decided that our unwelcome guests were almost certainly teenage boys from the town and, suspecting that their intentions were less than honourable, we agreed to alert the Duty Master at the boys' end.

Peter Arter was the Duty Master that evening and, needless to say, he was not happy about being woken up. However, once we had explained what we had heard and seen, he decided to phone the Headmaster and asked us to accompany him to the girls' dormitories to make sure that all was in order.

Who could possibly turn down an 'official' opportunity to explore the girls' dormitories at night!

By now it was at least one o'clock in the morning, and the three of us walked down the boys' staircase, along central corridor and up the stairs towards the girls' dormitory. It must have been a strange sight – the three of us, dressed in pyjamas and dressing gowns, creeping around in the middle of the night. Michael Fenton was over 6ft 4ins tall, Peter Arter was 5ft 4ins and I am just under 5ft 8ins. The only thing we had in common was a lack of ability to defend ourselves if presented with an intruder, so it was not clear what we would do if we did find anyone who shouldn't have been there.

By now the girls' Duty Mistress, Jean Stubbs, was also on the scene and, after checking a number of dormitories without event, together we approached the Barn Dormitory door. This was the only dormitory which can be easily accessed from the back of the school as its windows are just four or five feet above the top of the girls playroom lobby roof. It was obvious that, if we were to find intruders, this was going to be the place.

As we slowly opened the door mayhem pursued. We hit the lights to be presented with five or six teenage boys who, to our enormous relief, appeared more afraid of us than we did of them – little did they know! Four of them made a dive for the open window that they had entered from and quickly made their getaway. However, two of them in their moment of panic, decided to make a run for the dormitory door which involved passing within inches of where we were standing.

It was one of those situations where you simply could not believe what was happening. It all happened so fast. There was no time to think. It's a cliché but it was them or us.

Anyone who knew Michael would know that he would have difficulty harming a fly let alone another human being but, to my complete surprise, I saw a different side to him that night. He grabbed the two intruders, pinned them firmly but with restraint against the wall and suggested that it was in their interest to stand still or he might have to kill them. How exactly he intended to do this was less than clear but it had the desired affect and they stayed rooted to the spot looking up at this 6ft 4ins giant of a Sixth Former. For my part, I was ready to defend the honour of the School (not to mention the girls involved) but Michael had the situation covered, so fortunately my role was reduced to one of moral support only.

Fortunately, the lives of these intruders were saved by the arrival of the Headmaster (John Woods), supported by the local police. With the situation under control, the intruders were taken away and Michael and myself, feeling somewhat proud with ourselves, went back to bed.

In the morning, at breakfast, the excitement of the night before had somehow become common knowledge and, as Michael and I entered the Dining Hall, we were greeted by clapping – what heroes!

Questions like what these people were doing there in the first place, what their intentions were and what would have happened had they not been challenged remain unanswered to this day.

Buoyed up by our new hero status, Michael and I stood in that year's School Election, to coincide with the General Election, under the dream ticket of Batman and Robin. Obviously, our mandate involved the saving of teenage girls from the perils of uninvited guests as well as a wider platform of other super-hero attributes! Given Michael's 6ft 4ins frame and dark hair and my more compact dimensions and ginger hair I will leave it for you to decide who was Batman and who was Robin! To our surprise we came third behind the main two parties.

As far as we know, the youths questioned by the police were let off with a caution and the incident passed into the folklore of the school to rest with many other anecdotes, some of which appear in this excellent book.

Mark Bertram

Long, balmy, irresponsible summer evenings in the first year of the sixth form in the late 1950s. Four of us could not resist tweaking the tail of the cricketing establishment and our mischief fell on the venerable roller (still going strong, I notice). We would turn it upside down. Except that would be impossible. So we would make it appear to have been turned upside down. Out came the penetrating oil several nights running to be applied to the large rusty bolts joining the axle to the frame. Then one night out came some big spanners and the work of taking the frame off, turning it over and re-attaching it, upside down,

to the axle was quite quick. Next morning, gasps of horror and admiration, depending on cricketing orientation.

The Head, Kenneth Nicholson, complained to the whole sixth form about how the roller could have been broken by being turned upside down but he had the good sense not to go for the pranksters. I can now give their names, because they are written on the back of my commemorative photo: Ian Drummond, John Elsden, Peter Fraenkel and Mark Bertram. The Head asked philosophically why, if vandalism was going to become a problem, he should not mount machine guns watching over our activities. "Expense, Sir?" suggested Oliver Weaver.

James Hawkes

I was a scholar between 1985 and 1992, not sure I can recall any significant developments except staff cutbacks and after many years, J C Woods leaving. The school band (*Void*, I think) performed a deafening rendition of Go Jonny Go in assembly, preceded and followed by the silence of worship. I remember the Five Day Week being introduced. I think Collect for Assembly disappeared at this time for the younger years.

I was in the last group at Gibson House before it briefly turned into mixed accommodation for the first and second years. When it was abandoned we had to return there for a term during the sixth form as Hillcroft was made 'Fire Safe' which completely devalued it, only for it to be put on the market a year or two later. During the time I was at School many irreversible decisions were made, The land at Friends Walk (allotments by the Scout Hut), Most of the Young Farmers field, Robins Acre including its long garden an orchard and the old Bursar's House were sold off, probably without much long term gain. Hillcroft was superb as a mixed Boarding House although there was little hijinks between the 1st and 2nd floor - well, none that I participated in!

Scouts run by John Capper was great fun, and with just enough discipline, very beneficial. One of the more popular activities was lighting a fire in the boughs of a tree behind the scout hut and cooking baked beans and tea on it.

One superb anecdote concerned Jane Laing and Gavin Parnaby during the trip behind the Iron Curtain around 1991.

Jane Laing seeing the amount of drink in Gavin's glass (Gavin was a big chap) exclaimed as the lift doors separated them "Gavin, That's far too much Vodka!" By the time they met in the lobby (I think), Gavin having taken the stairs, the Glass was drained to avoid confiscation. Jane of course went on to be the Head Teacher (I am sure she was very sound).

The Present Generation

We invited six current Sixth Formers to tell us how they feel about the School as it is now and their hopes for the future. Two girls, both day scholars, and four boys, all boarders, took part in the survey. They are studying for their A Levels in subjects varying from the traditional English and History, Physics, Chemistry and Biology, to more modern courses such as General Studies, Key Skills, Sport, Drama and Film Studies. They are all active in sport and one hopes to make sport his career.

Two of our respondents followed siblings into the School and the decision to attend in all cases was taken jointly with their parents. Only one comes from a Quaker family whose parents are Old Scholars and one has decided to join the Society of Friends as a result of his experiences at the School and participating in such activities as the Quaker Pilgrimage.

An overwhelming impression to be gained from their answers is the importance to them of the Quaker ethos, also the fact that the School is co-educational and multi-ethnic. While some feel the limitations of being in a small community, they feel that their experiences of variety in their environment give them a good foundation for coping with adult life.

Here are the questions we asked with examples of the replies we received.

How does a Quaker school differ from others?

All obviously gain a sense of calm and community:

The silent assemblies and emphasis on silence and peace within a person. The small, close community spirit and feel *(girl)*. It has a distinct atmosphere which I have never explained satisfactorily, but it is there *(boy)*. The whole atmosphere and ethos of the School is calm and relaxed. There is little sense of hierarchy between the year groups *(girl)*. The relaxed atmosphere gives you a chance to develop completely, naturally. Nothing is forced down you *(boy)*. I believe that Friends' School, Saffron Walden, perhaps more than other Friends' Schools, holds to the Quaker ethos well. That is not to say that Quaker traditions are forced on to us. The Quaker ethos is seen running through the community of the School almost unnoticed *(boy)*. The sense of community *(boy)*.

Is it important that the School is co-educational?

This is extremely important to all:

One boy goes as far as to say single sex is artificial, surreal and full of cliques. Both girls feel they learn to co-operate with each other and reach levels of toleration which prepare them for later life, for university and the world of work, also to see how the opposite sex feels on certain issues. They also feel they will be better able to bond with people of both sexes.

It is important to achieve a well rounded and tolerant outlook to life and this must include interaction between the sexes *(boy)*. Other boys' comments: some of my best friends are women; a part of me wouldn't grow. You get to know how to treat women.

What about the School's location and setting?

What some see as calm, others see, perhaps, as dull:

In a traditional, small town with a Quaker following within, likened to the atmosphere of the School, fairly quiet and spacious setting and surroundings *(girl)*. The School's grounds give it a great setting *(boy)*.

'Beautiful' fails to sum up the School, both in its setting and ethos *(boy)*. The town of Saffron Walden may lack in excitement and verve, but makes up for it with a natural calm and friendly feeling in the community. The Friends' School grounds show their true beauty during the summer months *(boy)*. Fairly good – close to London, Bishops Stortford and Cambridge. Saffron Walden could have more stuff for people our age (bowling etc).

What do you think of the School's facilities, buildings etc.

. . . what some see as tradition, others regard as behind the times:

Mostly very old style and characteristic. Main building still holds an old and traditional feel, whilst the outbuildings are more modern and practical for modern day teaching *(girl)*. In general they are good – the buildings are nice *(girl)*.

The grounds are nice, facilities are

adequate for a small school. The School's facilities are adequate for such a small school. Its IT facilities are constantly improving as the School reacts to the need for young people to improve their capabilities in this area. Sports, good; Classes, good; Grounds, nice. Could do with a weights room but overall good. *(boys)*

Is this school multicultural?

All respondents agree that the School is multicultural and inclusive:

The girls... Yes, definitely! There are members of all cultures and nations from all over the world and all are easily mixed into the community and school life. Definitely – this school gives you a good opportunity to mix and interact with people from all over the world.

And the boys... Yes, it is multicultural. There are a large number of cultures represented and no tensions between them. Yes, the cultures come from all over the world, from Buddhists to Quakers to Jews, from every corner of the world. To say that Friends' is multicultural is an understatement. The presence of so many cultures gives the School a special, unique community. Each culture adds its theme to the community. Yes, you get to learn about different cultures.

Is being a boarder different from being a day scholar?

Not really much difference, although boarders tend to be closer to each other as they spend 24 hours a day together in the closed environment *(girl)*. In the Sixth Form there is not so much difference, but lower down the School there is a kind of a divide slightly between boarders and day pupils *(boy)*. I'm a day scholar and during lesson time there is not much of a divide, but at other times it is more noticeable *(girl)*. I have been both a day scholar and a boarder. There is a great difference. This is my home. I spend most of my time here. I care about it. There isn't a divide between the two but our approach is different *(boy)*. In general, boarders form closer relationships with each other than with day scholars. However, the Friends' community is a flowing entity that constantly changes with the people present at the time. Certainly being a boarder gives you the opportunity to be more involved with all of school life *(boy)*. In years Seven to Eleven there is more of a divide between the two. Boarding makes you more independent and prepares you for life out of school *(boy)*.

Is the Sixth Form experience different from that of lower years?

All are of one voice on this subject:

It is much nicer in the Sixth Form! You get more of a sense of freedom and being responsible for yourself, treated more 'grown-up'. There are many more privileges – recess, snacks, larger/better common room areas, getting lunch first – always *(girl)*. A far greater sense of freedom. This comes from private study periods as well as a greater level of privileges out of School *(boy)*. Sixth Form has given me more freedom to be how I want. It has also taught me to be more self-motivated and disciplined with my work *(girl)*. It's good. You become closer as a year. You're treated differently by the staff and lower years, mostly you gain respect *(boy)*. The Sixth Form is a vastly more enjoyable experience than lower years. Sixth Form students are allowed much more freedom of movement. We are allowed to leave the School grounds at recess, lunchtime and between 8.30 and 10.00. In the Sixth Form, the reduction in the size of year group really pulls together an already close community *(boy)*. You get a better relationship with Staff and more freedom. You have free periods and get into lunch early *(boy)*.

Leisure, time out of School?

Chatting to everybody – mostly my year group in Croydon House Common Room, watching videos, playing pool, computer room, mostly in groups of people, not on your own *(girl)*. Talking with other pupils and in spite of the small year groups, the social life is good *(boy)*. Either socialising with other members of the School, doing sport, work. The social life is quite good *(girl)*. Talking, drinking coffee and working and eating toast. My social life is good. It's a very tight community *(boy)*. I spend most of my free time gathering with other students in social areas of the School. The social life of the School is the successful factor that holds together its community *(boy)*. Social life good – lots of socialising done in town. Free time watching television, computer etc *(boy)*.

How are your relations with the Staff?

Generally they are quite good and there is a great deal of co-operation. Obviously it's not like that with every student teacher, but that's to be expected *(girl)*. Broadly they are very good and close *(boy)*. They get better in the Sixth Form *(girl)*. Very good – one of the best things about the School *(boy)*. The small class sizes allow student/staff relationships to reach a higher level of friendship whilst also keeping a degree of respect *(boy)*. Very good *(boy)*.

What have been the high points of your time at the School?

Mostly respondents cite good exam results, sporting achievements or achieving promotion within the School. Other highlights have been the School balls and entertainments, the Quaker Pilgrimage... and: seeing Sarah Evans fall over in Assembly! *(boy)*

...and the low points?
Not many, it seems, however:

Things have got a bit claustrophobic and difficult at times, due to the very small number of people in each year group *(girl)*. The way the Sixth Form is so small. Even though I truly love these guys, you can easily become claustrophobic *(boy)*. The School seems to reach its low point just after Christmas, the weather remains damp and cold and Christmas is long over *(boy)*.

What do you like most about the School?
All agree on this – words such as atmosphere, relaxed, calm and community abound. The Quaker ethos and multi ethnicity are cited, the wonderful environment of the grounds in summer and, as one boy says: All of it really.

What do you like least about the School?
It can get very cold in winter before the heating is turned on – especially in the older parts!! The limited number of subjects offered (especially at A-level) *(girl)*. Late in the terms it can become boring as everyone has said everything that want to say to each other and need a break *(boy)*. Because people are so close, it can get too claustrophobic (not physically) *(girl)*. If you have a secret, it is 90% sure to get out *(boy)*. The grounds in winter and the lack of personal space are the most irritating features of the School *(boy)*. And it seems there is still a problem which was experienced in the 40s – there are occasional incidents of theft.

How would you like the School to develop in the future?
I hope it continues to improve with age and keeps up to modern day standards. Also that the continuance of effectively dealing with issues such as bullying and difficult pupils is maintained as it is a school environment in which these have been and can be effectively controlled. Additions to and continued modernisation of facilities *(girl)*. I would like to see it grow and continue to prosper *(boy)*. I would maybe like to see pupils being able to express themselves more freely, ie through their dress *(girl)*. I would like the diversity to grow, mainly in the subjects taught, but also in the people attending Friends'. Oh, and of course, more boarders *(boy)*. I would like to see the School show more interaction with other schools, perhaps with other Friends' Schools. Ideas for an exchange with a school in Ireland being reinstated is just the thing that I believe the School needs. I would like the School to continue to develop but also to retain to the spirit of Quakerism in the community which, I feel, is the backbone of the School *(boy)*. The majority of students are happy here and it would be a shame if they were not. Sports teams to improve so I can play a good First Eleven as an Old Scholar *(boy)*.

How has the School changed since you have been here?
The turnover of staff during the years covered has been the biggest cause for concern among the respondents:

The uniform has changed and it has gone through phases of popularity (ie intake in students). Many new additions, facilities, improvements to Swimming Pool, Teachers *(girl)*. Head Teacher has changed three times. Subjects have moved many times, but broadly the School has retained the same feeling for me *(boy)*. The Headship has changed three times and therefore the feel of the School changes too *(girl)*. Staff have come and gone (mostly gone), refurbishment which was nice *(boy)*. The facilities of the School have improved all the time, including the Swimming Pool, Science Labs and IT facilities. The School also seems to have a high staff turnover *(boy)*. Stricter, interior has improved, different Teachers, Tennis Courts *(boy)*.

First Impressions in 2001

Having only been at Walden since January 2001, I know little about the School's rich history. However, while I may not know much about its past, I have certainly learned a lot about its present.

My husband, Brian, and I moved down from Scotland, having just left very long term teaching posts to take over responsibility for Boys' and Girls' House, as well as the duties of Boarding Co-ordinator. From the first day we arrived, we have been made to feel so welcome by absolutely everybody – every member of Staff, no matter what their station, and all the Pupils. The support and assistance we have received have been very much appreciated. People have tolerated our beginners' lack of knowledge and have helped us through more than one or two rather difficult situations.

The accommodation we have been given, as obviously we have to live on site, is wonderful. We live in the Tower Flat – what a misnomer! Well, yes, it is in the Tower of the School but, rest assured, it is anything but flat. From the living area, you have to climb 38 ever narrowing steps to the Guest Bedroom – I wonder if this is why guests rarely outstay their welcome?

When we first visited the School for our interview, we felt it had a warm and friendly atmosphere. We reckoned that we could be happy here, even though it meant leaving our children and grandchildren back in Scotland. Our initial impressions have been confirmed many times. The Quaker ethos helps new staff and pupils to feel at home very quickly and to feel valued, no matter what they are doing. This atmosphere is not present in all schools, but it is one which should certainly be encouraged everywhere – it really does make a difference.

Moira Thomson

Friends' Junior School – a recent venture with a new Head

Friends' Junior School opened as Gibson House in 1992 in the premises built originally as the school sanatorium in 1925. It was expanded in 1995 to include a Nursery.

Starting with an intake of just fifteen, there are now 171 children at the School and a two-form entry is planned for 2002.

As well as the traditional subjects, the curriculum takes in craft, design and technology, information computer technology and personal, social and health education. The range of sports is wide – football, netball, cross-country, hockey, swimming, cricket, rounders, athletics, tennis and new image rugby. Afternoon clubs take place after school and there are lunchtime activities including recorder, saxophone and string groups and a choir.

New Head, Andrew Holmes grew up in Norfolk and attended Hammonds Grammar School, Swaffham and Wymondham College before moving to Bath to complete a Cert Ed. His first appointment was at Kent College, a coeducational day and boarding school in Canterbury. While in Canterbury he took a BEd(Hons) at the University of Kent. He was then appointed Head of Mathematics at Oswestry Junior School, a prep-school in Shropshire and from here he moved to Dame Bradbury's School in Saffron Walden as Deputy Head. He took up the post of Head of Friends' Junior School in 2001.

He has been married to Sue, who is also a teacher in Saffron Walden, for 25 years. They have two children, Ben (eighteen) who is at University of Wales, and Beth (eleven) who is at Newport Grammar School.

Andrew has always been a keen sportsman and has regularly played rugby, football and golf. He has played cricket for Somerset Second Eleven, and other League teams. He still plays village cricket.

He arrives at FSSW at a challenging and exciting time – a new Head for the Senior School, an Inspection by the Independent Schools Inspectorate and the School's Tercentenary celebrations all coming within his first year.

He finds that the School has a very distinct ethos and a special sense of history which is being specially highlighted in the Tercentenary year. Together with everybody else at the School, he looks forward, with optimism and confidence to the next one hundred years.

Still Inclusive, Still Thriving

There are many ethnic groups in school at present: Asian (Hong Kong Chinese, mainland Chinese, Korean, Japanese, Sri Lankan, Thai, Indian, Pakistani); Afro Caribbean (Trinidad, Jamaica); African (Ghana, Cameroun, Kenya, Sudan, Guyana), Hispanic (Brazil, Mexico); European non-English (Ukrainian, Turkish, German, French). Many different religious backgrounds are also represented.

Twenty-nine pupils do not have English as their first language (9% of school population) and there are in total around 40 pupils (12% of pop.) from 21 countries other than the UK.

There are 162 children aged over eleven in the School of whom 75 are boarders. There are 172 children aged under eleven but none of these board.

Boarding nationally has been in decline until this year, when numbers ceased falling for the first time in a decade. There are many contributory factors; a cultural backlash against boarding in the late 80s and early 90s; many parents now have no experience of boarding and do not consider it as an option; improved transport systems and higher levels of car ownership make boarding less 'necessary' than before. Cost is also a factor – schools have been required by law (especially in *The Children Act 1989*) to make boarding provision more private, secure and luxurious, hence the costs have risen dramatically. A senior school boarding place at FSSW now costs in the region of £14,700 a year – over £100,000 for the seven years of Senior education. 'Flexible' boarding is now the norm in most schools, where a large number of boarding pupils are only in school from Monday night to Thursday night and are at home every weekend. This is particularly common in suburban/rural areas like Saffron Walden, where most London based boarders would be unable to go home on a daily basis but can comfortably make the journey in 90 minutes on a Friday night.

New Head, **Andy Waters**, feels that boarding may well have a slow return to popularity, especially amongst families where both partners work full-time in order (in many cases) to pay the school fees. 'Convenience' boarding is thus becoming a mini-phenomenon. He doubts, however, if boarding will *ever* return to the levels seen in the 50s and 60s when it was culturally acceptable to send your eight year old off to school. He doubts the validity of the so-called 'Harry Potter' effect (children choosing to board at a young age because of the books and films showing boarding in a good light). He would welcome some proper research into why children really choose to board – if, indeed, it is their choice and not that of their parents.

A New Head for a New Century

Andy Waters was born in Coventry in 1957 and was educated at a West London boys' grammar school. After studying languages at 'A' Level, he gained a B.Ed. (Hons) degree in Physical Education and History at Borough Road College before taking up his first teaching appointment (1980) in a large and challenging maintained school in Camberwell, London. In 1984 Andy moved to North Wales to become a management tutor and mountaineering specialist at the Outward Bound School (Aberdyfi), where he was also a member of the North Wales Mountain Rescue Organisation.

In 1987 Andy returned to teaching and became Head of Physical Education at St. Christopher School, (Letchworth). He and Hazel were married in 1988, and ran a succession of co-educational boarding houses whilst continuing to teach PE and History. Andy completed an in-service MA in Educational Management in 1996 and was appointed Deputy Headmaster of Oswestry School (Shropshire) in September 1997. After four years of valuable experience, during which time he was responsible for pastoral care, staff professional development and the day-to-day administration of the school, Andy was appointed to the Headship of Friends' School Saffron Walden in September 2001.

Andy and Hazel have two children, Bethan born in 1992 and Ryan in 1994. Both now enthusiastically attend the Junior School at Friends'; Hazel, a qualified primary school teacher, is currently working as a teaching assistant in Cambridge. Andy retains a love of music and has played guitars in a number of working ceilidh bands in the past fifteen years. He also competes in triathlon events over a range of distances, and escapes back to the mountains with his family to ski and climb whenever the opportunity arises.

Here he outlines his hopes for the future of the School.

A Vision for the Future

I am very proud to have been appointed Head of Friends' School at such an important time in its history. Andrew Holmes (the new Head of Junior House) and I have an exciting and challenging task ahead of us, but we have the security of knowing that the School has strong foundations underneath it, and a tangible ethos based on its Quaker roots which has stood the tests of time over the past three hundred years. The School already has a fine site, dedicated staff, supportive parents and governors, and a body of enthusiastic pupils; it will be our job to take these assets and shape them in such a way that the future of the School is assured.

My priorities for 2001/2002 have, to a great extent, been pre-determined. The School undergoes its Independent Schools' Inspectorate Inspection in February 2002, and will celebrate its Tercentenary in May and September. A new prospectus is planned, and modifications to the changing rooms to enhance the work done on the Swimming Pool will begin in the summer. Where, though, might we be in five years' time? On my appointment to the Headship I gave a presentation to the Governors outlining my vision for Friends' School, and I should like to share this with readers of this volume.

The School will continue to be both a day and boarding establishment, firmly guided by Quaker beliefs and principles, serving a diverse intake of around 380 children. These children will not be exclusively selected by academic ability, and will range in age from 3 to 18. The School will seek to harness the inner potential of every child through a wide variety of academic, creative, sporting and cultural opportunities, and it will be staffed by dedicated and committed educationalists who understand that teaching is a day-long, week-long, life long process. Pupils from every race, creed and cultural background will be equally welcomed and valued.

The School will be financially sound without being wasteful, and will have undergone a successful inspection and a positive reinforcement of its history and underlying principles during the Tercentenary celebrations. Its buildings will be enhanced, and its spaces better utilised for the benefit of pupils. It will be better known locally and nationally, and will seek to strengthen the bonds between current and past scholars as well as with local schools. It will be well informed about educational change, prepared to respond to new initiatives and capable of the flexibility which an ever-changing educational world requires. Vitally, it will stand ready and able to serve the needs of children as it has done since 1702.

I like to think of the School as a diamond; old and precious, and treasured by those who share ownership of it. Like all diamonds, though, it will benefit from some polishing and from being allowed to shine in a different setting. Andrew and I look forward to guiding the polishing, and enhancing the setting of our diamond as we lead it into its fourth century.

Andy Waters
February 2002

Postscript

I commend this fascinating book as a good read for all those who already have connections with FSSW, and as an excellent introduction for newcomers to our community. It adds substantially to an understanding of the history of the School, and our deep involvement with the Society of Friends. The personal stories and comments give us glimpses of the day to day reality of school life in the recent past, and I am sure they will act as a trigger to the memories of countless Old Scholars and Staff. We are truly grateful to all those who have been kind enough to contribute.

The idea for a new publication about the School came from a small steering group of Governors planning the Tercentenary Appeal and Celebrations with me, at least five years ago. We were all delighted when Hilary Halter with her wide experience of the world of publishing, agreed to take on the task of Editor, but I am sure she did not realise what a huge undertaking this would be.

Hilary has given this project countless hours and it is entirely due to her persistence in pursuing contributions, and her cheerful approach to overcoming all the difficulties surrounding publication, that we have such a wonderful finished product. It is a pleasure to know how much satisfaction Hilary has found in this work – it has indeed been a labour of love! I offer her heartfelt thanks on behalf of the School and all those who read this book.

The Old Scholars' Committee have supported the project throughout, providing practical assistance and the vital financial backing. I would like to thank them collectively for their enthusiastic help.

The publication of this book is a fitting tribute to the indefinable but enduring spirit of the School in its Tercentenary Year. We all look forward to the next instalment!

Jane Laing

Index of Names
[Nicknames in square brackets]

Abrey, Glynn, 1940-50
Alexander, Kenneth, 1927-32
Allward, James 1938-41
Allward, Maurice, 1938-40
Arman, Jennie, 1961-63
Armfield, John, 1839-44
Arundel, Frank Rivers 1875-77
Ashford, Joy *Dupont* (Staff), 1951-1972
Atkins, Michael, 1941-49
Atkinson, Don, 1948-54
Bader, Godric , 1935-41
Badger, Ranger *Behrendt* (Staff: Modern Langs), 1979-83
Baldwin, Walter (Staff), 1931-36
Ball, Margaret, 1945-49
Barber, Barry, 1941-51
Barrie, Jeanne (Staff), 1930-48
Bawden, Edward, 1918-20
Beecham, Henrietta *Edmundson* (Staff), 1922-35
Beeson, Lenon (Staff), 1950-56
Bennett, Roger, 1943-53
Benson, Donald (Staff), 1955-88
Berny, Jan, 1949-54
Bertram, Mark, 1955-60
Best, Richard M, 1938-43
Bird, Gladys (Staff), 1916-35
Black, Julian, 1976-80
Blake, Sylvia, 1943-45
Bolam, David, 1936-43
Bolton, John, 1927-30
Booth, Audrey *Williams*, 1935-38
Brereton, Arnold (Staff), 1909-47
Brereton, Iona *Dean*, 1939-45
Brinkworth, Margaret (Staff), 1974-92
Brooks, Anthony, 1936-46
Brown, Eric (Staff), 1946-76
Brown, Tessa (Staff), 1976-88
Burtt, Barbara *Phillips*, 1958-65
Bush, Roger, 1942-48
Buss, Roger, 1945-51
Butler, Daniel [Diffy], 1942-45
Cadman, John, 1944-50
Campbell, Patrick [Jim], 1938-40
Cane, Ivan (Staff), 1956-63
Carlton Smith, Alan, 1935-37
Cassuto, Fulvio, 1942-48
Castillejo, David, 1941-44
Chalk, Arthur, 1949-52
Chuter, Pat *Webb*, 1946-53
Clark, Edna *Kerney* (Staff), 1933-42

Clark, Sylvia (Staff), 1937-44
Clarke, Hugh, 1950-57
Clover, Owen, 1901-04
Clymo, Richard S, 1944-51
Colbeck, Ruth *Cole*, 1975-77
Collins, Mark
Collins, Mike (Staff), 1973-99
Collinson, Elisabeth *Francis*, 1944-49
Comber, Barbara *Bowyer* (Staff), 1943-56
Comber, Michael, 1942-51
Cottrell, Olive (Staff), 1946-50
Cuthbert, Mary (Staff), 1958-62
David, Irene *Matthews*, 1942-44
Dickinson, John (Staff), 1977-97
Duffill, Michael, 1957-64
Dunstan, Pete, 1951-57
Dunstan, Robert, 1945-54
Dutton, Bobby, 1946-53
Dutton, Jimmy, 1945-52
Dyer, Julia *Dent Dyer*, 1939-44
Edmunds, Albert J, 1966-73
Edwards, Jennifer *Richards*, 1947-53
Edwards, Owen, 1943-50
Eggleton, Mollie, 1939-45
Ellinor, Jennie (Staff), 1944-64
Ersksine, Ralph, 1925-31
Evans, John , 1972-79
Evans, John (Staff), 1958-65
Evans, Sarah (Staff), 1989-96
Fairbanks, David, 1944-49
Fairbanks, James, 1875-80
Follett, Jeff (Staff), 1946-58
Fordham, Paul, 1936-43
Foxley, Ann (Staff), 1974-88
Free, Dot (Staff)
Freelove, Eleanor J, 1887-91
Fry, Susan *Smith*, 1942-49
Fulford, Mary (Staff), 1941-44
Galbraith, Sheila *Shacklock* (Staff), 1943-45
Garcia, Delia *Baker*, 1939-42
Garcia, Elvio, 1939-42
Garcia, Helvecia, 1939
Gatward, Brian, 1944-56 (Staff), 1977-90
Gatward, Rebecca
Gatward, Jonathan
Gatward, Matthew
Gutwein, Tommy, 1948-51
Gee. Michael, 1945-50
Gelsthorpe, Brian (Staff), 1957-62
Gerstl, Uwe, 1942-50
Goddard, Pauline *Haigh*, 1938-46 (Staff) 1950-54

Goodrich, Jane *Gorman*, 1947-53
Graham, Mrs (Staff)
Green, Arnold, 1891-98
Grillet, Christophe, 1938-42
Grillet, Elisabeth *Seale*, 1937-41
Haggith, Toby , 1974-81
Harris, Joyce *Lingham-Lees* (Staff), 1931-46
Harvey, Malcolm, 1948-54
Haselgrove, Maurice (Staff), 40s
Hawkes, James , 1985-92
Hayler, Wilfrid, 1940-48
Heap (Staff)
Hembry, Sue (Staff), 1973-93
Hills, David, 1954-61
Hockley, Hilary *Halter*, 1941-47
Hockley, Muriel *Markham*, 1941-46
Hollingbery, Diane *Martin*, 1949-55
Holttum, Catherine *Smith*, 1946-50
Holttum, Deborah, 1946-50
Holttum, Richard Eric, 1907-11
Honigmann, Paul, 1944-51
Hopwood, Gillian *Godwin*, 1938-45
Horlick, Agnes (Staff), 1947-57
Houlder, Philip (Staff), 1957-59
How, Michael, 1942-50
Hudson, Robert (Staff), 1957-61
Hugall, Martin (Staff), 1972-
Jackson,Gwyneth *Dutton*, 1945-51 (Staff) 1954-58
Jackson, Hilary *Charlton*, 1946-54
Jacob, Bernard (Staff), 1935-63
Jeffery, Pat *Johnstone*, 1939-46
John, Iorwerth (Staff), 1956-74
Johnston, Graeme, 1955-61
Jones, Caroline, 1972-79
Jones, David, 1941-47
Jones, Diana *Burrow*, 1945-53
Jones, Rhoda (Staff)
Joselin, Peter, 1942-49
Kendon, Alice *Thomas*, 1942-49
Kenningham, Margaret (Staff), 1958-62
Kerrison, Irene, 1957-59
King Beer, G Stanley (Staff), 1917-39
King Beer, Mabel (Staff), 1943-49
Kohler, Charles, 1924-28
Laing, Jane, Deputy Head, 1989-95 Head, 1995-2001
Lamond, Pat *Lawrence*, 1943-47
Lampard, Gillian *Newell*, 1948-54
Lansdell, Marygold *Marsden-Smedley*, 1938-47

Lawson, Pat (Staff), 1998-2000
Lemere, Henry Bedford, 1879-80
Lenz, Eric (Staff), 1943-48
Lenz, Marie (Staff), 1943-46
Lewis, David (Staff), 1959-66
Lillie, Paul (Staff), 1991-92
Lindley, Albert (Staff), 1934-35
Littleboy, Gerald (Staff), 1914-15;1934-55
Lloyd Judith, (Staff) became Judith *Gelsthorpe* (Staff). 1958-60)
Lyell, Jean *Durrant*, 1940-46
MacDonald, Amanda (Staff), 2000-
Macdonald, Pat
Marriage, Eleanor *Soar*, 1942-51
Marriage, Sam, 1990-97
Marriage, Thomas, 1943-52
Marshall, Gladys (Housekeeper), -61;1965-66
Marty, Tom (Staff), 2000-
Matthews, David, 1949-52
Matthews, Michael, 1963-72
Mauger, Paul, 1906-13
McTear, Andrew , 1973-80
McTear, Nigel , 1973-80
Mercer, Mary (Staff), 1951-69
Michaelis, Martin, 1941-43
Michaelis, Ruth *Barnett*, 1941-43
Mileson, Mary *Noyce* (Staff) 1952-55; 1968-
Mileson, Timothy, 1969-74?
Milford, Pauline *Wilsdon*, 1941-43
Miller, Anthony, 1939-49
Miller, Mark (Staff), 1971-77
Miller, Olga (Staff), 1954-72
Moore, Kathleen *Stierer*, 1937-47
Morland, Betty (Staff), 1942-44
Morland, M Ethel *Crawshaw*, 1885-92
Morley, Nurse Anne (Staff), 1958-61
Mould, Barbara Elaine *Bass* (Staff) 1962-64
Mummery, Cyril A (Staff), 1943-80
Mummery, Joan (Staff), 1946-48
Murray, Annie (Staff), 1913-46
Nash, Peter, 1946-54
Newton, Tony, 1948-55
Nicholson, Kenneth (Staff), 1928-29; 1955-67
Osborn, Kelvin (Staff), 1944-63
Page, Ursula *Duerden*, 1943-49

iv